Measuring L2 Proficiency

SECOND LANGUAGE ACQUISITION

Series Editor: Professor David Singleton, *University of Pannonia, Hungary and Fellow Emeritus, Trinity College, Dublin, Ireland*

This series brings together titles dealing with a variety of aspects of language acquisition and processing in situations where a language or languages other than the native language is involved. Second language is thus interpreted in its broadest possible sense. The volumes included in the series all offer in their different ways, on the one hand, exposition and discussion of empirical findings and, on the other, some degree of theoretical reflection. In this latter connection, no particular theoretical stance is privileged in the series; nor is any relevant perspective – sociolinguistic, psycholinguistic, neurolinguistic, etc. – deemed out of place. The intended readership of the series includes final-year undergraduates working on second language acquisition projects, postgraduate students involved in second language acquisition research, and researchers and teachers in general whose interests include a second language acquisition component.

Full details of all the books in this series and of all our other publications can be found on http://www.multilingual-matters.com, or by writing to Multilingual Matters, St Nicholas House, 31–34 High Street, Bristol BS1 2AW, UK.

SECOND LANGUAGE ACQUISTION: 78

Measuring L2 Proficiency
Perspectives from SLA

Edited by
**Pascale Leclercq, Amanda Edmonds
and Heather Hilton**

MULTILINGUAL MATTERS
Bristol • Buffalo • Toronto

Library of Congress Cataloging in Publication Data
Measuring L2 Proficiency Perspectives from SLA/Edited by Pascale Leclercq, Amanda Edmonds and Heather Hilton.
Second Language Acquisition: 78
Includes bibliographical references and index.
1. Second language acquisition—Evaluation. 2. Second language acquisition—Research—Methodology. 3. Language and languages—Research—Methodology. 4. Literacy—Research—Methodology. I. Leclercq, Pascale, 1977- editor of compilation. II. Edmonds, Amanda, 1979- editor of compilation. III. Hilton, Heather, editor of compilation.
P118.M396 2014
401'.93–dc23 2014004896

British Library Cataloguing in Publication Data
A catalogue entry for this book is available from the British Library.

ISBN-13: 978-1-78309-228-4 (hbk)
ISBN-13: 978-1-78309-227-7 (pbk)

Multilingual Matters
UK: St Nicholas House, 31-34 High Street, Bristol BS1 2AW, UK.
USA: UTP, 2250 Military Road, Tonawanda, NY 14150, USA.
Canada: UTP, 5201 Dufferin Street, North York, Ontario M3H 5T8, Canada.

Website: www.multilingual-matters.com
Twitter: Multi_Ling_Mat
Facebook: https://www.facebook.com/multilingualmatters
Blog: www.channelviewpublications.wordpress.com

Copyright © 2014 Pascale Leclercq, Amanda Edmonds, Heather Hilton and the authors of individual chapters.

All rights reserved. No part of this work may be reproduced in any form or by any means without permission in writing from the publisher.

In the manufacturing process of our books, and to further support our policy, preference is given to printers that have FSC and PEFC Chain of Custody certification. The FSC and/or PEFC logos will appear on those books where full certification has been granted to the printer concerned.

Typeset by Techset Composition India (P) Ltd., Bangalore and Chennai, India.

Contents

Contributors		vii
Acknowledgments		xiii
Preface		xv

Introduction

1 How to Assess L2 Proficiency? An Overview of Proficiency
      Assessment Research   3
   Pascale Leclercq and Amanda Edmonds

Part 1: General Considerations for L2 Assessment

2 Oral Fluency and Spoken Proficiency: Considerations for
      Research and Testing   27
   Heather Hilton

3 Multiple Assessments of Oral Proficiency: Evidence from
      a Collaborative Platform   54
   John Osborne

4 Using Learner Corpora for Testing and Assessing L2 Proficiency   71
   Marcus Callies, María Belén Díez-Bedmar and Ekaterina Zaytseva

Part 2: Language Processing and L2 Proficiency

5 Listening Comprehension: Processing Demands
      and Assessment Issues   93
   Peter Prince

6 A Psycholinguistic Measurement of Second Language
      Proficiency: The Coefficient of Variation   109
   Carrie A. Ankerstein

7 Evaluating the Workings of Bilingual Memory with a
    Translation Recognition Task   122
    *Dominique Bairstow, Jean-Marc Lavaur, Jannika Laxén
    and Xavier Aparicio*

Part 3: Focused Assessment Instruments

8 'Repeat as Much as You Can': Elicited Imitation as a Measure of
    Oral Proficiency in L2 French   143
    *Nicole Tracy-Ventura, Kevin McManus, John M. Norris and
    Lourdes Ortega*

9 Exploring the Acquisition of the French Subjunctive: Local
    Syntactic Context or Oral Proficiency?   167
    *Kevin McManus, Nicole Tracy-Ventura, Rosamond Mitchell,
    Laurence Richard and Patricia Romero de Mills*

10 Testing L2 Listening Proficiency: Reviewing Standardized Tests
    Within a Competence-Based Framework   191
    Naouel Zoghlami

11 Assessing Language Dominance with the Bilingual
    Language Profile   208
    Libby M. Gertken, Mark Amengual and David Birdsong

   Epilogue   226
   Index   228

Contributors

Editors

Pascale Leclercq is currently a Lecturer (maître de conférences) in the English Studies department of Université Paul Valéry Montpellier 3 (France). She teaches EFL, SLA and L2 pedagogy to undergraduate and postgraduate students, and trains future language teachers. Her research interests include the acquisition of temporality by adult L2 learners, the use of nominal anaphora in learner discourse, the role of typology in SLA, L1/L2 comparisons, and research methodology (with a particular focus on the role of proficiency assessment in SLA research).

Amanda Edmonds (PhD, Indiana University) is a Lecturer (maître de conferences) in French as a Foreign Language at the Université de Pau et des Pays de l'Adour (France). She is currently director of the Master's program in French as a Foreign Language, and her teaching includes courses on FFL, SLA and language pedagogy. Her current research has three main focuses: the acquisition of a phraseological competence in an L2, the L2 acquisition of variable structures, and proficiency assessment.

After working as a French teacher and completing a doctorate in the US (Emory University), **Heather Hilton** moved to France, spending 25 years at the Université de Savoie, before moving on to a research position in Paris and now at the Université de Lyon. Her research in foreign language teaching methodology and language acquisition is strongly grounded in socio-cognitive theories of learning and in psycholinguistic theories of language processing and use.

Authors

Mark Amengual (PhD, University of Texas at Austin) is an Assistant Professor in the Department of Languages and Applied Linguistics at the

University of California at Santa Cruz. His research interests focus primarily on experimental phonology and phonetics, cognitive and linguistic aspects of bilingualism, sociolinguistics and language variation.

Carrie Ankerstein is currently a Senior Lecturer in Applied Linguistics in the English Department at Saarland University, Saarbrücken, Germany. She holds a PhD in Psycholinguistics from the University of Sheffield, an MPhil in Applied Linguistics from the University of Cambridge and a BA in German Linguistics from the University of Wisconsin-Madison and the Albert-Ludwigs Universität in Freiburg, Germany. Her research interests include implicit and explicit language processing and SLA.

Xavier Aparicio is currently a Post-doctoral researcher and has a PhD in Cognitive Psychology. His research interests focus on how multilinguals access their mental lexicons, and he is specifically interested in issues of language switching. His applied research focuses, on the one hand, on the benefits of bilingualism with regards to brain functioning and executive functions and, on the other hand, on the processing of audiovisual multilingual information.

Dominique Bairstow received her PhD in cognitive psychology from the University of Montpellier 3 in 2012. Her research focuses mainly on the perception, comprehension and memorization of movies depending on the presence (or not) of subtitles, but also on the type of subtitles used (i.e. different language combinations). Her work takes into account many factors, such as the languages presented on the screen, the viewers' knowledge and the information provided by the movie. Her other line of work explores possibilities of language acquisition through movies and is based on research regarding the multilingual lexicon.

David Birdsong is Professor of French Linguistics and Chair of the Department of French and Italian at The University of Texas at Austin. His research interests include SLA, bilingualism and psycholinguistics. He has published in such journals as *Language, Journal of Memory & Language, Language Learning, Studies in Second Language Acquisition* and *International Review of Applied Linguistics*. Birdsong has also contributed to *The New Handbook of Second Language Acquisition, Handbook of Bilingualism: Psycholinguistic Approaches, The Handbook of Applied Linguistics* and *The Handbook of Educational Linguistics*.

Marcus Callies is Full Professor and Chair of English Linguistics at the University of Bremen, Germany. He received his PhD in English Linguistics with a study on *Information Highlighting in Advanced Learner English* (Benjamins, 2009). He is co-editor of the *International Journal of Learner Corpus Research*, published starting from 2015 with John Benjamins. His main research interests are learner corpus research, discourse-functional and pragmatic aspects of advanced learner varieties, lexico-grammatical variation and English for academic purposes. He is director of the research project 'Lexico-grammatical variation in advanced learner varieties' and compiler of the *Corpus of Academic Learner English* (CALE).

María Belén Díez-Bedmar is Associate Professor at the University of Jaén (Spain). Her research interests include the compilation, analysis and exploitation of learner corpora, language testing and assessment, the learning of English as a foreign language and CMC. She is co-editor of the book *Linking up Contrastive and Learner Corpus Research* (Rodopi, 2008) and a special issue of the *International Journal of Corpus Linguistics* (2014) on the corpus-based description of high-school EFL students' written language. She is involved in international corpus projects such as the *International Corpus of Crosslinguistic Interlanguage* (ICCI) and the *Corpus of Language and Nature* (CLAN).

Libby M. Gertken holds a Research Affiliate-Post Doctoral position in the Department of French and Italian at the University of Texas at Austin. She researches adult SLA and bilingualism. She is particularly interested in syntactic processing in first and second languages, as well as priming methods.

Jean-Marc Lavaur lectures and carries out research in cognitive and media psychology at the University of Montpellier 3, France. His basic research relates to the organization and functioning of the multilingual lexicon (recognition and integration of written and oral forms). His applied research examines the cognitive processing of audiovisual information (particularly in the case of audiovisual programs with subtitles) with respect to the understanding and retention of audiovisual information. His research also focuses on the possibilities of learning languages through movies and, in more general terms, attempts to estimate theoretical, methodological and empirical contributions of cognitive science to the field of film studies and media accessibility.

Jannika Laxén lectures in psychology and communication at the University of Montpellier 2, France, and carries out research in cognitive psychology on the bilingual semantic memory, child bilingualism, and emotion and memory. Her basic research examines the influence of numerous semantic factors on the quality and the speed of translation. Her research focuses also on methodological issues in multilingual research.

Kevin McManus received his PhD in French Linguistics and Second Language Acquisition from Newcastle University and is currently a British Academy Postdoctoral Fellow in the Centre for Language Learning Research,

Department of Education, University of York. His research focuses on second language learning, particularly French, especially form-meaning mapping, crosslinguistic influence, and the role of context in learning. His current research project is a classroom intervention study on French tense and aspect, funded by a British Academy Postdoctoral Fellowship.

Rosamond Mitchell is Professor of Applied Linguistics at the University of Southampton. She trained originally as a teacher of Irish and French but has taught aspects of applied linguistics for many years, at universities in Scotland and England. Her research interests include corpus-based research on SLA, classroom L2 teaching and learning, and foreign language education policy in Anglophone contexts. She is co-author of *Second Language Learning Theories* (3rd edn, 2013), with Florence Myles and Emma Marsden.

John Norris works in the areas of language testing, program evaluation and language pedagogy, and he is particularly interested in task-based language education, meta-analysis, and educational assessment. His recent books explore language teaching (*Task-based Language Teaching: A Reader*), evaluation (*Toward Useful Program Evaluation in College Foreign Language Education*), assessment (*Validity Evaluation in Language Assessment*) and research synthesis (*Synthesizing Research on Language Learning and Teaching*). He speaks and conducts research in German, Spanish and Portuguese, as well as English.

Lourdes Ortega is Professor in the Department of Linguistics at Georgetown University. Her main area of research is in SLA, particularly bilingual, usage-based and educational dimensions of adult language learning in classroom settings. Her most recent book is *Understanding Second Language Acquisition* (revised edn, 2014). She can be contacted at lo3@georgetown.edu.

John Osborne teaches English language and linguistics at the University of Savoie, in Chambéry. His research focuses on the use of learner corpus data in analyzing fluency, complexity and propositional content in L2 oral production. He has recently participated in several European life-long learning projects (WebCEF, CEFcult, IEREST) aimed at developing resources for the assessment of oral proficiency and for intercultural education.

Peter Prince is a Senior Lecturer in Applied Linguistics at the University of Aix-Marseille, where he is also in charge of the listening comprehension course for students in Applied Foreign Languages. He set up the university's self-access centre, which he ran for 12 years until 2009, developing as a result, an interest in autonomy and motivation in second language learning. His other main research interest is second language vocabulary acquisition, with special attention to the development of online resources designed to help students improve their English vocabulary.

Laurence Richard, after finishing an MPhil in SLA at the University of Southampton (looking at NS–NNS interactions in the French undergraduate oral class), continued working there as a Language Teaching Fellow, and is now the Director of the Centre for Language Study in the same institution.

Patricia Romero de Mills received her PhD in Applied Linguistics from the University of Southampton where she currently is a Senior Teaching Fellow (Spanish Language). Her main research interests are centered on pedagogical and philosophical issues concerning language teaching and learning in higher education and, in particular, on the contribution of the Year Abroad to Modern Languages programs and the role of this experience in the development of language students as language specialists and critical beings.

Nicole Tracy-Ventura (PhD, Northern Arizona University) is an Assistant Professor in the Department of World Languages at the University of South Florida (US) where she teaches courses and conducts research on SLA and L2 pedagogy. Much of her work has analyzed language use using methods from corpus linguistics, and she also helped manage the creation of two freely available learner corpora: Langsnap (langsnap.soton.ac.uk: L2 French & Spanish) and SPLLOC 2 (splloc.soton.ac.uk: L2 Spanish). Her work can be found in journals such as *Bilingualism: Language and Cognition, Corpora, System* and in edited collections.

Ekaterina Zaytseva obtained a BA in Linguistics & Intercultural Communication and Methodology of Teaching Foreign Languages at Orel State University, Russia, and a Master of Arts in European Linguistics from Albert-Ludwigs-Universität Freiburg, Germany. She is currently a doctoral researcher in the project 'Lexico-grammatical variation in advanced learner varieties' at the University of Bremen, Germany, working on a PhD dissertation on the expression of contrast in L1 and L2 writing. Her research interests include learner corpus research, English for academic purposes, phraseology, and text linguistics.

Naouel Zoghlami is currently a Lecturer and research assistant at the Human Arts and Sciences Campus of the University of Lorraine, France. She has been involved in English teaching programs in Tunisia and France for almost eight years. She was the coordinator of the listening/speaking courses at the Higher Institute of Languages in Tunis for three years. She has an MA in Applied English Linguistics and her specific research interests include the teaching and testing of L2 listening, strategy instruction and metacognition. She is now pursuing a PhD at the University of Paris 8.

Acknowledgments

We wish to thank Lucile Cadet, Saveria Colonna, Jean-Yves Dommergues, Jonas Granfeldt, Henrik Gyllstad, Florence Myles, Rebekah Rast, Claire Renaud, Andrea Révész and Daniel Véronique for their valuable comments on the work presented here, as well as Inge Bartning for her insightful comments and continuous support for the project. We are also indebted to the EMMA (Etudes Montpelliéraines du Monde Anglophone) research team at University Paul Valéry Montpellier 3, France, who provided the right conditions for the development of this project.

Preface

Language 'proficiency' is a concept that language teachers have been grappling with directly for the past 30 years: how can we help students improve their proficiency (both productive and receptive) in communicative or 'task-based' classrooms, and how can we 'measure' this type of improvement? During this same period, second language acquisition (SLA) researchers have been interested in the emergence of proficiency in a second or foreign language (L2), its characteristics, and possible stages that language learners pass through on their way towards plurilingual competence. And, of course, the assessment of receptive and productive proficiency, both in the oral and written modes, is the bread and butter of the language testing industry, and lies at the heart of the *Common European Reference Framework for Languages*.

This book is an attempt to bring together concrete ideas on identifying and measuring L2 proficiency, from different branches of SLA research. The authors are not testing specialists, but researchers interested in different facets of foreign- and second-language (L2) proficiency, and most particularly in indicators of receptive or productive proficiency that are valid, reliable and easily implemented. We believe that this is the contribution of our volume – a renewal of interest in the criteria of reliability and feasibility in the assessment of L2 proficiency, both of which were sidelined in the performance-testing wave that swept in with the Communicative Approach. The authors of the *European Framework*, for example, declare quite openly that validity is the unique construct used to define the European language 'reference levels': '*Validity* is the concept with which the *Framework* is concerned' (Council of Europe, 2001: 177). Dismissing *reliability* as a mere 'technical term', the authors maintain (rather circuitously) that 'accuracy' of assessment decisions can only be determined by the 'validity of the criteria used' and of the procedures used to determine these criteria (Council of Europe, 2001: 177).

Certainly the *Framework*'s reference levels were painstakingly established (Council of Europe, 2001: 205–216), in an attempt to guarantee the accuracy/validity of the descriptors, but it has not been so easy for language teachers and language-teaching institutions to dismiss questions relating to the reliability and feasibility of implementing these performance-based descriptors. These questions have been addressed at numerous international conferences, and various European projects have been set up in an attempt to improve the reliability of the 'Reference Level' scales or their implementation, including the WebCEF project (summarized in this volume by John Osborne), the SLATE project, CEFLING, as well as projects such as 'What is speaking proficiency?' (WISP, coordinated by the Amsterdam Center for Language and Communication at the Universiteit van Amsterdam).

It therefore seems timely to assemble investigations into L2 proficiency emanating from the various branches of SLA research: psycholinguistic, sociolinguistic, corpus-based and applied linguistics. The chapters that follow are all concerned with indicators of productive or receptive proficiency in a second or foreign language that are precise and valid (often validated experimentally), but also practical to implement – and therefore useful. What can be measured, precisely and objectively, in L2 production and reception? What can one reliably propose in the form of self-assessment questionnaires? Which, among the reliable measures, best reflect overall proficiency? Are there subcomponents of proficiency that constitute particularly valid indicators of L2 level, and, if so, which of these can be easily measured? These chapters offer insights from the SLA research agenda that can also be useful to teachers, and may inspire new avenues of investigation for language-testing specialists.

Heather Hilton
November 2013

Introduction

1 How to Assess L2 Proficiency? An Overview of Proficiency Assessment Research

Pascale Leclercq and Amanda Edmonds

This volume addresses an area of great interest to both language teachers and researchers interested in pedagogy and second language acquisition (SLA), namely how to assess *proficiency* in a second language (L2). For teachers, it is important to be able to assess accurately and reliably the L2 proficiency of their learners, whether for formative evaluation, summative evaluation or within the context of language certification. For researchers, valid proficiency assessment measures are crucial, as without them meaningful interpretation of research results remains elusive (Norris & Ortega, 2003: 717; Pallotti, 2009). In her thorough review of the assessment practices in more than 150 articles published in four major SLA journals, Thomas forcefully argues this point, concluding that 'there is evidence that L2 proficiency is sometimes inadequately assessed in current second language acquisition research. In certain cases, this compromises empirical claims; in many cases, it limits the generalizability of research results' (Thomas, 1994: 330). According to Thomas, and many others, it is important that proficiency assessment measures be *valid* (i.e. testing what they purport to test), *reliable* (i.e. providing trustworthy information) and *practical* (i.e. fitting the needs of their users in terms of ease of implementation). However, two decades after Thomas's call for a better control of the proficiency variable in the field of SLA, authors continue to highlight the difficulties associated with proficiency assessment. Hulstijn *et al.*, for example, point to the lack of reliable level assignment as a general problem in SLA research:

> SLA [...] has frequently simply taken groups of learners at supposedly different levels of ability, conducted cross-sectional research and claimed that the results show development. Yet the levels have been woefully undefined, often crudely labelled 'intermediate' or 'advanced', or 'first

and second year university students' – which means little if anything in developmental terms – and which cannot therefore be interpreted in any meaningful way. (Hulstijn *et al.*, 2010: 16)

Carlsen (2012: 2) deplores the fact that proficiency level remains a 'fuzzy variable' in digital learner corpora: although she admits that most learner corpora developers report on the different levels of proficiency included in their material, she claims, like Hulstijn *et al.*, that 'the levels of proficiency are not always carefully defined, and the claims about proficiency levels are seldom supported by empirical evidence.' (For discussions of proficiency levels, see the chapters in this volume by Tracy-Ventura, McManus, Norris & Ortega, and Callies, Díez-Bedmar & Zaytseva.) Carlsen moreover argues that the reliability of corpus-based research is jeopardized by the fuzziness of the proficiency variable. Thus, despite the clear need for valid, reliable and practical methods of assessing L2 proficiency, it seems that research agendas do not always grant sufficient attention to this issue.

Our volume attempts to respond to this need for additional attention with a presentation of recent research concerning L2 proficiency assessment in L2 English and L2 French. Our aim is to provide a variety of perspectives on L2 proficiency assessment, reflecting the multiple approaches that contribute to the field of SLA research. Some of the chapters present measures of receptive proficiency (those by Prince, Zoghlami, Ankerstein and Bairstow *et al.*, this volume), while others focus on the assessment of productive proficiency (those by Hilton, Osborne, Callies *et al.*, Tracy-Ventura *et al.* & McManus *et al.*, this volume). Although most of the studies presented in this volume deal with L2 learners, Gertken *et al.* and Bairstow *et al.* take a slightly different perspective and present assessment tools for bilingual populations. This volume also includes testing instruments designed to be used in an educative setting (Prince, Zoghlami, Osborne, Gertken *et al.* & Callies *et al.*, this volume), and a range of assessment instruments more specifically designed for SLA researchers: coefficient of variation (Ankerstein, this volume), translation recognition task (Bairstow *et al.*, this volume), elicited imitation (Tracy-Ventura *et al.*, this volume), measurement of oral fluency (Hilton, this volume), and cluster analysis (Callies *et al.*, this volume).

This first chapter is intended to serve as a general introduction to proficiency assessment research within the larger field of SLA and to situate the different contributions to the volume. Our presentation is necessarily brief, and we refer interested readers to Norris and Ortega (2003), Bachman and Palmer (1996), McNamara (2000), Housen and Kuiken (2009) and Hulstijn (2010a, 2010b, 2011) for more complete treatments of the topic. Our own presentation will begin with a contextualization of the issue of L2 proficiency, followed by a discussion of the key concepts used in the fields of SLA and L2 proficiency research. We will then provide a preview of the different contributions to the present volume.

L2 Proficiency: A Moving Target

One of the challenges facing teachers, researchers, language testers and students interested in L2 proficiency is the defining of what it actually means to be proficient in an L2. Many proposals have been put forth, each of which is tied to a particular theoretical stance on language acquisition. The relationship between SLA theory and proficiency is clearly highlighted by Norris and Ortega (2003: 723–729) in their review of L2 proficiency from a generative, an interactionist and an emergentist perspective. As noted by these authors, 'what counts as acquisition is so dependent on the theoretical premises of the research domain that the same measurement data may be interpreted as evidence of acquisition or the lack thereof, depending on the theoretical approach adopted' (2003: 728). In addition to theoretical stance, conceptions of L2 proficiency are dependent on what we believe knowing an L2 actually entails (i.e. model of L2 competence).

Conceptions of L2 proficiency

Models of L2 competence – that is, models of what constitutes L2 proficiency – have undergone numerous changes over the past several decades. In the realm of language testing and assessment, Lado's (1961: 25–29) model of language proficiency prepared the way for language teaching and testing for decades to come. In it, he describes the intersections between four language 'elements' (pronunciation, grammatical structure, lexicon and cultural meaning) and four language 'skills' (speaking, listening, writing and reading). He acknowledges that learners' language development may occur at a different pace in the four skills, and considers 'the degree of achievement' in each of these separate skills as a variable to be tested. He also mentions 'the ability to translate' as a fifth skill, but one that should be tested 'as an end in itself and not as a way to test the mastery of language' (1961: 26). Most language textbooks and language tests are still organized today around these concepts. The year 1961 also saw the first publication of the now classic article by Carroll (1961), in which he identified fundamental considerations for the testing of L2 proficiency. In that article, Carroll argued that L2 competence included both *knowledge* of the language system and *facility* in its use, and he championed the use of both discrete-point and integrative test items in order to test both aspects (see later for a definition of these concepts). The inclusion of *facility* in his conception of L2 proficiency is particularly noteworthy, as it foreshadows the focus on learners' language-processing capacities that has recently come back to the forefront in language-learning theory.

In the field of linguistics and, later, in the field of SLA research, numerous models of language competence have been proposed. If, in the middle of the 20th century, certain linguists focused quasi-exclusively on the knowledge of grammatical structures as an indication of the mastery of a language (influenced by Chomsky's 1965 term *linguistic competence*), the publication of Hymes' (1972) article on communicative competence called this narrow interpretation of the notion of 'competence' into question, insisting on the pragmatic aspects of language use. Canale and Swain (1980) attempted a typology of the skills involved in communicative competence in a second or foreign language, particularly emphasizing its pragmatic and strategic sub-components. For them, communicative L2 competence involves grammatical and sociolinguistic competence, as well as strategic competence ('the compensatory communication strategies to be used when there is a breakdown in one of the other competencies' [1980: 27]). The importance of social and communicative (in addition to purely linguistic) competence has been more recently stressed in the *Common European Framework of Reference for Languages* (CEFR, Council of Europe, 2001), a highly influential statement of European language policy, which is solidly grounded in these early sociolinguistic models of communicative competence. Indeed, it contains functional descriptors of 'general and communicative language competences' (2001: 9), including descriptors covering what Canale and Swain (1980) referred to as strategic competence (Council of Europe, 2001: Ch. 4), as well as numerous proficiency scales examining aspects of grammatical, sociolinguistic, pragmatic and cultural competence (Council of Europe, 2001: Ch. 3 and 5) to describe learners' ability to produce, comprehend, interact in, and mediate their L2. (See Hulstijn, 2010b, and the recent *EUROSLA Monographs Series* edited by Bartning *et al.*, 2010, for numerous studies examining the CEFR.) This document has given rise to interest and debate among policy makers, testers, teachers and researchers alike, and in many European countries, the widespread application of the CEFR has constituted a turning point in teaching and assessment practices.

This brief review mentions but a sampling of some of the different conceptions of language competence. It is important to note that the changes described here have been felt far beyond the restricted circle of those researchers interested in modeling L2 competence: they have modified our conception of what deserves our attention in language classrooms and, more importantly for the current volume, they have required changes in our conception of what it means to be proficient in an L2 and how to assess such proficiency (see Richer, 2012: 38, for a presentation of the evolution of the concept of *competence* as it relates to language teaching).

Defining proficiency

Higgs (1984: 12, cited by Kramsch, 1987: 356) defined proficiency as 'the ability to function effectively in the language in real-life contexts,' whereas Thomas (1994: 330, note 1) considered proficiency to correspond to 'a person's overall competence and ability to perform in L2'. More recently, Hulstijn (2010b: 186) has taken issue with the definition proposed by Thomas, finding it ambiguous because it raises the question of how to define *competence* and *ability*. In his 2010 articles and in subsequent publications, Hulstijn (2011, 2012) has set about the task of providing a more comprehensive definition of the notion of language proficiency. His 2011 article, in particular, contains a detailed discussion of this concept. What is particularly interesting is that Hulstijn's definition covers both native speakers' and learners' language proficiency, including linguistic as well as cognitive competences. The definition begins as follows:

> ...*language proficiency* is the extent to which an individual possesses the linguistic cognition necessary to function in a given communicative situation, in a given modality (listening, speaking, reading, or writing). Linguistic cognition is the combination of the representation of linguistic information (knowledge of form-meaning mappings) and the ease with which linguistic information can be processed (skill). Form-meaning mappings pertain to both the literal and pragmatic meanings of forms (in decontextualized and socially-situated language use, respectively). (Italics in the original, Hulstijn, 2011: 242)

He goes on to specify that language proficiency comprises peripheral and core components. Peripheral components include metacognitive competences, such as metalinguistic knowledge and strategic competence, whereas core components refer to linguistic cognition (in the domains of phonetics, phonology, morphosyntax etc.). He moreover claims that linguistic cognition (for native and non-native speakers alike) can be divided into basic language cognition (BLC) and higher language cognition (HLC), which he defines as follows.

(1) *Basic language cognition*: '(a) the largely implicit, unconscious knowledge in the domains of phonetics, prosody, phonology, morphology and syntax; (b) the largely explicit, conscious knowledge in the lexical domain (form-meaning mappings), *in combination with* (c) the automaticity with which these types of knowledge can be processed. BLC is restricted to frequent lexical items and frequent grammatical structures, that is, to lexical items and morphosyntactic structures that may occur in any communicative situation, common to all adult L1-ers, regardless of age, literacy, or educational level.' (Italics in the original, 2011: 230)
(2) *Higher language cognition*: 'the complement or extension of BLC. HLC is identical to BLC, except that (a) in HLC, utterances that can be understood or produced contain low-frequency lexical items or uncommon morphosyntactic structures, and (b) HLC utterances pertain to written as well as spoken language. In other words, HLC utterances are lexically and grammatically more complex (and often longer) than BLC utterances and they need not be spoken.' (2011: 231)

Hulstijn's definition of language proficiency, encompassing peripheral and core (HLC + BLC) elements, and covering the competence of both L1 and L2 speakers, is the one we feel to be most relevant for the current volume. It should be noted that in the different contributions, the term *proficiency* will sometimes be used to refer to overall language proficiency, as in Hulstijn's definition, and at other times to proficiency with respect to a specific component (e.g. listening proficiency).

Evidence used to evaluate L2 proficiency: Different practices and approaches

Discussions of L2 proficiency also vary as a function of the types of evidence that teachers and researchers have used to evaluate it. One recent and influential SLA-oriented approach focuses on the components of complexity, accuracy and fluency (CAF) in L2 proficiency (Housen & Kuiken, 2009; Housen et al., 2012). These variables have been used to measure progress in language learning and have been under close scrutiny in applied linguistics research since the early 1980s. Skehan (1989, cited by Housen & Kuiken, 2009: 461) was the first to propose CAF as three key features of L2 proficiency. The following definitions are provided by Housen and Kuiken (2009: 461):

> Complexity has thus been commonly characterized as 'the extent to which the language produced in performing a task is elaborate and varied' (Ellis, 2003: 340), accuracy as the ability to produce error-free speech, and fluency as the ability to process the L2 with 'native-like rapidity' (Lennon, 1990: 390) or 'the extent to which the language produced in performing a task manifests pausing, hesitation, or reformulation' (Ellis, 2003: 342).

Housen and Kuiken (2009: 463) note that the use of these notions to assess L2 proficiency is not uncontroversial. If accuracy is an easily comprehended concept, and a widely used one in educative contexts, its operationalization as a proficiency measure remains problematic, in so far as it implies a comparison with a native speaker norm (which is a fuzzy notion in itself, native speakers' speech being extremely variable and influenced by speakers' literacy, as pointed out by Lado, 1961: 26; Davies, 2003 and Hulstijn, 2011). Complexity is an ambiguous concept that can be applied variously to the task (task difficulty being more or less equated with task complexity), to the linguistic properties of the language being used (but it remains unclear to what extent complex linguistic structures entail greater processing complexity) or to language processing itself. Fluency, the third member of this trilogy, covers a variety of dimensions related to the ease with which a speaker uses a language. However, a consensus as to which of the many dimensions involved should be taken into consideration in judging L2 proficiency has yet to be reached (but see Hilton, this volume, for a promising proposal on this issue). Moreover, in interlanguage development, accuracy, complexity and fluency (linguistic and cognitive) may interfere with one another: the focus a learner places on fluency may be detrimental to accuracy, or vice versa. The implementation of CAF indicators for L2 proficiency assessment may therefore be difficult for teachers, researchers and learners, although Martin et al. (2010) propose a model of analysis ('DEMfad') that seeks to trace changes in developmental patterns by looking at the developmental route in a given domain [D] from emergence [E] to mastery [M] with respect to the frequency [f], accuracy [a] and distribution [d] of forms.

In addition to the CAF features, other types of evidence have been used to investigate L2 proficiency. In SLA research, corpus-based analyses of learner varieties have led to fine-grained descriptions of indicators of developmental stages in SLA. Although these descriptions are aimed at characterizing the interlanguage of learners (or learner varieties) for research, rather than for assessment purposes, pedagogical applications are welcome: Perdue (1993: 3) states that one of the aims of the European Science Foundation project was to 'describe and explain the acquisition process in an everyday social setting, so that pedagogical intervention may be better informed.' He also invites readers to use the longitudinal studies proposed in the two volumes that gathered together the results of the project as a basis for language training programmes (Perdue, 1993: xiii). Bartning and Schlyter (2004: 297) conclude their presentation of the six stages of L2 acquisition (based on the morphosyntactic analysis of a corpus of productions by Swedish learners of French) by stating that these stages could be useful to researchers and teachers who want to determine learners' grammatical level.[1]

Studies focusing on L2 processing have proposed various performance features that may constitute reliable indicators of L2 proficiency level, including working memory capacity in the L2 (Cook, 2001), reaction times in lexical decision tasks (Ankerstein; Bairstow et al., this volume), and brain activation patterns, as measured by evoked potentials (van Hell & Tokowicz, 2010). The L2 mental lexicon has also received a good deal of attention, with researchers examining the potential for measures such as vocabulary size (Laufer et al., 2004: 224; Meara, 1996) and lexical diversity (Malvern & Richards, 2002: 95) to serve as reliable indicators of overall L2 proficiency.

Defining Key Concepts

There are many concepts that are of importance when it comes to discussing L2 proficiency. In this section, we set out to define several such concepts, many of which will be taken up by one or more of the contributions to this volume.

Validity, reliability and practicality

In the introduction to this chapter, we mentioned the meta-analysis conducted by Thomas (1994), and her conclusion that L2 proficiency measures and tests need to be valid, reliable and practical. These concepts have and will come up numerous times over the course of our presentation, and will continue to be evoked throughout the volume. Validity, reliability and practicality are indeed central concerns in L2 proficiency assessment. In the SLA context, the question of validity – that is, that an instrument measures what it purports to measure – has particular importance, in so far as judgments of validity condition the trustworthiness of SLA research (Hulstijn, 2010b: 187). In the field of language testing, Carroll describes the ideal English language proficiency test as one that

> [...] should make it possible to differentiate, to the greatest possible extent, levels of performance in those dimensions of performance which are relevant to the kinds of situations in which the examinees will find themselves after being selected on the basis of the test. The validity of the test can be established not solely on the basis of whether it appears to involve a good sample of the English language but more on the basis of whether it predicts success in the learning tasks and social situations to which the examinees will be exposed. (Carroll, 1972 [1961]: 319)

Valid L2 proficiency assessment practices should ideally predict the capacity of a learner to perform a given task in a given social context. However, in practice, questions of validity are not always addressed by testers, teachers and researchers. For example, Carlsen (2012: 3) observes that '[w]e cannot take for granted that a given proficiency scale is a valid representation of the underlying theoretical construct, or that the way language proficiency is described at different levels actually represents stages of second language acquisition.' In the current volume, Zoghlami's article specifically addresses the issue of construct validity; working within a competence-based framework, she sets out to assess the validity of the listening portions of two well-known norm-referenced measures of English proficiency.

While it is essential that the validity of assessment measures not simply be taken for granted, Bachman and Palmer (1996: 19) also point to the crucial importance of test reliability, which they define as 'consistency of measurement' across testing conditions; a test-taker should obtain a similar score with different versions of the same test, or with different raters, in order for the test to be reliable. Bachman and Palmer nevertheless remind us that if test reliability is essential for a test to be valid and useful, it is not a sufficient condition for either:

> Suppose, for example, that we needed a test for placing individuals into different levels in an academic writing course. A multiple-choice test of

grammatical knowledge might yield very consistent or reliable scores, but this would not be sufficient to justify using this test as a placement test for a writing course. This is because grammatical knowledge is only one aspect of the ability to use language to perform academic writing tasks. (Bachman & Palmer, 1996: 23)

The issue of reliability is tackled in various chapters included in this volume, and in particular in the chapter by Osborne, which reports on a collaborative platform for L2 oral proficiency assessment.

Another key feature of language assessment is practicality, defined by Bachman and Palmer (1996: 35) as the ratio between available resources and required resources. If required resources exceed available resources, the test cannot be considered practical. Resources include human resources (scorers, raters, clerical support), material resources (rooms, equipment, materials), time (development time and time for specific tasks such as designing, writing, administering, scoring, analyzing), as well as the associated cost. Practicality is often the most immediate concern for teachers and researchers, and is taken into account in several of the contributions to this volume (see, in particular, those by Gertken *et al.*, this volume and Tracy-Ventura *et al.*, this volume for presentations of assessment measures designed with particular attention paid to practicality).

Assessment, measurement and testing

As seen earlier in this chapter, *proficiency* refers to a multicomponent phenomenon underlying one's knowledge of and ability to use a language, making it particularly difficult to evaluate. Proficiency evaluation is further complicated by differences in evaluative scope (e.g. general versus specific performances or knowledge) and differences in context (e.g. research versus classroom contexts). In terms of scope, teachers and researchers may either need a general proficiency measure covering all components that make up language proficiency, or a specific proficiency measure to assess a particular skill. This is often the case for SLA researchers, who for example do not use the same kinds of measurements for a project analyzing speaking versus one in which listening is the object of study. The evaluation of L2 proficiency also depends on testing objectives, and the context in which it is carried out; proficiency evaluation in an institutional or academic context may not involve the same stakes or objectives as proficiency evaluation in a research context or in an immigration policy context (see Clahsen, 1985, for a reflection on the segregative power of language testing). The question then is how to refer to the evaluation of language proficiency, with the terms *assessment*, *measurement* and *testing* all being used in the literature.

Of these three terms, *assessment* is the most general, and we will use it as an umbrella term referring to the different types of proficiency evaluation.

Within assessment, we will distinguish between *measurement*, on the one hand, and *testing*, on the other. We consider *measurement* to be concerned with the quantification of a knowledge or skill, which may involve determining the size and/or extent of a change (often in response to a treatment, usually in an experimental – SLA – context). Although Chapelle and Plakans (2012: 241) claim that 'both the terms "test" and "assessment" are used to denote the systematic gathering of language-related behavior in order to make inferences about language ability and capacity for language use on other occasions', we will use *testing* to refer to assessment processes involving institutionalized instruments and procedures (such as the TOEFL for L2 English or the DELF/DALF for L2 French). Such tests are often, but not always, norm-referenced.

Defining assessment practices

Assessment practices aim at testing one or several components of language proficiency. Taken by itself, any single assessment practice has its limits, and can only tell us so much about the L2 proficiency of a given speaker. As stated by Byrnes (1987: 45), 'since human behavior eludes exhaustive treatment, each assessment tool makes its own limiting statements about criteria'. It is important, then, to know what any given assessment tool can demonstrate, as well as the limits and drawbacks of each. Lado (1961: 27) and Hulstijn (2010b) both discussed opposing sets of features for test format (see points (3) a. and b. below) and test scoring and administration (points (3) c. and d. below) that can be useful in defining assessment practices:

(3) a. discrete-point versus integrative assessment
 b. direct versus indirect assessment
 c. objective versus subjective assessment
 d. group testing versus individual assessment

The first two of these features concern the types of items selected for a given assessment tool. Discrete-point items, which 'aim at profiling the learner's language performance in terms of differential linguistic patternings' (De Jong & Verhoeven, 1992: 8) are opposed to integrative ones, which target 'a global interpretation of language performance' (De Jong & Verhoeven, 1992: 9). This distinction was already present in both Carroll (1972 [1961]) and Lado (1961), with Lado speaking of testing 'integrated skills versus [separate] elements of language' (1961: 27). As pointed out by Hulstijn (2010b), discrete-point tests claim to measure a single type of knowledge, whereas integrative ones are designed to evaluate a mixture of knowledge or abilities. Hulstijn (2010b: 188) also highlights a distinction between direct and indirect testing (3b), which concerns to what extent the assessment type places restrictions on the participant's response. According to Hulstijn, 'direct tests leave test-takers more freedom in responding than indirect tests; they are called "direct" because performance is less mediated by response constraints.'

Cloze tests, which heavily constrain the test-takers' answers, are an example of indirect tests (and they are also good means of assessing a speaker's lexical, collocational, grammatical and pragmatic knowledge, as advocated by Tremblay, 2011), while 'writing an essay on a self-chosen topic' constitutes a direct test (as well as a form of integrative testing).

Assessment practices also differ in terms of scoring (3c). When scoring requires a judgment on the part of the assessor, Lado (1961: 28), for example, speaks of subjective tests, which he opposes to objective ones, for which scoring can be done mechanically without the subjective intervention of a rater. Self-assessment constitutes one example of subjective assessment (see Oscarson, 1989, for a detailed review, and Gertken *et al.*, this volume, for a discussion of self-assessment procedures to evaluate language dominance). Although the scoring of objective tests is often reliable and relatively efficient, it is crucial that the items that make up the test be valid. Unfortunately, the validity of items (particularly discrete-point, indirect ones, which can in general be objectively scored) is not always established. Lado sums up the sometimes tense relationship between objectivity and validity in the following way: 'often we have to choose between more apparent validity but less objectivity and more objectivity but less apparent validity' (1961: 29). The final feature mentioned concerns test administration, and opposes group testing to individual assessment (3d). Choice of test administration type is in part driven by practical considerations. As mentioned by Lado (1961: 28–30), the constraints of the educative system impose group testing most of the time. The same is often true for researchers who want to assess the proficiency level of the participants in their studies: individual testing is time-consuming and cannot always be implemented.

Examples of assessment practices

Although proficiency assessment can take many forms, in this section, we will turn our attention to two assessment practices that have received significant attention: proficiency rating scales (such as the CEFR) and corpus-based language assessment practices. According to Carlsen (2012: 3), a proficiency rating scale may be defined as

> a series of ascending bands of proficiency. It may cover the whole conceptual range of learner proficiency, or it may just cover the range of proficiency relevant to the sector or institution concerned' [Council of Europe (CoE) 2001: 40]. The bottom and top, as well as the different bands on the scale, such as 'beginner', 'intermediate', or 'advanced' need to be defined in terms of language descriptors for different formal or functional traits in order to yield meaningful information, and to represent a basis for reliable level assignment. A proficiency level is a band which allows some variation, but still, a given level has some characteristics that distinguish it from the level below and the one above.

As Hulstijn (2007) has highlighted, the CEFR descriptors are fairly subjective, and have given rise to assessment tools that require a subjective interpretation on the part of the judges (the learners themselves in the case of self-evaluation[2], or an external assessor – a teacher, for example) to decide whether the criteria for a particular level have been met by the learner in his or her performance. As is the case for any subjective assessment practice, the question then arises as to whether different raters assess a given performance in the same way. In other words, how reliably do multiple raters assess a given performance? In the case of the collaborative assessment of oral proficiency with respect to CEFR levels, Osborne (this volume) argues that inter-rater reliability can be measured in terms of both *consistency* (do different raters independently assign similar rankings among learners?) and *consensus* (does a group of raters agree as to which level to assign a given performance?), and he points out that reliability in the application of the CEFR is a long-standing concern for teachers and researchers who are involved in using the framework.

Although not the case for the CEFR (see Fulcher, 2004, for a detailed presentation and critique of its development), a proficiency scale should ideally be based on extensive corpus work that describes stages and paths of (instructed and natural) L2 development for reception and production skills. There has, moreover, been much recent attention given to the use of corpora in language proficiency assessment (e.g. Carlsen, 2012). In their contribution to this volume, Callies *et al.* highlight the role corpora can play in language testing and assessment and show that there are three main approaches using corpora in proficiency assessment: those that are corpus-informed, corpus-based or corpus-driven.

Corpus-based work on developmental stages and pathways has been – and continues to be – one of the central preoccupations of many researchers in the field of SLA, particularly with respect to the L2 development of morphosyntax. For L2 French, Bartning and Schlyter (2004) described six stages of development in Swedish learners' L2 French (see also Bartning *et al.*, 2009, for a proposal for two additional stages). Of the many projects on L2 English, we will mention the recent English Profile project[3], the aim of which is to create a 'profile' or set of Reference Level Descriptions for English linked to the CEFR using the Cambridge English Profile corpus. Hawkins and Buttery (2009), for example, attempt to define learner profiles by identifying the correct and incorrect linguistic properties (or positive and negative 'criterial features') associated with a given L2 level, with the intention of adding grammatical and lexical details to the largely functional CEFR descriptors.

The English Profile project is one of many projects associated with the recently created SLATE (Second Language Acquisition and Testing in Europe) research network.[4] According to their website, SLATE brings together researchers interested in 'the relationship between second/foreign language development, levels of second-language proficiency, and language testing research.' Their research currently focuses on matching the CEFR levels with a description of learners' interlanguage at various stages of acquisition, in order to address the following research question: which linguistic features of learner performance (for a given target language) are typical at each of the six CEF levels? Thus, many of the various SLATE-affiliated research projects integrate proficiency scales (in the form of the CEFR) with corpus-based research, in an attempt to further analyze the CEFR, in order to make the reference levels more reliably identifiable. Examples of such projects include the Norwegian Profile, linguistic features of the communicative CEFR levels in written L2 French, the English Profile, CEFLING – Linguistic Basis of the Common European Framework for L2 English and L2 Finnish, and so on (see contributions in Bartning et al., 2010, for descriptions of and results from the various projects).[5] Although this research is promising, authors such as Hulstijn have expressed reservations about the feasibility of equating the CEFR levels with the developmental paths followed by L2 learners:

> [T]he levels in the CEFR are associated with both proficiency and development. It is crucial, however, to keep proficiency and development apart. A close examination of the definitions of the B2, C1 and C2 levels in the activity and the competence scales reveals that performance at these higher levels requires higher intellectual skills. (Hulstijn, 2011: 240).

Indeed, the descriptors for the B2, C1 and C2 levels imply competence that may only be attained – in the L1 and L2 alike – by highly educated individuals with higher intellectual skills. Researchers are only just beginning to explore the implications of such observations with respect to L2 proficiency assessment (Bartning et al., 2010).

What the Current Volume Contributes

As conceptions of L2 proficiency continue to be reshaped over time, new evaluation tools must inevitably be proposed to accommodate the various definitions of what it means to be proficient in an L2. These tools will need to respect concerns of construct validity and reliability, but also be easy to administer and grade, in order to respond to the needs of language teachers and researchers alike. Thus, the principal aim of this volume is to narrow the gap between SLA research and language teaching by proposing concrete applications of advancements in SLA research for both pedagogical and research-based applications. The different contributions to this volume adopt different standpoints (including both more general and very focused considerations, as well as clearly psycholinguistic concerns) and suggest various types of tools – some complex, some much simpler – all used to assess different aspects of L2 proficiency.

16 Introduction

As evoked in the previous sections, the evaluation of language proficiency raises numerous questions (relevant chapters in this volume are indicated in parentheses):

- Can a single measure significantly predict overall L2 proficiency? (see Tracy-Ventura *et al.* on elicited imitation).
- Which linguistic and psycholinguistic criteria constitute valid indicators of learners' proficiency? (Ankerstein; Bairstow *et al.*; McManus *et al.*).
- Is it possible to provide a description of/to profile learners' productions at various proficiency levels? (Callies *et al.*; Hilton; Osborne).
- How does proficiency relate to language dominance in bilingual populations? (Gertken *et al.*).
- What kind of language test is appropriate for the assessment L2 learners' comprehension and production skills in a broad, competence-based framework? (Osborne; Prince; Zoghlami).
- What constructs do norm-referenced language tests tap into? (Zoghlami).

Such are the questions, among others, that are involved when it comes to assessing, measuring and testing language proficiency, and that are addressed by the chapters included in this volume. We have organized the current volume into three main parts, highlighting the variety of perspectives on L2 proficiency assessment adopted by the contributors. The first part (*General considerations for L2 assessment*) groups three chapters (Hilton; Osborne; Callies *et al.*) that use examples of assessment instruments to take a wider methodological perspective on L2 proficiency assessment. The second part (*Language processing and L2 proficiency*) includes three chapters (Prince; Ankerstein; Bairstow *et al.*) focusing on language processing and what it entails for L2 proficiency assessment. Finally, the third part (*Focused assessment instruments*) combines four chapters that explore specific second-language proficiency assessment tools (McManus *et al.* on the subjunctive; Tracy Ventura *et al.* on elicited imitation; Zoghlami on standardized tests; Gertken *et al.* on the Bilingual Language Profile).

Part 1: General Considerations for L2 Assessment

Part 1, *General Considerations for L2 Assessment*, includes three chapters that use various assessment methodologies as a basis for a larger reflection on the evaluation of L2 proficiency and what it entails for SLA researchers and L2 teachers.

Hilton

Hilton's chapter aims at showing how a detailed analysis of real-time speech by L2 speakers with different overall proficiency levels can contribute to the debate on the *reliable* evaluation of spoken production. Hilton provides a thorough and informative presentation of fluency in L2 oral production, supported by well-documented theoretical arguments and numerous concrete examples, as well as an inventory of the characteristics of oral production as recorded in a parallel oral corpus of L1 and L2 French and English. The rigorous analysis of the corpus data highlights several characteristics that may be used as indications of spoken proficiency level. Of the numerous temporal fluency measurements examined, it was clause-internal hesitations that were found to be the most promising in order to distinguish among the different fluency levels contained in the corpus.

Osborne

Osborne's chapter addresses the issue of inter-rater agreement in proficiency assessment, with a report on WebCEF, a large-scale collaborative project on the assessment of oral and written production in a foreign language, using the proficiency scales provided by the CEFR. Osborne explores whether evaluators understand the CEFR descriptors in the same way. He questions the possibility of reliable assessment when the given proficiency scale includes descriptors that require a subjective judgment on the part of the assessor. The chapter presents two analyses: one that looks at the question of inter-rater reliability with respect to a subset of productions that have been rated by multiple raters, and a second that examines how more and less experienced raters may change their ratings of the same production.

Callies, Díez-Bedmar and Zaytseva

In this chapter, Callies and colleagues present the ways in which learner corpora can be used in the assessment of L2 proficiency in writing tasks. After a review of learner corpora research (LCR) and the *corpus-informed, corpus-based* and *corpus-driven* approaches, the authors present two examples of what LCR can bring to the larger field of language testing and assessment. The first example presents a learner corpus of English essays written by Spanish learners in the University Entrance Examination at the University of Jaén, Spain. The corpus was error-tagged and the essays were graded by two expert raters with the CEFR proficiency scales. The authors outline the variety of proficiency levels within the same institutional status, and focus on the negative linguistic properties defining each level. The second example describes how the Corpus of Academic Learner English (CALE) can be used to operationalize 'positive linguistic properties' (in this case, language- and register-specific linguistic descriptors) to assess writing proficiency in an academic context. The authors focus on the use of reporting verbs as a feature of written academic prose. They detail how they select the relevant linguistic descriptors within the corpus, and apply a cluster analysis to assign a proficiency level to individual papers.

Part 2: Language Processing and L2 Proficiency

Part 2, *Language Processing and L2 Proficiency*, includes three chapters that examine L2 processing, both in terms of the demands it places on the learners (see, in particular, Prince's chapter), but also with respect to how measures of L2 processing may be used to devise innovative L2 proficiency assessment tools.

Prince

Prince's study is classroom-based and examines two comprehension restitution tasks (dictogloss and summarizing a news bulletin) to determine their respective processing demands, so as to decide which is best suited to assess the listening proficiency of students in a French university. After a discussion of the criteria to be taken into account when selecting a valid listening test, Prince proposes a thorough description of the nature of the listening proficiency construct. He then presents his study, involving ten students who were tested with the dictogloss and the summarizing tasks, as well as a word recognition task, to examine the contribution of word recognition to performance. His results show that the dictogloss task places particularly high demands on working memory, and that the summarizing task, which uses higher-order cognitive skills, is more appropriate to assess the listening proficiency of higher-education students.

Ankerstein

In her chapter, Ankerstein examines the automaticity of lexical access in an L1 and an L2. According to the author, it is likely that L2 proficiency will impact the automaticity with which an L2 speaker accesses an L2 lexical item. In other words, with more experience and greater proficiency, a learner's lexical retrieval should become both faster and more efficient. In order to test this hypothesis, Ankerstein administered a semantically primed visual lexical decision task to native speakers and to higher-proficiency L2 speakers of English, and compared not only their response times and error rates, but also the coefficient of variation (as a measure of efficiency) between participant groups. The coefficient of variation for response times is the standard deviation divided by mean response time and has been argued to reflect qualitative differences in language processing (namely, automatization). Ankerstein's results showed that the higher-proficiency L2 speakers demonstrated coefficients of variation that were not statistically different from those found for the native speakers. Coefficient of variation as a measurement of L2 language-processing efficiency appears to be a potentially promising tool for SLA researchers.

Bairstow, Lavaur, Laxén and Aparicio

The chapter by Bairstow and her colleagues begins with an overview of several models of bilingual memory. They then present the results from a pilot study for a translation recognition task, which the authors hypothesize should be sensitive to different levels of bilingual proficiency. For the translation recognition task, a participant saw two words on a computer screen and then had to decide whether they were translation equivalents. Twenty-five

French L1–English L2 speakers were recruited for the task, and the results showed that the ability to create links within memory between two languages (as measured by accuracy scores) was significantly correlated with self-reported L2 proficiency.

Part 3: Focused Assessment Instruments

In Part 3, *Focused Assessment Instruments*, four chapters detail various proficiency assessment tools used in various contexts, including SLA research, the language testing/educative field and wider social contexts.

Tracy-Ventura, McManus, Norris and Ortega

Tracy-Ventura and her co-authors present an elicited imitation task designed to assess global L2 French proficiency in SLA research contexts. The authors begin with a thorough review of the use of elicited imitation in SLA research before presenting the validation procedure devised for the French version of an elicited imitation task developed by Ortega *et al.* (1999). Twenty-nine non-native speakers of French completed the 30-item task. Administration time was 9 minutes, 15 seconds, and scoring time ranged from 10 to 15 minutes per task, making the task relatively fast to administer and easy to score. In addition to meeting the criterion of practicality, the results indicated that the task was reasonably valid and reliable. It is also of note that this French elicited imitation task is the newest in a series of similar measures that have already been developed and tested for five other L2s, thus allowing for crosslinguistic comparisons of L2 proficiency.

McManus, Tracy-Ventura, Mitchell, Richard and Romero de Mills

McManus and his colleagues present an SLA study in which they examined an aspect of French morphosyntax that shows some variation, namely the subjunctive. The authors looked into the role of proficiency level (as measured by the elicited imitation task presented in Tracy-Ventura *et al.*, this volume) and of local syntactic context on the acquisition of the French subjunctive by 23 English-speaking learners. Participants completed three different tasks, and the results showed that although local syntactic context was not significant, subjunctive use in elicited production could be taken as a positive indicator of advanced proficiency.

Zoghlami

Zoghlami directly examines questions of construct validity for the listening comprehension sections of two norm-referenced tests of L2 English proficiency (the *Oxford Placement Test*, OPT, and the *First Certificate in English*, FCE). She uses a competence-based framework inspired from Buck (2001) to see to what extent the listening sections of these two tests can function as predictors of overall listening proficiency. The first part of her analysis is dedicated to defining the listening constructs underlying both tests, so as to determine which test best suits the needs of test users in a competence-based framework.

Her results show that the FCE measures a larger set of listening skills than the OPT, which mainly focuses on segmenting and sound discrimination skills, without accounting for higher-order listening skills. Her analysis therefore favors the FCE over the OPT as a measure of proficiency as it requires linguistic, but also discursive, pragmatic and sociolinguistic knowledge.

Gertken, Amengual and Birdsong

In the last chapter of this volume, Gertken and her colleagues present the BLP (Bilingual Language Profile), a self-report questionnaire used to assess language dominance in bilinguals in a large variety of contexts. Gertken *et al.* define language dominance as a construct including proficiency-related components, such as the differences in a bilingual person's competence and processing ability in two languages, as well as psychosocial factors (attitude to language.) The BLP instrument seeks to assess language dominance, which is conceived of as a continuum, by tapping into these three components. After describing the existing self-report language dominance questionnaires (the Bilingual Dominance Scale (BDS), the Language Experience and Proficiency Questionnaire (LEAP-Q), and the Self-Report Classification Tool (SRCT)), the authors describe the piloting, testing and validation procedure for their instrument.

Conclusion

We hope that the different contributions brought together in this volume will provide language teachers and researchers with new insight into what it means to be proficient in a language, not only with respect to morphosyntax and lexis, but also in relation to language processing. The variety of tools and guidelines for the assessment of L2 proficiency contained in the following chapters should serve to enhance the reliability of SLA research, as well as to improve assessment practices in pedagogical and broader social contexts. Nonetheless, the selection of a L2 proficiency assessment tool is to be undertaken with caution, as so clearly expressed by Hulstijn:

> choosing an LP [language proficiency] test for an SLA study is not a simple matter. Given the goal, research questions and theoretical embedding of their SLA studies, researchers must reflect on how to define LP as a human attribute, taking central notions from psychometrics, linguistics and psychology into account, before choosing an LP test. (Hulstijn, 2010b: 185)

Notes

(1) 'We also think that, whatever their status, these stages will be very useful for researchers and teachers who would like to determine the grammatical level of a given learner.' (Bartning & Schlyter, 2004: 297, our translation.)

(2) See in particular the self-assessment tool developed in the Portfolio, which allows learners to self-assess by responding to a selection of can-do descriptors in the first person (see http://elp.ecml.at/UsingtheELP/tabid/2323/language/en-GB/Default.aspx).
(3) See http://www.englishprofile.org/
(4) See http://www.slate.eu.org/index.htm
(5) For a full list and description of projects, see http://www.slate.eu.org/index.htm

References

Bachman, L.F. and Palmer, A.S. (1996) *Language Testing in Practice*. Oxford: Oxford University Press.
Bartning, I. and Schlyter, S. (2004) Itinéraires acquisitionnels et stades de développement en français L2. *Journal of French Language Studies* 14, 281–299.
Bartning, I., Forsberg Lundell, F. and Hancock, V. (2009) Resources and obstacles in very advanced L2 French: Formulaic language, information structure and morphosyntax. *EUROSLA Yearbook* 9, 185–211.
Bartning, I., Martin, M. and Vedder, I. (eds) (2010) *Communicative Proficiency and Linguistic Development: Intersections Between SLA and Language Testing Research*. EUROSLA Monographs Series 1. See http://eurosla.org/monographs/EM01/EM01home.php (accessed 3 March 2014).
Buck, G. (2001) *Assessing Listening*. New York: Cambridge University Press.
Byrnes, H. (1987) Proficiency as a framework for research in second language acquisition. *The Modern Language Journal* 71, 44–49.
Canale, M. and Swain, M. (1980) The theoretical bases of communicative approaches to second language teaching and testing. *Applied Linguistics* 1, 1–47.
Carlsen, C. (2012) Proficiency level – a fuzzy variable in computer learner corpora. *Applied Linguistics* 33, 161–183.
Carroll, J.B. (1961) Fundamental considerations in testing for English language proficiency of foreign students. In *Testing the English Proficiency of Foreign Students*. Washington, DC: Center for Applied Linguistics. [Reprinted in Allen, H.B. & Campbell, R.N. (eds) (1972) *Teaching English as a Second Language: A Book of Readings* (pp. 313–320). New York: McGraw-Hill.]
Chapelle, C.A. and Plakans, L. (2012) Assessment and testing: Overview. In C.A. Chapelle (ed.) *The Encyclopedia of Applied Linguistics* (pp. 241–244). New York: Blackwell.
Chomsky, N. (1965) *Aspects of the Theory of Syntax*. Cambridge: MIT Press.
Clahsen, H. (1985) Profiling second language development: A procedure for assessing L2 proficiency. In K. Hyltenstam and M. Pienemann (eds) *Modelling and Assessing Second Language Acquisition* (pp. 283–332). Clevedon: Multilingual Matters.
Cook, V. (2001) *Second Language Learning and Language Teaching*. London: Hodder Arnold.
Council of Europe (2001) *Common European Framework of Reference for Languages: Learning, teaching, assessment*. Cambridge: Cambridge University Press.
Davies, A. (2003) *The Native Speaker: Myth or Reality?* Clevedon: Multilingual Matters.
De Jong, J.H.A.L. and Verhoeven, L.T. (1992) Modeling and assessing language proficiency. In J.H.A.L. De Jong and L.T. Verhoeven (eds) *The Construct of Language Proficiency: Applications of Psychological Models to Language Assessment* (pp. 3–22). Amsterdam: Benjamins.
Fulcher, G. (2004) Deluded by artifices? The Common European Framework and harmonization. *Language Assessment Quarterly* 1, 253–266.
Hawkins, J.A. and Buttery, P. (2009) Using learner language from corpora to profile levels of proficiency: Insights from the English Profile Programme. In *Language Testing Matters: Investigating the Wider Social and Educational Impact of Assessment – Proceedings of the ALTE*

Cambridge Conference, 2008. See http://linguistics.ucdavis.edu/People/jhawkins/past-activities/Hawkins-ALTE2008.pdf/view (accessed 5 August 2011).

Housen, A. and Kuiken, F. (2009) Complexity, accuracy, and fluency in second language acquisition. *Applied Linguistics* 30, 461–473.

Housen, A., Kuiken, F. and Vedder, I. (2012) *Dimensions of L2 Performance and Proficiency: Complexity, accuracy and fluency in SLA*. Amsterdam: Benjamins.

Hulstijn, J.H. (2007) The shaky ground beneath the CEFR: Quantitative and qualitative dimensions of language proficiency. *Modern Language Journal* 91 (4), 663–667.

Hulstijn, J.H. (2010a) Linking L2 proficiency to L2 acquisition: Opportunities and challenges of profiling research. In I. Bartning, M. Martin, and I. Vedder (eds) *Communicative Proficiency and Linguistic Development: Intersections between SLA and language testing research* (pp. 233–238). EUROSLA Monographs Series 1. See http://eurosla.org/monographs/EM01/233-238Hulstijn.pdf (accessed 3 March 2014).

Hulstijn, J.H. (2010b) Measuring second language proficiency. In E. Blom and S. Unsworth (eds) *Experimental Methods in Language Acquisition Research* (pp. 185–200). Amsterdam: Benjamins.

Hulstijn, J.H. (2011) Language proficiency in native and non-native speakers: An agenda for research and suggestions for second-language assessment. *Language Assessment Quarterly* 8, 229–249.

Hulstijn, J.H. (2012) The construct of language proficiency in the study of bilingualism from a cognitive perspective. *Bilingualism: Language and Cognition* 15, 422–433.

Hulstijn, J., Alderson, C. and Schroonen, R. (2010) Developmental stages in second-language acquisition and levels of second-language proficiency: Are there links between them? In I. Bartning, M. Martin and I. Vedder (eds) *Communicative Proficiency and Linguistic Development: Intersections between SLA and language testing research* (pp. 11–20). EUROSLA Monographs Series 1. See http://eurosla.org/monographs/EM01/11-20Hulstijn_et_al.pdf (last accessed 3 March 2014).

Hymes, D. (1972) On communicative competence. In J.B. Pride and J. Holmes (eds) *Sociolinguistics* (pp. 269–293). Harmondsworth: Penguin Books.

Kramsch, C. (1987) The proficiency movement: Second language acquisition perspectives. *Studies in Second language Acquisition* 9, 355–362.

Lado, R. (1961) *Language Testing*. New York: McGraw-Hill.

Laufer, B., Elder, C., Hill, K. and Congdon, P. (2004) Size and strength: Do we need both to measure vocabulary knowledge? *Language Testing* 21, 202–226.

Malvern, D. and Richards, B. (2002) Investigating accommodation in language proficiency interviews using a new measure of lexical diversity. *Language Testing* 19, 85–104.

Martin, M., Mustonen, S., Reiman, N. and Seilonen, M. (2010) On becoming an independent user. In I. Bartning, M. Martin and I. Vedder (eds) *Communicative Proficiency and Linguistic Development: Intersections between SLA and language testing research* (pp. 57–80). EUROSLA Monographs Series 1. See http://eurosla.org/monographs/EM01/57-80Martin_et_al.pdf (last accessed 3 March 2014).

McNamara, T. (2000) *Language Testing*. Oxford: Oxford University Press.

Meara, P. (1996) The dimensions of lexical competence. In G. Brown, K. Malmkjaer and J. Williams (eds) *Performance and Competence in Second Language Acquisition* (pp. 35–52). Cambridge: Cambridge University Press.

Norris, J. and Ortega, L. (2003) Defining and measuring SLA. In C.J. Doughty and M.H. Long (eds) *The Handbook of Second Language Acquisition* (pp. 717–761). Oxford: Blackwell Publishing.

Ortega, L., Iwashita, N., Rabie, S. and Norris, J.M. (1999) *A Multilanguage Comparison of Measures of Syntactic Complexity* [Funded Project]. Honolulu, HI: University of Hawaii, National Foreign Language Resource Center.

Oscarson, M. (1989) Self-assessment of language proficiency: Rationale and applications. *Language Testing* 6, 1–13.

Pallotti, G. (2009) CAF: Defining, refining and differentiating constructs. *Applied Linguistics* 30, 590–601.
Perdue, C. (ed.) (1993) *Adult Language Acquisition: Cross-linguistic perspectives. Volume 1, Field Methods*. Cambridge: Cambridge University Press.
Richer, J.-J. (2012) *La Didactique des langues interrogée par les compétences*. Brussels: EME.
Thomas, M. (1994) Assessment of L2 proficiency in second language acquisition research. *Language Learning* 44, 307–336.
Tremblay, A. (2011) Proficiency assessment standards in second language acquisition research: 'Clozing' the gap. *Studies in Second Language Acquisition* 33, 339–372.
van Hell, J.G. and Tokowicz, N. (2010) Event-related brain potentials and second language learning: Syntactic processing in late L2 learners at different L2 proficiency levels. *Second Language Research* 26, 43–74.

Part 1
General Considerations for L2 Assessment

2 Oral Fluency and Spoken Proficiency: Considerations for Research and Testing

Heather Hilton

The titles of this volume and this chapter contain the word *proficiency*, a somewhat treacherous concept in the contemporary world of second language (L2) teaching methodology (and a notoriously difficult word to translate). According to the *Oxford English Dictionary*, the Latin etymon of the adjective *proficient* has the meaning of *going forward, making progress*. The first definition given is 'Going forward or advancing towards perfection', and the second is 'Advanced in the acquirement of some kind of skill; skilled, expert' (1971: 2317). Yet this idea of expertise is at odds with current European texts defining a 'plurilingual' policy for language teaching and assessment:

> [T]he aim of language education is [...] no longer seen as simply to achieve 'mastery' of one or two, or even three languages, [...] with the 'ideal native speaker' as the ultimate model. Instead, the aim is to develop a linguistic repertory, in which all linguistic abilities have a place. (Council of Europe, 2000: 5)

In a similar generalizing vein, the American Council of Teachers of Foreign Languages (ACTFL) – one of the first organizations to implement wide-scale oral proficiency testing in the wake of the Communicative movement in language teaching back in the 1980s – has recently altered its definition of oral proficiency from 'the ability to accomplish linguistic tasks' (ACTFL, 1999: 1) to the broader 'functional language ability' (ACTFL, 2012: 3).

A vast amount of experimental and applied research has been devoted to exploring exactly what 'functional language ability' actually consists of, and how a teacher, an examiner or a researcher can describe or identify varying levels of this ability. Most of it tends to equate 'proficiency' with ability to *produce* spoken or written language, and unfortunately neglecting the more reliably measured ability to *comprehend* spoken language as a robust proficiency indicator (Feyten, 1991; see also the chapters by Zoghlami and Prince in this volume for a detailed presentation of the construct of listening comprehension). For reasons linked to the epistemology of language acquisition research (emerging from applied *linguistics*, Hilton, 2011a), much of this work on productive proficiency has focused on the morphosyntactic and discursive characteristics of foreign-language speech and writing (Hulstijn, 2010: 236; see McManus *et al.*, this volume), with a recent shift of scientific interest towards the lexical, phraseological and phonological components of proficient expression. This chapter will be devoted to an inventory of the characteristics of oral production in a parallel corpus of native and non-native speech in French and English. Following two recent models of L2 production (Kormos, 2006; Segalowitz, 2010), I will be considering 'functional language ability' more from a *language processing* perspective than a linguistic or acquisitional point of view. Online language-processing experiments rarely deal with spoken language at a discursive level, and L2 oral corpora have rarely been examined as illustrations of processing phenomena.[1] The point of this chapter is to see what careful analysis of real-time speech by speakers of differing 'language ability' can contribute to the on-going proficiency debate, and more specifically to the *reliable* evaluation of spoken production.

Current L2 Production Models

Two interesting books have recently attempted to augment and update the famous 'blueprint for speaking' developed by psycholinguist Willem Levelt during the 1990s (Levelt, 1989, 1999): Judit Kormos' (2006) *Speech Production and Second Language Acquisition* and Norman Segalowitz's (2010) *Cognitive Bases of Second Language Fluency*. As their titles indicate, both books examine the particularities of second- or foreign-language speech production, using Levelt's meticulously documented first language (L1) model as their starting point. The book titles also indicate the different focus adopted by each author: Segalowitz considers *fluency*, a 'multidimensional construct' (2010: 7) that is a sub-component (or indicator) of overall speaking proficiency, whereas Kormos explores all aspects of L2 speech production, including fluency. Both Kormos and Segalowitz avoid the pedagogically unfashionable etymological nuances of the word 'proficiency' by adopting (respectively) the more generic term 'production' or focusing on the more limited 'fluency' construct. Oral *production* can be at any level of expertise; this is one of the four basic language skills, the one we spend about 30% of our L1 processing time engaged in (Feyten, 1991: 174). The adjective *fluent* is often used in conversational English as a synonym of *proficient*, but the notion of *fluency* has taken on a more restricted meaning in the field of language acquisition research, referring to the temporal characteristics of spoken discourse (speech rate, hesitation rates, numbers of words or syllables between pauses, and so on; for overviews, see Griffiths, 1991; Kaponen & Riggenbach, 2000; Lennon, 1990; and especially Segalowitz, 2010: Ch. 2). The prevalence of the term *fluency* in recent second language acquisition (SLA) research illustrates a scientific interest in objective, quantifiable – and therefore reliable – indicators of oral performance (Segalowitz, 2010: 31); this preoccupation should not be mistaken for a reductionist view of language proficiency. Temporal characteristics – and more precisely various hesitation phenomena (silent and filled pauses, stutters, repetitions and repairs) – are seen as important keys to understanding the complex processes (pragmatic, cognitive and linguistic) that make L2 communication possible. Fluency is 'a performance phenomenon' (Kormos, 2006: 155); fluency indicators would be those that reliably reveal 'how efficiently the speaker is able to mobilize and temporally integrate, in a nearly simultaneous way, the underlying processes of planning and assembling an utterance in order to perform a communicatively acceptable speech act' (Segalowitz, 2010: 47).

As cognitive and social psychology advance, psycholinguistic models become more and more complex, and Kormos' 'model of bilingual speech production' (2006: 168; reproduced in Figure 2.1) is no exception. Those familiar with Levelt's 'blueprint' will recognize the three experimentally established 'encoding modules' (on the left of the diagram) that interact in cascading fashion in L1 production – the conceptualizer (which generates a 'preverbal message'), the formulator (which 'encodes' this message in words and phrases) and the articulator (which prepares the motor processes involved in uttering the message). These are fed by knowledge and procedures stored in a speaker's long-term memory, at the center of the diagram (De Jong *et al.*, 2012: 10–11; Kormos, 2006: 166–167). The particularities of L2 production are reflected by a set of 'L2 declarative rules' that have been added to the long-term store: these are the not-yet automatized 'syntactic and phonological rules' that much L2 classroom time is devoted to describing (Kormos, 2006: 167). It is a pity that this model does not illustrate more clearly an important difference between the L1 and L2 lexical store, which Kormos clearly develops in her eighth chapter – that is, the fact that much of the language manipulated in L1 speech is composed of plurilexical 'formulaic sequences' (Erman & Warren, 2000; Sinclair, 1991; Wray, 2000, 2002), whereas less-proficient L2 production involves the conscious[2] arrangement of individual lexemes into syntactic units, a concerted, serial process that is qualitatively different from highly automatized L1 speech (Kormos, 2006: 166). Segalowitz develops similar themes in his consideration of L2 fluency; his model also situates Levelt's 'cognitive-perceptual' modules within a larger system that includes the social and personal aspects of language processing, such as motivation to communicate, personal experience, and interactive context (Segalowitz, 2010: 21, 131).

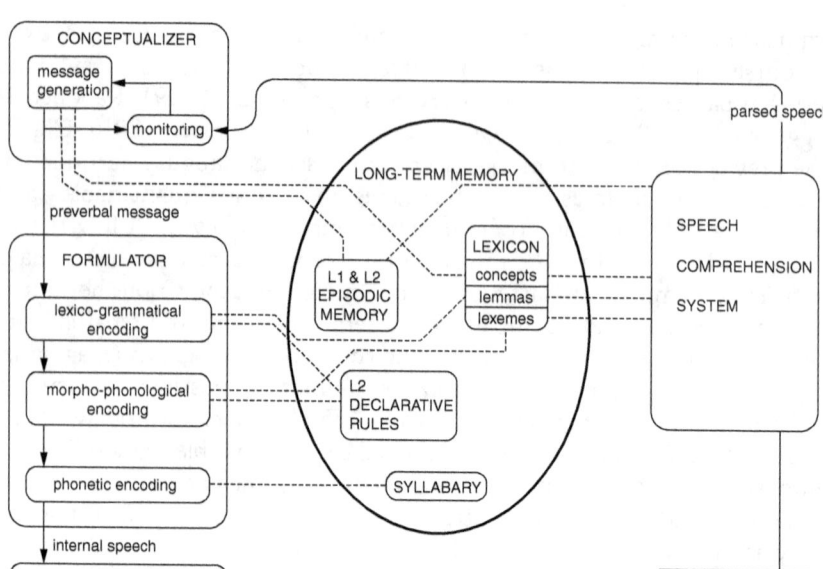

Figure 2.1 Kormos' 'model of bilingual speech production' (Kormos, 2006: 168)

Using Kormos' model as its theoretical framework, the next section of this chapter will look more closely at temporal features of L2 speech, and the characteristics of temporally fluent and less-fluent productions. It is hoped that by considering temporal features of productive *fluency*, and by examining the linguistic and discursive phenomena observed at different, objectively identifiable fluency levels, we can come to a clearer understanding of just what makes a speaker *proficient*.

Analysis of the PAROLE Corpus

Corpus design

As more extensively reported elsewhere (Hilton, 2009, 2011b; Osborne, 2011), the *Corpus PARallèle Oral en Langue Etrangère* (PAROLE Corpus) compiled at the Université de Savoie in Chambéry, France (Hilton *et al.*, 2008), is a relatively classic learner corpus (young adults carrying out quasi-monological descriptive tasks in either L2 English or French). The 45 subjects (33 learners of English and 12 learners of French) were recruited as paid volunteers from groups hypothesized to have different overall proficiency levels: first-year language or business majors, compared with students in a Master's program preparing for a competitive foreign-language teaching qualification.

Spoken proficiency was *not* measured prior to the project, but each subject completed a series of complementary tests and questionnaires, providing further information on L2 listening level, lexical and grammatical knowledge, as well as motivation for L2 learning, grammatical inferencing ability, phonological memory and linguistic profile (Hilton, 2008c: 8–10). The actual productions in the English L2 sub-corpus were evaluated by two expert raters, who determined each learner's European reference level for both fluency and overall speaking proficiency (Council of Europe, 2000: 28–29); inter-rater reliability was high for these criterion-referenced judgments of oral performance (Spearman rank correlation coefficients of 0.84 for fluency and 0.73 for overall speaking proficiency).

PAROLE was originally designed for linguistic analysis (morpho-syntactic and lexical characteristics of L2 speech) within the conventions of the *Child Language Data Exchange System* (CHILDES, MacWhinney, 2007), but the research team rapidly became interested in the temporal characteristics of the L2 speech samples obtained, and during the transcription process all hesitations of over 200 ms were timed and carefully coded (Hilton, 2009). In order to obtain L1 fluency values for comparison, 17 native speakers (NSs) of the project languages (nine English, eight French) performing the same tasks were recorded, and these productions were also transcribed and coded. The findings presented here are compiled from two summary tasks (describing short video sequences immediately after viewing, with minimal intervention from the interviewer). The L2 subset of the corpus totals 9087 words (1 hour and 15 minutes), and the L1 subset 3732 words (22 minutes). According to the transcription conventions developed for CHILDES, an utterance in PAROLE is defined as an independent clause and all its dependent clauses (basically, a T-unit); all errors, stutters, drawls and retracings, as well as silent and filled pauses and other hesitation phenomena, have been coded conventionally, with a few project-specific adaptations. We are fully aware of the limitations of the T-unit as the basis for spoken discourse analysis (Foster *et al.*, 2000), but in order to take advantage of the various programs developed for the CLAN (Computerized Language ANalysis) component of CHILDES, we were obliged to structure our transcriptions in this traditional way. In addition to the reliable tagging programs available in CLAN for the project languages, we were interested in the programs for lexical analysis (the useful 'D' statistic of lexical diversity, the automatic generation of regular and lemmatized frequency lists), the automated calculations of mean length of utterance and total speaker talking time, as well as classic search possibilities (for any string or coded element). The timing and coding of hesitations (silent and filled pauses) is relatively easy in the 'sonic mode' of CLAN, but further calculations of hesitation time values are relatively laborious, involving importing the results of symbol searches into a spreadsheet, and manipulating them to obtain totals, task by task. Information on hesitation times is, however, the key to quantifying fluency features in the speaker's productions, and this process enabled us to calculate measures including mean length of hesitation, hesitation rates (per utterance, per 1000 words), the percentage of speaking time spent in hesitation, and mean length of run (MLR, the number of words between two hesitations). Speech rate (measured as words per minute) was also calculated, based on totals easily obtained in CLAN: total speaker talking time, total number of words produced, including ('unpruned') or excluding ('pruned') retracings and L1 words.

As in any corpus project, we found it necessary to clarify the criteria used to define various speech phenomena, and notably the typology used to code errors, hesitations and retracings (for full detail, see Hilton, 2008c). Five general error categories were coded: phonological, lexical, morphological, syntactic and referential. Four different types of retracing were coded: simple repetitions, reformulations (in which only one element of the repeated material has been changed), restarts (more than one element changed) and false starts (utterance abandoned; these last two categories were collapsed into a single 'restart' category for statistical analysis). Raw numbers of retracings and errors were converted to rate of retracing and error (per 1000 words). All silent or filled pauses of 200 milliseconds or more (Butterworth, 1980: 156) were timed and coded in PAROLE, and sequences of silent and filled pauses occurring between two words (or attempted words) were timed as a single 'hesitation group' (see Hilton, 2009, for details; Roberts & Kirsner, 2000: 137; see Campione & Véronis, 2004, for a similar treatment of hesitation sequences). The position of every hesitation (isolated pauses or hesitation groups) was manually coded according to three possible locations: at an utterance boundary, a clause boundary or within a clause.

Other non-temporal characteristics of the subjects' productions were also manually coded. The syntactic components of each utterance were categorized as either a *main clause* (simple, coordinate or superordinate), a *subordinate clause* (finite or non-finite), a *non-verbal phrase* or what we are calling a *'support clause'* (existential or complement clause). These syntactic measures enabled us to calculate various indicators of syntactic density, such as the number of syntactic units per utterance, per 100 words, per minute, or the ratio of subordinate to main clauses. The informational content of the participants' productions was quantified as the number of 'information units' expressed: a list was drawn up, compiling all of the information conveyed by the PAROLE speakers (native and non-native) for each of the two descriptive tasks; these lists were then used to tabulate the amount of information encoded by each speaker (Appendix 2A provides the list for one summary task). Information units were categorized as *frames* (introducing or concluding a section of discourse), *events* (with macro- and micro-events totalled in a single category) or *attributes* (information concerning the objects or participants in these events, such as *being large/plump/nasty/with his mother/named 'Dumbo'*, and so on). Raw numbers of information units encoded by each speaker were then used to calculate various measures of information delivery: mean length of information unit (in words), information units per utterance, information units per minute and information units per 100 words. A measure of relative 'granularity' (Osborne, 2011) indicates the percentage of total statements (corpus-wide) that an individual speaker chose (or managed) to encode.

Fluency sub-groups in PAROLE

The lengthy process of transcribing and coding the PAROLE production data has enabled us to identify, in an objective fashion, three *fluency* levels – using the temporal characteristics of the corpus productions as a basis for our classification. A closer look at some of the characteristics of the speech produced by more and less fluent learners (as well as comparisons with the native speaker group) will illustrate some of the processing characteristics of L2 speech, and potential useful indicators of spoken L2 proficiency.

In L1 acquisition research, mean length of utterance (MLU, measured in words or morphemes per utterance) is a classic indicator of developmental level, and speech rate (measured as words, syllables or phonemes per minute) is the standard temporal fluency measure. In L2 research, pause rate, mean length of pause and mean length of run have been shown to be the most significant fluency indicators (Towell *et al.*, 1996; Trofimovich & Baker, 2006; see Segalowitz, 2010: Ch. 2, for a comprehensive review). The PAROLE Fluency Index (FI) is a cumulative measure in which three fluency indicators – speech rate (in words per minute), percentage of production time spent hesitating and mean length of run – have been given a coefficient value (in relation to the native speaker average for each), and combined into a single index (Osborne, 2011: 2–3). Using this index, we have identified three learner sub-groups – the first quartile of learners' FI scores (low FI), the fourth quartile of learners' FI scores (high FI) and a mid-range group (the 12 learners grouped around the FI median, or mid FI). Table 2.1 presents the PAROLE FI measures for each of these sub-groups, as well as for the entire learner and native speaker populations. Sample size, age and years of L2 study are also given. The table also presents the median level of the learner groups for L2 listening and grammatical competence, expressed using the European reference levels, as measured by the DIALANG diagnostic tests.[3]

The figures in Table 2.1 show greater variation in the FI for more fluent learners and for native speakers (standard deviation, minima, maxima); there is no overlap (minima/ maxima) between the three learner sub-groups, indicating the potentially sensitive nature of this composite measure. The Spearman rank correlation coefficient comparing the FI with the range of expert spoken proficiency ratings established for the English learner corpus is high: $r_s = 0.89$, $p < 0.0001$. Table 2.2 provides a closer look at the temporal characteristics of the different fluency levels (learner, native, FI sub-groups), which echo L2 fluency findings by other researchers: overall, our L2 learners

Table 2.1 PAROLE Fluency Index (FI) values and fluency sub-groups

Corpus characteristics	Learner corpus				NSs
	Total	Low FI	Mid FI	High FI	
Total number	45	12	12	12	17
English sub-corpus	33	10	9	8	9
French sub-corpus	12	2	3	4	8
Age (years)	21.4	18.5	22.1	23.3	21.3
Years L2 study	8.1	6.4	8.6	9.7	–
L2 listening level	B2	A2	B2	C2–	–
L2 grammar level	B1	B1	B2	C2	–
FI mean	0.51	0.24	0.52	0.76	1.0
FI median	0.53	0.25	0.53	0.74	0.99
SD, FI	0.207	0.070	0.040	0.102	0.175
FI minimum	0.120	0.120	0.450	0.650	0.690
FI maximum	0.940	0.350	0.570	0.940	1.350

Table 2.2 Fluency differences between learners, native speakers and FI learner sub-groups (median values)

Fluency indicators	Learner corpus				NSs
	Total ($n = 45$)	Low FI ($n = 12$)	Mid FI ($n = 12$)	High FI ($n = 12$)	($n = 17$)
Words per minute	105.5	56.6	103.8	136.5	183.5
MLR (in words)	3.70	2.35	3.70	5.60	8.30
Variance, MLR	2.146	0.119	0.196	1.370	3.687
Production time hesitating (%)	40.6	58	40.2	29.5	21.2
Median length of hesitation (ms)	697	976	634	575	499
Variance, length hesitations	1.734	3.715	0.681	0.296	0.191
Maximum hesitation (s)	21.34	21.34	8.41	6.37	5.56
Retracing rate (per 1000 words)	83.3	130.1	76.0	50.8	39.8
Stutter rate (per 1000 words)	27.9	31.3	27.9	27.3	12.1

Note: MLR, mean length of run.

hesitate almost twice as much as native speakers. Their hesitations last longer and cut the speech stream into much smaller fluent runs (fewer than four words between hesitations, as opposed to over eight for L1 speech). Retracings and stutters are also more frequent in learner speech. Table 2.2 shows greater variance in median length of hesitation in learner speech, and less variance for mean length of run.

Quantitative results: Characteristics of group productions

The PAROLE FI provides an objective (quantitatively determined) measure of the ease with which the project participants are able to encode their ideas into oral speech. It is therefore interesting to look at the linguistic and informational characteristics of the speech that the different learner groups produce, as compared with the native speaker productions. Appendix 2B presents group and sub-group values observed in the corpus, for mean length of utterance, lexical diversity, rates of error, and syntactic and informational delivery. The PAROLE data show all native speakers producing longer, more lexically diverse utterances than the learners as a whole, with more syntactic units per utterance, but shorter information units. Native speakers manage to encode more ideas with fewer words, putting more information into each utterance. It is interesting to note that, despite a significantly higher error rate overall (more difficulty with formal encoding), the PAROLE L2 learners manage to communicate about as much information as the native speakers, in terms of the number of information units they mention – although the low-fluency learners do encode significantly less information than the fluent sub-groups. Chi-square analyses of frequency and distribution show that the types of information encoded by the different groups of PAROLE speakers do not differ according to group ($p > 0.45$): Native speakers and learners (whatever their fluency level) include similar numbers of frames, events and attributes. This discursive consistency may be due to the nature of summary tasks, in which all participants attempt to encode the same propositional content, and it would be interesting to compare the types of information units found when less constrained content is encoded.

If amounts and types of information conveyed remain essentially the same throughout PAROLE, interesting differences exist in the syntactic structure of discourse by speakers at different fluency levels ($p < 0.001$): native speakers produce distinctly more noun phrases and fewer support clauses than L2 learners, and high-fluency learners produce proportionally more subordinate clauses than less-fluent learners or native speakers. There is only a marginal difference in the types of errors that the three fluency sub-groups produce ($p = 0.02$), with only a slight tendency for less fluent learners to make proportionally more pronunciation errors, moderately fluent learners to make more lexical errors, and fluent learners to make proportionally more syntactic errors.

Similar analyses of the length and distribution of hesitations in PAROLE furnish further evidence of processing differences between different fluency levels. Native speakers produce proportionally more short pauses (from 200 to 500 ms), and learners produce more hesitations lasting over 1100 ms, and all but one of the 120 'outlier' hesitations lasting over 3s in the corpus.[4] Native speakers also produce proportionally more hesitations lasting 800–900 ms, and it would be interesting to conduct a study designed to probe the processing significance of this particular time band, which seems to correspond to a similar peak at 1100–1200 ms in L2 production. Analysis of the length of hesitations produced by the fluency sub-groups show that long hesitations (over 1700 ms) are a characteristic of low-fluency L2 speech, which also contains proportionally more hesitations in the 1000–1100 ms range, and fewer short pauses (200–400 ms). High-fluency learners produce proportionally more hesitations in the 500–700 ms range, and again it would be interesting to conduct online investigations into the types of processing associated with these time bands. Early 'pausology' research associates hesitation location and length, interpreting longer hesitations at utterance boundaries as being devoted to metalinguistic 'planning' processes, and short clause-internal hesitations to lexical retrieval processes (e.g. Goldman-Eisler, 1958), but we did not find such an association in our native-speaker corpus or in the speech of the low-fluency learners, possibly because of our technique of grouping sequences of silent and filled pauses (the traditional conclusions being based on analyses of silent pauses alone). In the learner corpus overall, shorter pauses (200–500 ms) are associated with clause boundaries, and hesitations of 1200–2000 ms are proportionally more frequent at utterance and clause boundaries in high-fluency L2 speech. Most importantly, the distribution of pauses is not the same in L1 and L2 speech ($p < 0.0001$): native speakers in PAROLE (as in other fluency studies) pause 70% of the time at a discursive or syntactic boundary, whereas over half of the hesitations in the L2 corpus (54%) occur within a clause. The distribution of hesitations differs within the learner population according to fluency level, with low- and mid-fluency learners hesitating proportionally more frequently within clauses, and high-fluency learners approaching – but not equalling – native-speaker proportions of boundary clauses. Numbers of clause-internal hesitations may in fact be a reliable indicator of fluency level, as illustrated in Figure 2.2, which shows the increasing proportions of within-clause hesitations as fluency level decreases. The differences in proportions are significant between each sub-group (all at $p < 0.0001$), making clause-internal hesitation a means of distinguishing native from near-native and intermediate from more elementary or advanced learners.

The complex hesitation groups that we coded in PAROLE (sequences of filled and unfilled pauses) also turn out to be a characteristic feature of L2 speech, comprising two-thirds (64%) of learner hesitations – and up to 77% for the low-fluency group – compared with 54% of native-speaker hesitations.[5] We did find in PAROLE that native speakers of French produced more hesitation groups than our Anglophone subjects (59% versus 47%), which might be related to the nature of processing a language with more complex noun or verb morphology, or may simply be an artefact of the perceived formality of the situation by the Francophone participants (who seemed less comfortable in a one-on-one interview than the Anglophone subjects, possibly because of the competitive nature of oral examinations in the French education system).

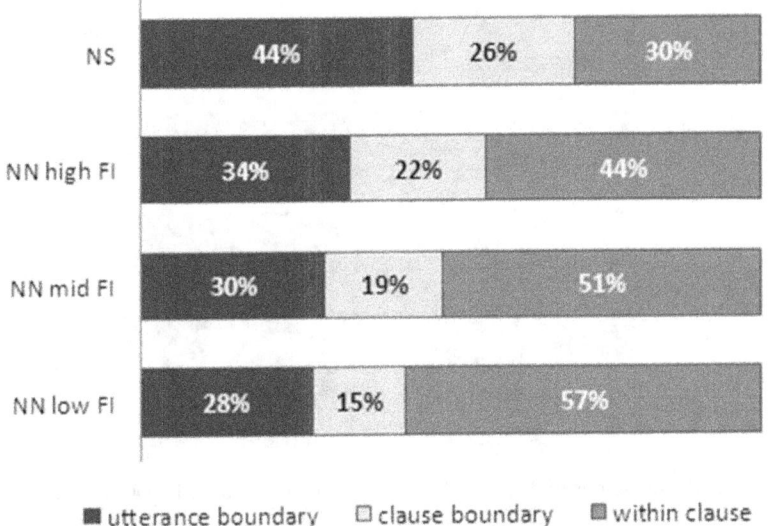

Figure 2.2 Proportions of hesitations at different discourse locations according to group

Retracings are another fluency feature showing interesting distributional differences between PAROLE sub-groups ($p < 0.0001$), as summarized in Figure 2.3. Between-group analysis shows that the difference lies not between native speakers and learners overall, but between the lower-fluency sub-groups and the others. Native speakers produce proportionally more reformulations and restarts, whereas low-fluency learners not only produce far more simple repetitions, but also distinctly fewer reformulations and, perhaps counter-intuitively, fewer restarts (changing or abandoning an utterance).

Qualitative findings: Links between processing and fluency

These quantitative findings from the PAROLE corpus indicate that – in addition to the predictable higher rate of formal errors in L2 encoding – the characteristic features of L2 learner speech are complex hesitation groups, clause-internal hesitations, simple repetitions, longer information units and more frequent subordinate and support clauses. A qualitative consideration of the connections between these phenomena will enable us to establish the link between fluency and proficiency – that is, to understand the processing issues associated with spoken production in first or foreign languages.

It is, of course, predictable that formal encoding – which is largely automatic in L1 production – will require attentional effort when a speaker is attempting to express ideas in a foreign language, where some formal

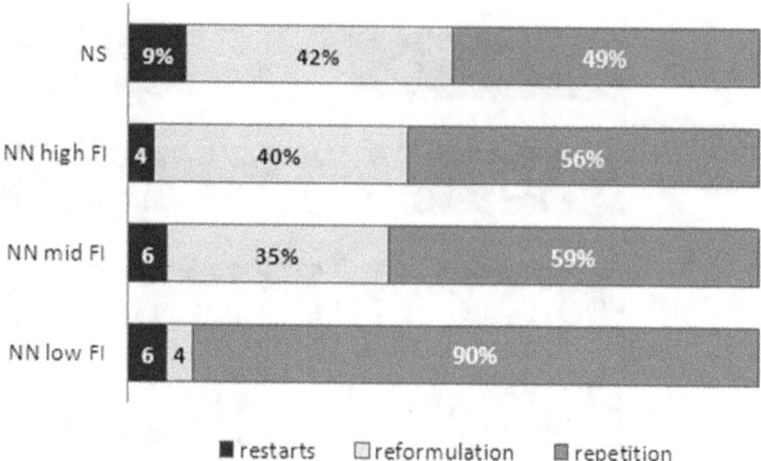

Figure 2.3 Proportions of different types of retracing produced by PAROLE sub-groups

knowledge and routines in long-term memory are bound to be lacking (Ellis, 2000). The fluency characteristics observed in the PAROLE L2 corpus are eloquent indicators of the greater cognitive effort required to summarize information when formal automatisms are lacking, with increasing temporal disruption as encoding problems increase. Previous studies have established the link between clause-internal hesitations, simple repetition and problems with lexical encoding in L1 speech (Butterworth, 1975: 84; Deese, 1980: 84; Goldman-Eisler, 1958: 67; Maclay & Osgood, 1959: 39; Rochester, 1973), and we find interesting examples of these phenomena in our L1 sub-corpus (native-speaker examples (1a–c); pause times are coded after the '#' symbol, simple repetitions are coded '[/]', and drawls ':'):

(1) a. *N46: [...] donc on voit en fait **une [/] u:h [#0_348] une grue** [...]
(repetition, including a drawled filled pause lasting 348 ms; ['so in fact we see a crane'])

b. *N01: [...] there's **a: #0_372 crane** maneuvering a fridge up to a window [...]
(drawled function word plus silent pause lasting 372 ms before the same low-frequency lexical item in English)

c. *N03: [...] it's an ad fo:r Rolos **the: #0_876 caramelly chocolatey** lollies
(drawled function word and 876 ms silent pause)

It is interesting to note that native-speaker activation of the less-frequent French and English words *grue/crane* (1a and 1b) both generate a drawled syllable and a pause of around 350 ms, and the assembly of a nonce adjective group *'caramelly chocolatey'* (example (1c)) generates a silent pause that lasts over twice as long, attesting, no doubt, to the explicit metalinguistic effort necessary for this creative coinage.

Similar features accompany much more frequent problems of lexical encoding in the L2 corpus: in example (2a), a filled pause lasting 342 ms precedes the substitution of an anglicized L1 word (French *caïd*) to encode the idea 'bully', while in examples (2b) and (2c), more effortful attempts at finding an appropriate English word generate longer hesitations – lasting almost 3 s in example (2c), as the speaker searches for the word *trunk*, before supplying the hyperonym *nose*. In example (2d), a disfluent hesitation group is followed by a metalinguistic commentary on the unavailability of a lexical item in the L2.

(2) a. *001: #0_569 a:nd uh it's a young **u:h [#0_342] caid@n** [...]
(mid-fluency learner; the @n coding suffix designating a lexical coinage/neologism)

b. *015: uh we can see **a: [/] #1_034 a skyscraper**
(low-fluency learner; *skyscraper* is referentially inappropriate for a three-storey apartment building)

c. *033: [...] you see: **the: #1_347 ti:pf@n** #0_836 of: [...] the elepha:nt's **<u:m #> [#2_804] nose** [...]
(mid-fluency learner, NS of German; lexical approximation *tipf* for *tip*)

d. *002: a fridge #0_511 which <u:m # um #> [#7_581]+...
(be)cause I [/] I don't know uh how [...] **we say uh *monter*.**
(low-fluency learner; complex hesitation lasting over 7 s, followed by a request for the English equivalent of the French verb *monter*, here, to rise or be hoisted)

A detailed analysis of all of the clause-internal hesitations lasting over 3 s in PAROLE showed that over three-quarters of them are followed by lexical encoding problems of this type, and that problems with verbs, as in example (2d), are particularly disruptive to spoken production (Hilton, 2008a). The higher rate of stuttering in L2 speech also appears to be linked to effortful lexical retrieval or articulation, as in example (3) (where '&' is used to code word fragments and stutters):

(3) *407: e:t [...] peut+être c' est le **&pruperit #0_325 &pri: #0_488 propri(é)tai:re** uh de la voiture [...]
(Chinese learner, assembling the phonologically complex French word *propriétaire*; ['and maybe it's the owner of the car'])

Table 2.3 Spearman rank correlations between (dis)fluency and production measures, and lexical diversity

Measure	D (lexical diversity)
Indicators of disfluency	
Number of clause-internal hesitations	−0.801 ***
Mean length of clause-internal hesitation	−0.742 ***
Mean length of hesitation	−0.773 ***
Percentage production time hesitating	−0.870 ***
Indicators of fluency and production	
Mean length of run	0.900 ***
Words per minute	0.890 ***
Fluency index	0.899 ***
Mean length of utterance	0.816 ***
Syntactic units per utterance	0.832 ***
Information units per utterance	0.735 ***

*** $p < 0.001$.

The link between lexical knowledge, spoken fluency and proficient production may be further illustrated by the high correlations that occur between our temporal measurements and the 'D' statistic of lexical diversity (Malvern & Richards, 1997), which are listed in Table 2.3. Here, we see negative correlations between D and several indicators of disfluency (numbers and duration of clause-internal hesitations, percentage of time spent hesitating), and positive correlations between lexical diversity and spoken fluency (mean length of run, words per minute) as well as productive efficiency (information units per utterance).

Effortful morphological encoding also generates turbulence in L2 fluency, although the hesitations do not last as long as the most disfluent lexical searches. Reformulations (coded '[//]') produced by a mid-fluency and low-fluency learner (examples (4b) and (4c), respectively), attest to an explicit metalinguistic search for memorized verb forms; a more fluent learner (4a) trips over the infamous English third-person singular, but manages to produce the appropriate form quickly:

(4) a. *020: [...] and #0_383 the elephant actually **slap** [/] #0_220 slap [//] **slaps** him #0_493 in the face [...].

b. *001: [...] the: fridge <u:h #> [#1_347] **felled** [//] <# u:h> [#0_530] **felt** #0_528 on a car [...]
(attempt at producing the irregular verb form *fell*)

c. *406: eu:h [#0_836] <**je vois**> [//] uh [#0_250] **j' ai vu** [...]. ('I see [//] I saw')

Grammatical reformulations of this type account for over half of the reformulations in the learner corpus (63% in the disfluent sub-corpus) and only 36% of those in the NS corpus, where reformulations are more characteristically linked to lexical replacement – either for greater precision (5a and 5b) or a more appropriate register (5c) – or to an increase in the amount information being communicated (5d and 5e):

(5) a. *N03: [...] a:nd just as they got their hands on it it slipped out of **the: [/] #0_343 the hold [//] the: [/] the rope** that was around it [...]

b. *N47: [...] donc un objet uh en haut <d' un> [/] **<d' un bâtiment> [//] d' un immeuble**. ('so an object uh at the top of a [/] of a building [//] of an apartment building')

c. *N46: [...] **<le gars d' en dessous> [//] (en)fi:n #0_459 le: [/] le monsieur du dessous** est en train de crier [...]. ('so the guy down below [//] we:ll # the: [/] the man below')

d. *N11: [...] he was taunting **<an elephant> [//] a baby elephant** #1_086 with it [...]

e. *N10: and **he &ta [//] well with his trunk he taps** the: now man #0_232 on the shoulder [...]

The higher proportions of semantic reformulations of this type in more fluent spoken production (both fluent learners and native speakers) illustrate the essence of proficient language processing. The PAROLE team was initially surprised to discover that native speakers produce proportionally more restarts (coded '[///]' or '[/-]') than learners, yet a closer analysis shows why this is the case. Restarts by native speakers seem to be linked to semantic or discursive operations, whereas those produced by less-fluent learners appear to be connected with problems of lexical or syntactic encoding (6a–6c):

(6) a. *005: [...] the man <u:h #> [#1_620] (h)ave <u:h #> [#2_066] [///] [...] it's not [...] a boy.
(low-fluency learner; restart to paraphrase the idea *the boy has grown up*)

b. *010: [...] (h)e is really <u:h # u:m #> [#4_487] [///] (en)fin@l1 [...] he want so this that he cried.
(lower-intermediate learner; restart to paraphrase the idea that the elephant is *disappointed*)

c. *021: [...] the fridge is being [///] <# uh> [#3_570] going up.
(fluent learner; abandoning a passive structure for an intransitive coding of the idea of *being lifted/ hoisted*)

As with the reformulations in (5), the restarts in (7a) and (7b) show two native speakers adjusting their utterance plans for greater referential clarity. It is interesting to note that these examples are found at the beginning of a summary or of a new episode in the video; the speaker seems to be taking the listener into account at these narrative 'hinge' points:

(7) a. *N13: so it seems that they were [////] #0_244 that people are trying to move into 0det apartment [...].

b. *N01: [...] th(e) next scene is the [//] <um #> [#1_440] is on a [///] he's the same #0_656 boy but a: grown man at a parade.

As suggested by Kormos (2006: 166), L2 speech may be characterized by effortful formal encoding, which can only operate in serial fashion, and indeed the very short runs produced by the less-fluent learners illustrate just such a laborious, word-by-word process. Seventeen of the PAROLE learners produce runs of fewer than three words on average; examples (8a) and (8b) illustrate the disfluency of such effortful formal encoding (see also example (4b)):

(8) a. *004: [...] and u:h [#0_232] the: [/] #0_854 the man <uh #> [#1_103] <that [/] <u:h #> [#1_115] that <uh #> [#1_904]> [//] who <u:h #> [#2_148] is the car <# uh> [#1_602] is u:h [#0_458] very <u:h #> [#1_230] [///] is not happy.

b. *002: and <u:h #> [#2_415] the result is <e:r #> [#0_981] that uh the: fridge <# &=bouche #> [#8_203]+...
*002: I uh don't know uh [...] tomber@l1. [...]
*INV: falls down. [...]
*002: <u:h # u:m> [#6_242] falls down <u:h #> [#2_182] sur@l1 <# &=bouche #> [#4_876]+...
*INV: onto.
*002: +, on [/] on the: [/] <# &=bouche> [#0_702] the car.
('&=bouche' codes a paralinguistic noise, such as tongue clacks, sighs, etc.)

These lower-fluency learners have both been studying English for over seven years; the first (8a) adopts a paraphrase strategy to compensate for two missing lexical items (the verb *to own* and the emotion adjective *furious, upset*). The second speaker (8b) relies on a time-consuming translation strategy, assuming that the interviewer will supply the missing words. Despite the temporal inefficiency of these laborious formal processes, speaker 002 manages to encode 21 information units during the two project summary tasks – this is equal to the learner average, and less than one standard deviation below the native-speaker average of 25. The difference is, of course, in the rate of delivery, and the 'packaging' of this information: with only 3.5 information units communicated per minute, it takes this learner three to four times longer to impart this information than a more fluent learner, and six times longer than a native speaker. Example (8a) also illustrates why learner speech contains proportionally more subordinate clauses than the native-speaker summaries; here, a relative clause is used to paraphrase what more fluent speakers (example (9a)) will put into a simple noun phrase, *the car's owner*:

(9) a. *025: and I think the car's owner was screaming he was uh raising his hands and he was uh screaming +'/.
+' what happened to my car?

The extreme efficiency of automatic formal encoding in this example of fluent-learner speech is clear: two filled pauses of less than 200 ms barely cause a ripple in the delivery of information. The attentional effort necessary for the metalinguistic operations involved in word-by-word formal encoding (as in (8)) seems to saturate the speaker's working memory, making 'higher-level' management of the referential aspects of the narration difficult. In (8b), for example, the definite article 'the' is used to introduce a car that has not been previously mentioned by the speaker – an indefinite article (as well as some information concerning the location of the car, such as 'in the street' or 'down below') would make the situation being described more comprehensible. Higher numbers of support clauses (of the type *we can see a..., there is a...*), followed by a complement clause or a restrictive relative are characteristic of less-fluent learner speech (Osborne, 2011: 291). This type of discourse arrangement may be a by-product of the serial encoding processes we have observed at the phrase level in disfluent speech:

(9) b. *015: [...] at the end u:h [#0_272] of this film #0_354 we can see <u:m #> [#1_445] the: [//] #0_313 a man.
[...] maybe [... #5_453] the man <u:h #> [#1_045] who: [/] who (h)a(s) the car.
[...] and [...] he's [/] [...] #1_298 he's <u:m #> [#1_910] sad.

Such reliance on support and subordinate clauses explains why information units in L2 speech are longer than in native speech. The greater informational density of L1 speech can be traced in part to the more frequent use of noun phrases and a greater proportion of main clauses – syntactic possibilities that seem to rely on a rich lexical base. Compare example (10a) (an intermediate-fluency learner, who valiantly compensates for her encoding difficulties) with (10b) (a native speaker):

(10) a. *020: [...] two or three people ↑ #0_888 at a wi:ndo:w on the: second floor o:f [///] #0_424 well I don't know which floor.
#0_546 a:nd they are trying to: [/] <um #> [#4_086] [...]
#0_435 okay: they try to: <u:m # &=snap #> [#4_969] <have a refrigerator reaching> the window [//] +/.
+, to have the refrigerator going #0_285 through the window.

b. *N11: so there's a crane hoisting a refrigerator #0_279 up into: uh it looked like a [/] u:m [#0_418] a: third + storey window.

Initially postulated by Pawley and Syder (1983), and included in both Kormos' (2006: 154–165) and Segalowitz's (2010: 116–119) theories of L2 speech, is the idea that differences in fluency level can be attributed to a qualitative difference in the language units that speakers activate to encode their ideas (Hilton, 2008b, 2011b). As we have seen in examples (6), (8) and (9), the very short runs of less-fluent speech illustrate the fact that these learners have very few multiword sequences available for effective encoding. It is interesting to compare the nature of the retracings produced by learners in examples (4) and (6) with the reformulations and restarts produced by native speakers in (11), below. Here, the bits of language being juggled and substituted are not individual words, but phrases – entire chunks of language:

(11) a. *N13: […] a:nd <uh #> [#0_720] (be)cause I guess they don't want (t)o: [///] it won't fit up [///] they won't [//] don't want to take it <up the elevator> [//] up the stairs […].

b. *N01: […] there's a: #0_372 crane maneuvering a fridge up to a window #0_698 trying to: uh get it in through the window <of the:> [///] #0_424 to the apartment <# u:m #> [#1_031] trying to maneuver it.

The theory that fluent language processing is made possible by the direct activation of multi-word chunks in long-term memory is compatible with classic 'chunking' accounts of expertise (Chase & Simon, 1973; Miller, 1956), and with 'instance' theories of automaticity (Logan 1988, 1991). Freed from effortful processing at the lexical and syntactic levels, the attentional capacity of proficient speakers can be devoted to higher-order processes of managing discourse cohesion, perspective and referential structures, with the listener in mind; this no doubt explains why more proficient discourse contains certain linking words and grammatical indicators of perspective-taking (Forsberg & Bartning, 2010; Wei, 2011). From a processing point of view, proficiency can be simply defined as ease of processing; and various fluency features give a clear and objective indicator of the ease or difficulty experienced by a particular speaker or learner.

Temporal Fluency and L2 Proficiency: Considerations for Research and Assessment

The study reported here illustrates some of the methodological weaknesses that future SLA research should attempt to avoid (Lieven, 2010;

MacWhinney, 2010; Myles, 2005): university students of assumed proficiency levels performing non-standardized speaking tasks; our analyses use the same production samples to examine both the components and the determinants of proficiency (compare De Jong *et al.*, 2012). Despite these limitations, we feel that our exploration of spoken production at various levels and in different languages enables us to formulate a certain number of suggestions for oral proficiency testing and research.

Hulstijn (2010) points out that automatic scoring of L2 *written* samples is already possible for some European languages, and may soon be generally available, based on the automatic recognition of certain morphemes or lexical items, without the necessity for the laborious tagging of the texts produced. The transcription and tagging of an *oral* corpus is, however, a long and difficult task. Voice-recognition software offers some hope of automatic transcription, but problems of pace, accent and intonation mean that it is still too soon to use this technology for reliable transcription of spontaneous L2 speech.[6] It does not, therefore, currently seem realistic to assess *untranscribed* spoken discourse – the type of discourse classroom teachers and testers must regularly assess – based on the types of morphosyntactic or lexical analyses that are available for written texts.

For both research and testing purposes, temporal fluency measurements would appear to be a good way of obtaining objective indicators of 'ease of processing', and therefore of general spoken proficiency. As we have seen here, the proportion of clause-internal hesitations is a sensitive indicator of fluency level, with significant differences between each of the fluency subgroups considered in PAROLE, including fluent L2 and native speakers. It would certainly be useful for testers, researchers and teachers to have at their disposal a simple application for easily marking up sound files: hesitations could be selected, and tagged when occurring within a clause. An automatic count of numbers and lengths of hesitations would give a clear, quantitative picture of the processing effort required by the task – particularly useful for SLA and pedagogical research (to measure longitudinal change, or the impact of a certain teaching technique on the ease of spoken production). Applications already exist for the automatic measurement of silence in a sound file (in Praat, for example: Boersma & Weenink, 2009; De Jong & Wempe, 2007), but this process counts filled pauses as syllables, and would significantly underestimate hesitation by certain disfluent speakers (Hilton, 2009: 655). The application I have in mind would also involve a much simpler user interface, for purposes of classroom assessment and action research.

Another finding from PAROLE that seems important for performance testing specialists to keep in mind is the fact that native and fluent speakers in PAROLE produce *shorter* information units than the less-fluent speakers. Influenced, no doubt, by analyses of written text, many criterion-referenced descriptors characterize proficient learners as being able to 'explain complex matters in detail, and provide lengthy and coherent narration' (ACTFL, 2012:

5), to 'produce clear, well-structured, detailed text on complex subjects' (Council of Europe, 2000: 24). In fact, L2 learners of all levels attempt to include details in their descriptions in PAROLE – sometimes overlooking essential information that more fluent speakers include. This may be due either to avoidance strategies (Osborne, 2011: 291–292), or because of working memory overload. Management of discourse perspective and referential systems that take the listener into account seem to be more important characteristics of proficient spoken production than the amount of detail communicated.

Notes

(1) Notable exceptions being the work on L1 and L2 'pausology' initiated by Goldman-Eisler in the 1950s, and recent research on L2 fluency (for example, Derwing *et al.*, 2009; Serrano *et al.*, 2012; Trenchs-Parera, 2009), which illustrates renewed SLA interest in the processing paradigm.
(2) Involving attentional effort in working memory.
(3) A1–A2 indicating 'basic users', B1–B2 'independent users', and C1–C2 'proficient users' (Council of Europe, 2001: 23–24). The European diagnostic tests in DIALANG were available at www.dialang.org.
(4) 'Outlier' not because we eliminated them from our analyses, but because this is a hesitation length rarely occurring in spoken interaction, speech partners tending to intervene to keep the conversation moving after about 2.5 s (Griffiths, 1991; Rieger, 2003: 43); the behaviour of the PAROLE interviewers (instructed *not* to help out) was pragmatically unusual.
(5) The remaining hesitations being 'simple', i.e. a single silent or filled pause. These figures are lower than the results presented by Campione and Véronis (2004), who found that 91% of the silent pauses in an L1 French corpus were accompanied by a filled pause. The difference must stem from the fact that PAROLE calculations include hesitations from 200 ms, whereas the cut-off used by the Aix-en-Provence team was 300 ms.
(6) Although it can be reliably used to assess L1 and L2 oral reading skill (Bolaños *et al.*, 2013; de Wet *et al.*, 2009), or the phonological quality of highly constrained responses (Zechner *et al.*, 2007).

References

American Council on the Teaching of Foreign Languages (1999) *ACTFL Proficiency Guidelines, Speaking: Revised*. Alexandria, VA: ACTFL.
American Council on the Teaching of Foreign Languages (2012) *ACTFL Proficiency Guidelines* (3rd edn). Alexandria, VA: ACTFL. See http://actflproficiencyguidelines 2012.org/ (accessed 18 September 2012).
Boersma, P. and Weenink, D. (2009) *Praat: Doing Phonetics by Computer*. See http://www.praat.org.
Bolaños, D., Cole, R.A., Ward, W.H., Tindal, G.A., Schwanenflugel, P.J. and Kuhn, M.R. (2013) Automatic assessment of expressive oral reading. *Speech Communication* 55, 221–236.
Butterworth, B.L. (1975) Hesitation and semantic planning in speech. *Journal of Psycholinguistic Research* 4 (1), 75–87.
Butterworth, B. (1980) Evidence from pauses in speech. In B. Butterworth (ed.) *Language Production (vol. 1): Speech and Talk* (pp. 155–175). London: Academic Press.

Campione, E. and Véronis, J. (2004) Pauses et hésitations en français spontané. In B. Bel and I. Marlien (eds) *Actes des XXVèmes Journées d'Etude sur la Parole* (pp. 109–112). Fès: Association francophone de la Communication parlée.

Chase, W.G. and Simon, H.A. (1973) Perception in chess. *Cognitive Psychology* 4, 55–81.

Council of Europe (2000) *The Common European Framework of Reference for Languages.* Cambridge: Cambridge University Press.

De Jong, N.H. and Wempe, T. (2007) Automatic measurement of speech rate in spoken Dutch. *ACLC Working Papers* 2 (2), 51–60.

De Jong, N.H., Steinel, M.P., Florijn, A.F., Schoonen, R. and Hulstijn, J.H. (2012) Facets of speaking proficiency. *Studies in Second Language Acquisition* 34 (1), 5–34.

de Wet, F., Van der Walt, C. and Niesler, T.R. (2009) Automatic assessment of oral language proficiency and listening comprehension. *Speech Communication* 51, 864–874.

Deese, J. (1980). Pauses, prosody, and the demands of production in language. In H.W. Dechert and M. Raupach (eds) *Temporal Variables in Speech* (pp. 69–84). den Haag: Mouton.

Derwing, T.M., Munro, M.J., Thomson, R.I. and Rossiter, M.J. (2009) The relationship between L1 fluency and L2 fluency development. *Studies in Second Language Acquisition* 31 (4), 533–558.

Ellis, N.C. (2000) Memory for language. In P. Robinson (ed.) *Cognition and Second Language Instruction* (pp. 33–68). Cambridge: Cambridge University Press.

Erman, B. and Warren, B. (2000) The idiom principle and the open choice principle. *Text* 20, 29–62.

Feyten, C.M. (1991) The power of listening ability: An overlooked dimension in language acquisition. *Modern Language Journal* 75 (2), 173–180.

Forsberg, F. and Bartning, I. (2010) Can linguistic features discriminate between the communicative CEFR-levels? A pilot study of written L2 French. In I. Bartning, M. Martin and I. Vedder (eds) *Communicative Proficiency and Linguistic Development* (pp. 133–158). EUROSLA Monograph Series. See http://eurosla.org/monographs/EM01/EM01home.php (accessed 23 September 2012).

Foster, P., Tonkyn, A. and Wigglesworth, G. (2000) Measuring spoken language: A unit for all reasons. *Applied Linguistics* 21 (3), 354–375.

Goldman-Eisler, F. (1958) Speech analysis and mental processes. *Language and Speech* 1, 59–75.

Griffiths, R. (1991) Pausological research in an L2 context: A rationale, and review of selected studies. *Applied Linguistics* 12 (4), 345–362.

Hilton, H.E. (2008a) The link between vocabulary knowledge and spoken L2 fluency. *Language Learning Journal* 36 (2), 153–166.

Hilton, H.E. (2008b) Connaissances, procédures et productions orales en L2. *Acquisition et interaction en langue étrangère* 27, 63–91.

Hilton, H.E. (2008c) *Le corpus PAROLE: Architecture du corpus et conventions de transcription.* Pittsburgh, PA: Carnegie Mellon University. See http://talkbank.org/BilingBank/

Hilton, H.E. (2009) Annotation and analyses of temporal aspects of spoken fluency. *CALICO Journal* 26 (3), 644–661.

Hilton, H.E. (2011a) L'influence des théories d'acquisition sur la didactique des langues: perspectives historiques. In P. Trévisiol-Okamura and G. Komur-Thilloy (eds) *Discours, acquisition et didactique des langues* (pp. 37–52). Paris: Orizons.

Hilton, H.E. (2011b) What is implicit and what is explicit in L2 speech? Findings from an oral corpus. In C. Sanz and R.P. Leow (eds) *Implicit and Explicit Language Learning: Conditions, processes, and knowledge in SLA and bilingualism* (pp. 145–158). Washington DC: Georgetown University Press.

Hilton, H.E., Osborne, N.J., Derive, M.-J., Suco, N., O'Donnell, J. and Rutigliano, S. (2008) *Corpus PAROLE* (Chambéry: Université de Savoie). TalkBank: SLABank. Pittsburgh: Carnegie Mellon University. http://talkbank.org/BilingBank/

Hulstijn, J.H. (2010) Linking L2 proficiency to L2 acquisition: Opportunities and challenges of profiling research. In I. Bartning, M. Martin and I. Vedder (eds) *Communicative Proficiency and Linguistic Development* (pp. 233–238). *EUROSLA Monographs Series*. See http://eurosla.org/monographs/EM01/EM01home.php (accessed 23 September 2012).

Kaponen, M. and Riggenbach, H. (2000) Overview: Varying perspectives on fluency. In H. Riggenbach (ed.) *Perspectives on Fluency* (pp. 5–24). Ann Arbor, MI: University of Michigan Press.

Kormos, J. (2006) *Speech Production and Second Language Acquisition*. Mahwah, NJ: Lawrence Erlbaum.

Lennon, P. (1990) Investigating fluency in EFL: A quantitative approach. *Language Learning* 40 (3), 387–417.

Levelt, W.J.M. (1989) *Speaking: From intention to articulation*. Cambridge, MA: MIT Press.

Levelt, W.J.M. (1999) Producing spoken language: A blueprint of the speaker. In C.M. Brown and P. Hagoort (eds) *The Neurocognition of Language* (pp. 83–122). Oxford: Oxford University Press.

Lieven, E. (2010) Language development in a cross-linguistic context. In M. Kail and M. Hickmann (eds) *Language Acquisition across Linguistic and Cognitive Systems* (pp. 91–108). Amsterdam: John Benjamins.

Logan, G.D. (1988) Toward an instance theory of automatization. *Psychological Review* 95 (4), 492–527.

Logan, G.D. (1991) Automaticity and memory. In W.E. Hockley and S. Lewandowski (eds) *Relating Theory and Data* (pp. 347–367). Hillsdale, NJ: Laurence Erlbaum.

Maclay, H. and Osgood, C.E. (1959) Hesitation phenomena in spontaneous English speech. *Word* 15, 19–44.

MacWhinney, B. (2007) *The CHILDES Project: Tools for Analysing Talk, electronic edition*. Pittsburgh, PA: Carnegie Mellon University. See http://childes.psy.cmu.edu/manuals/ (accessed 7 August 2007).

MacWhinney, B. (2010) A tale of two paradigms. In M. Kail and M. Hickmann (eds) *Language Acquisition across Linguistic and Cognitive Systems* (pp. 17–32). Amsterdam: John Benjamins.

Malvern, D. and Richards, B. (1997) A new measure of lexical diversity. In A. Ryan and A. Wray (eds) *Evolving Models of Language* (pp. 58–71). Clevedon: Multilingual Matters.

Miller, G.A. (1956) The magical number seven, plus or minus two: Some limits on our capacity for processing information. *Psychological Review* 63, 81–97.

Myles, F. (2005) Interlanguage corpora and second language acquisition research. *Second Language Research* 21 (4), 373–391.

Osborne, N.J. (2011) Fluency, complexity and informativeness in native and non-native speech. *International Journal of Corpus Linguistics* 16 (2), 276–298.

Oxford English Dictionary: Compact Edition (1971). Oxford: Oxford University Press.

Pawley, A. and Syder, F.H. (1983) Two puzzles for linguistic theory: Nativelike selection and nativelike fluency. In J.C. Richards and R.W. Schmidt (eds) *Language and Communication* (pp. 191–226). London: Longman.

Rieger, C.L. (2003) Disfluencies and hesitation strategies in oral L2 tests. In R. Ecklund (ed.) *Gothenburg Papers in Theoretical Linguistics* 90 (pp. 41–44). Göteborg: Göteborg University

Roberts, B. and Kirsner, K. (2000) Temporal cycles in speech production. *Language and Cognitive Processes* 15 (2), 129–157.

Rochester, S.R. (1973) The significance of pauses in spontaneous speech. *Journal of Psycholinguistic Research* 2, 51–81.

Segalowitz, N. (2010) *Cognitive Bases of Second Language Fluency*. New York, NY: Routledge.

Serrano, R., Tragant, E. and Llanes, A. (2012) A longitudinal analysis of the effects of one year abroad. *Canadian Modern Language Review* 68 (2), 136–163.

Sinclair, J.M. (1991) *Corpus, Concordance, Collocation*. Oxford: Oxford University Press.

Towell, R., Hawkins, R. and Bazergui, N. (1996) The development of fluency in advanced learners of French. *Applied Linguistics* 17 (1), 84–119.

Trenchs-Parera, M. (2009) Effects of formal instruction and a stay abroad on the acquisition of native-like oral fluency. *Canadian Modern Language Review* 65 (3), 365–393.

Trofimovich, P. and Baker, W. (2006) Learning second language suprasegmentals: Effects of L2 experience on prosody and fluency characteristics of L2 speech. *Studies in Second Language Acquisition* 28 (1), 1–30.

Wei, M. (2011) Investigating the oral proficiency of English learners in China: A comparative study of the use of pragmatic markers. *Journal of Pragmatics* 43, 3455–3472.

Wray, A. (2000) Formulaic sequences in second language teaching: principle and practice. *Applied Linguistics* 21 (4), 463–489.

Wray, A. (2002) *Formulaic Language and the Lexicon*. Cambridge: Cambridge University Press.

Zechner, K., Higgins, D. and Xi, X. (2007) SpeechRaterTM: A construct-driven approach to scoring spontaneous non-native speech. In *Proceedings of the 2007 Workshop of the International Speech Communication Association Special Interest Group on Speech and Language Technology in Education* (pp. 128–131). Pittsburgh, PA: Carnegie-Mellon University.

Appendix 2A

Propositional content ('information units') for one video description task in PAROLE (summary of a two-part advertisement for Rolo sweets)

Information units	Frames	Events	Attributes
Initial framing (presentation)			
F1: an ad for chocolate			
EVENT 1: (the boy teases the elephant)			
F2a: framing: flashback/in B + W			
macro-event: a boy teases an elephant			
A1: attributes			
boy (*young/obnoxious/plump/pullover/shorts*)			
elephant (*baby/with mother/Dumbo*)			
chocolate (*Rolo/his last one*)			
Micro-events or statements			
E1 he is in a zoo			
E2 he has/is eating chocolates			
E3 unwraps a Rolo			
E4 is about to eat the (last) Rolo			
E5 he sees an elephant			
E6 he calls the elephant			
E7 offers a chocolate			
E8 elephant approaches			
E9 stretches out its trunk			
E10 wants/tries to take the Rolo			
E11 boy takes back the chocolate			
E12 puts it in his mouth			
E13 eats it himself			
E14 laughs/says 'na na na na na'			
E15 elephant is sad/furious			
EVENT 2: (the elephant gets its revenge)			
F2b: framing: years later/in colour/flash forward			
macro-event: revenge of the elephant			
A2: (new) attributes			
boy (*adult/same pullover/hair*)			
elephant (*adult, grown-up*)			
Micro-events or statements			
E16 he is in the street			

	Frames	Events	Attributes
E17 there is a parade/circus			
E18 there are camels etc.			
E19 he is eating a Rolo again			
E20 the elephant walks by			
E21 recognizes/remembers the man			
E22 taps the man on his shoulder			
E23 he looks up			
E24 (E25) hits/slaps him (with his trunk)			
E26 man staggers/falls			
E27 elephant walks away			
E28 trumpets 'na na na na na'			
Final framing (conclusion)			
F3: elephant never forgets/revenge of elephant/think twice			
Total, information units, subject #_____			
	Frames	*Events*	*Attributes*

Appendix 2B

Significant production measures for all learners (NNs), for learner fluency sub-groups (low, mid and high FI) and for native speakers (NSs)

Production measures	Average	Median	Min	Max	SD	Comparisons
Pruned MLU						
NN (all)	11.0	11.1	5.9	17.2	3.06	
Low FI	7.8	7.6	5.9	9.9	1.26	***
Mid FI	11.4	11.6	7.6	15.9	2.75	Low < mid < high
High FI	13.9	13.4	9.6	17.2	2.37	
NSs	17.1	16.3	12.9	27.1	3.49	NS > NN***
Lexical diversity						
NN (all)	81.4	80.9	41.3	127.9	25.31	
Low FI	53.4	52.0	41.3	73.1	9.86	***
Mid FI	86.6	83.2	50.2	121.4	20.43	Low < mid < high
High FI	106.1	107.4	87.3	127.9	13.92	
NFs	142.8	137.7	96.7	208.1	29.13	NS > NN***
Error rate (per 1000 words)						
NN (all)	111.9	93.2	23.5	284.3	61.2	
Low FI	167.4	164.9	87.0	284.3	62.9	**
Mid FI	101.5	80.3	44.0	172.0	52.5	Low > mid > high
High FI	68.0	74.1	23.5	131.3	30.6	
NSs	11.4	10.6	0.0	25.6	6.8	NS < NN***
Syntactic units/utterance						
NN (all)	1.8	1.8	1.0	3.1	0.5	
Low FI	1.4	1.3	1.0	1.9	0.3	***
Mid FI	1.9	1.7	1.2	2.7	0.5	Low < mid < high

High FI	2.3	2.2	1.7	3.1	0.4	
NSs	2.9	2.8	2.4	4.0	0.4	NS > NN***
Information units/utterance						
NN (all)	1.2	1.1	0.53	2.1	0.40	
Low FI	0.8	0.8	0.53	1.33	0.23	*
Mid FI	1.2	1.1	0.60	1.92	0.44	Low < mid < high
High FI	1.5	1.4	0.92	2.1	0.39	
NSs	2.0	1.9	1.31	3.4	0.49	NS > NN***
Mean length of information unit						
NN (all)	11.5	10.9	7.6	17.9	2.60	
Low FI	11.9	12.0	7.6	15.5	2.47	
Mid FI	11.4	11.3	7.8	17.9	2.82	n.s.
High FI	10.9	10.1	8.4	15.6	2.46	
NSs	9.4	8.6	5.7	17.3	2.85	NS < NN*
% Information units mentioned						
NN (all)	32.9	32	14	56	9.29	
Low FI	26.3	26	16	40	7.18	*
Mid FI	34.7	35	14	56	11.89	Low < mid = high
High FI	37.7	38	28	48	6.14	
NSs	39.3	40	24	56	9.35	NS = NN (m)
Syntactic units/minute						
NN (all)	14.7	14.6	6.2	27.9	5.48	
NSs	29.8	29.3	19.3	37.3	5.31	NS > NN***
Information units/minute						
NN (all)	9.2	8.7	3.2	16.2	3.89	
NSs	20.9	20.8	11.7	32	6.00	NS > NN***

Note: Comparisons reported in the right-hand column are based on Mann–Whitney *U* test or Kruskall–Wallis one-way analysis of variance: *$p < 0.01$, **$p < 0.001$, ***$p < 0.0001$, (m) $p = 0.05$.

3 Multiple Assessments of Oral Proficiency: Evidence from a Collaborative Platform

John Osborne

Introduction

'How do I know that my Level B1 is your Level B1?' This question, originally formulated by Charles Alderson (see Figueras *et al.*, 2003: 2), is a long-standing concern for anyone involved in implementing or using the *Common European Framework of Reference* (CEFR). It is a question that can apply at any level of comparison: between countries, across languages, from one institution or from one assessor to another. In the assessment of writing or speaking, particularly, to what extent do assessors have the same understanding of the CEFR scales and descriptors, and how do they relate them to specific features in an individual learner's production? A good deal of work has already been done to provide guidelines, illustrative examples and commentaries that can help to answer the question: examples of secondary-level learners' spoken proficiency in English, French, German, Italian and Spanish are available on the Centre international d'études pédagogiques (CIEP) website[1]; the Council of Europe has prepared DVDs illustrating the spoken proficiency of young adult learners[2]; and the CEFtrain project[3] offers practice, for English only, in evaluating samples at all levels. All these materials allow individuals to compare their perception of the sample productions with assessments made by a panel of experienced teachers/assessors, but they present an apparently consensual view of assessment, in which hesitations, doubts or divergences on the part of the assessors have been ironed out. Such doubts and divergences are nevertheless a real concern for teachers who need to position their students' performance against the CEFR scales and who may wonder to what extent their interpretation of the descriptors converges with that of colleagues elsewhere. For this reason, it is useful to complement the consensual illustrations of CEFR levels with a resource that allows users to compare assessments – including their own – in order to see for themselves where there are areas of agreement or disagreement.

Collaborative Assessment

The WebCEF platform[4] (see Baten et al., 2012) was developed to provide an online tool for this kind of collaborative assessment of oral language proficiency. The platform is structured around collaboration within groups, which can be student groups (typically a group of language learners plus one or more teachers) or trainer groups (groups of teachers or of trainee teachers and teacher trainers). Within a group, the platform can be used for self- or peer-assessment by learners and/or 'expert' assessment by teachers. Briefly, the steps in making an assessment are as follows (for a more complete description see Osborne et al., 2009):

(1) Steps in making an assessment
   a. Create a task. New tasks can be created from scratch, with the instructions and supporting documents being uploaded to the server, or an existing task can be duplicated, modified as necessary, and assigned to a new group.
   b. Record a learner (or pair of learners) doing the task, and upload the recording onto the server. This can be done either by a teacher or by learners making and uploading their own recordings.
   c. Publish the recording so that it can be seen by other members of the group (and only by them). By default, since the platform is primarily designed for collaborative assessment, published recordings and any associated assessments are visible to the whole group, but a group can be configured so that only the learner and his/her teacher can access them.
   d. Assess the learner's performance and/or invite other members of the group to assess it, using the online grids. These are taken from the principal illustrative scales of the CEFR (see below) and include an annotation facility that assessors can use to explain or to detail their assessments; if the annotations refer to specific features in the learner's production, they can be time-stamped to link them to the corresponding point in the recording.

Once an assessment has been completed and published, it will appear alongside any other assessments that have been made of the same recording. The system does not average out multiple assessments to produce an aggregate score, as it was intended precisely to enable users to compare raw assessments. Clicking on a given assessment will display all the annotations and comments made by that assessor.

The samples and assessments made with WebCEF are stored on the project server, which thus constitutes a constantly growing database for those interested in the characteristics of learner productions and in the assessment of oral proficiency. The metadata for all samples can be downloaded and imported into a spreadsheet for the purposes of analysis. To date – early 2014 – the server has 1396 samples and 3116 completed assessments (plus an unknown number of partial or unpublished assessments, which do not appear in the metadata). The principal languages are English, French, Spanish, Italian, Dutch and German, plus a handful of samples in Finnish, Mandarin, Polish and Russian. A subsequent platform, CEFcult[5], added a scenario-building facility for creating tasks, additional scales for intercultural competence based on the INCA project (Prechtl & Davidson Lund, 2007), and an individual 'invite' function to give assessors access to samples, in place of the group structure used in WebCEF. The invite function gives learners more control over who sees their productions, but comparison of assessments is easier within a group structure. For this reason, the examples discussed below are all taken from the WebCEF platform.

The CEFR Scales and Descriptors

Because the purpose was to provide a platform for collaborative assessment using the Common European Framework, the assessment scales and descriptors are taken directly from the tables in the CEFR, without any modifications or additions. However, the CEFR contains more than 30 different scales that can be applied to spoken production: overall scales, analytic scales for qualitative aspects of oral production, and scales for specific competences. It is clearly not practical, and probably not useful, to include all of these in an online application, so the WebCEF assessment tool displays only the overall scale for oral production or for oral interaction (according to the task) and the basic qualitative scales: those for range, accuracy, fluency, interaction (when appropriate) and coherence (Council of Europe, 2001: 28–29). The descriptors are available on the platform in eight languages – Dutch, English, Finnish, French, German, Italian, Polish and Spanish – and will be displayed in whichever of these languages is chosen as the working language of a group at the time of its creation.

It has been observed (see Alderson, 2007: 660) that the translated versions of the CEFR are 'much clearer than the original English version'. Clarity is one of the criteria listed by the CEFR authors in their guidelines for developing descriptors, along with positiveness, definiteness, brevity and independence (Council of Europe, 2001: 206–207). By clarity, though, they mostly mean lack of jargon, and it is the second of their criteria, definiteness, that is likely to be a decisive element in reducing discrepancies between individual interpretations of the descriptors. The CEFR cites two requirements for definiteness:

> Firstly, the descriptor should avoid vagueness, like, for example 'Can use a range of appropriate strategies'. What is meant by strategy? Appropriate to what? How should we interpret 'range'? The problem with vague descriptors is that they can read quite nicely, but an apparent ease of acceptance can mask the fact that everyone is interpreting them differently. Secondly, since the 1940s, it has been a principle that distinctions between steps on a scale should not be dependent on replacing a qualifier like 'some' or 'a few' with 'many' or 'most' or by replacing 'fairly broad' with 'very broad' or 'moderate' with 'good' at the next level up. (Council of Europe, 2001: 206)

While these are sensible requirements, in practice it may not be so easy to meet them. CEFR descriptors typically combine user-oriented specifications of *what* learners can do in the target language and assessor-oriented specifications of *how well* they can perform. In addition, the characterization of how well a learner can do things may be formulated in quantitative terms ('errors are rare'), in functional terms ('does not make errors which cause misunderstanding') or in subjective perceptual terms ('there are few noticeably long pauses').

Scaling these criteria in a series of brief descriptors inevitably calls on a relatively small stock of words – not only qualifiers, but words of all categories – and however carefully the descriptors are phrased, it is sometimes difficult to avoid the impression that successive descriptors for a given aspect of language proficiency are recombinations of each other, with minor substitutions. The descriptors for fluency, for example, at the lower levels (A1 to B1) are essentially constructed around three points: the presence of pause phenomena (*pausing* or *pauses/false starts*), their degree of salience (*very noticeable* or *very evident*) and their putative causes (*to search for expressions* or *for grammatical and lexical planning and repair*):

(2) much pausing to search for expressions (A1);
very noticeable hesitation and false starts (A2);
pauses, false starts and reformulation are very evident (A2+);
pausing for grammatical and lexical planning and repair is very evident (B1).

While many teachers might well understand a difference between 'searching for expressions' and 'grammatical and lexical planning and repair,' the other distinctions, between 'pausing' and 'pauses' or between 'very noticeable' and 'very evident,' are likely to appear somewhat random. At the upper levels (B2+ to C2), the descriptors also evoke three main characteristics, this time spontaneity, lack of effort, and fluidity, combined respectively as follows:

(3) Can communicate spontaneously, often showing remarkable fluency and ease of expression (B2+);
Can express him/herself fluently and spontaneously, almost effortlessly (C1);
Can express him/herself at length with a with a natural, effortless, unhesitating flow (C2).

Assuming that fluency distinctions are actually meaningful beyond B2 level, despite the extent of individual differences in speech rate, pausing and retracing, it is not immediately obvious that 'remarkable fluency and ease of expression' characterizes a lower degree of fluency than 'a natural, effortless, unhesitating flow'. Of course words take their meanings from context, and the descriptors from which these fragments are taken were each designed to be read as a whole. They were also extensively tested, and according to the authors of the CEFR,

> [h]ave been found transparent, useful and relevant by groups of non-native and native speaker teachers from a variety of educational sectors with very different profiles in terms of linguistic training and teaching experience. Teachers appear to understand the descriptors in the set, which has been refined in workshops with them from an initial pool of some thousands of examples. (Council of Europe, 2001: 30)

For practical purposes, then, the question is whether teachers not only appear to understand the descriptors, but also apply them in similar ways in assessing spoken production. Given the increasing use of the CEFR as a European-wide benchmark for language proficiency, it is useful to know how much spontaneous agreement there is between raters in interpreting CEFR descriptors and whether the scales for oral production constitute a rubric that is applied consistently by different assessors, whether they come from similar or from different backgrounds.

Inter-Rater Agreement

The assessments stored on the WebCEF platform have mostly been carried out in the context of informal collaborative assessment. This is a different situation from that of formal testing, particularly for the purposes of certification, where test items will have been carefully selected, where the target level is known and where the examiners have been trained to apply common criteria consistently. In the less formal and less controlled context of collaborative assessment, one would expect more divergence; the question is whether some kinds of divergence are greater than others. The data available on the server are those that have accumulated naturally as a result of piloting and of regular use of the platform. There are groups where a relatively large number of samples have been rated by a small number of assessors, and others where there are numerous assessments of just one or two samples. The first example discussed here is an intermediate case: a set of 19 productions with multiple assessments, in which there is a subset of eight productions each assessed by the same five people. The productions come from an open-ended interactive task (exchanging information and opinions about mobile phones), potentially usable at all levels. The samples, in English, were rated for each of the CEFR scales used in the online assessment tool: overall spoken interaction, range, accuracy, fluency, interaction and coherence. The assessors, all experienced users of the CEFR, were teachers in secondary or higher education in Belgium, Finland, France, Germany and Poland; the learners were upper-secondary and university students, aged 17–24 years, with Dutch, Finnish, French, German or Polish as their L1.

Inter-rater agreement can be measured both in terms of consistency (i.e. the extent to which different raters establish similar rankings when comparing learners) and in terms of consensus (i.e. the extent to which they agree on assigning learners to a specific category, in this instance a given CEFR level). It would be possible for two assessors to show strong consistency but weak consensus, if for example they tend to agree that one speaker has a higher level than another, but disagree in their interpretation of which specific CEFR levels are appropriate for the speakers in question.

For the assessments discussed here, consistency and consensus were measured between each pair of raters (10 pairs in total), using Spearman rank correlation and weighted Kappa respectively. Table 3.1 shows the strongest and weakest agreement between pairs, for each of the six CEFR scales, and the median for all 10 pairs of raters. Generally, whether in terms of consistency or consensus, agreements tended to be stronger for accuracy and for interaction, and weakest for range and for coherence.

Table 3.1 Inter-rater agreement

CEF scale	Consistency (r)			Consensus (k)		
	Max.	Min.	Median	Max.	Min.	Median
Overall	0.956	0.426	0.777	0.822	0.407	0.565
Range	0.883	0.53	0.643	0.714	0.282	0.438
Accuracy	0.962	0.72	0.863	0.739	0.51	0.63
Fluency	0.892	0.511	0.722	0.68	0.455	0.585
Interaction	0.993	0.51	0.838	0.882	0.351	0.684
Coherence	0.928	0.29	0.689	0.83	0.184	0.509

Agreement on the 'overall' scale does not differ markedly from that for the analytic scales. An interesting question for users of the CEFR is how this overall scale is to be related to the scales for accuracy, range and so on. Does an overall rating of B1 suppose that the learner is also at a B1 level on each of the qualitative scales? Does a B2 rating for fluency and an A2 for accuracy somehow average out at an overall B1? The CEFR is not a numerical scoring system, so there is no reason in principle why this kind of calculation should apply, but if the ratings on the qualitative scales do not uniformly confirm the initial overall rating, then should this be moved down accordingly? The presentation of the descriptors in the CEFR suggests that it should:

> Each level should be taken to subsume the levels below it on the scale. That is to say, someone at B1 (*Threshold*) is considered also to be able to do whatever is stated at A2 (*Waystage*), to be better than what is stated at A2 (*Waystage*). (Council of Europe, 2001: 36–37)

If 'whatever' is taken to be all-inclusive, then presumably a learner who is rated overall at B1 should be rated at better than A2 for every aspect of his/her production. The ambiguity turns around whether 'able to do whatever is stated' refers only to quantitative aspects of production, or also includes qualitative aspects. In practice, assessors appear to adopt varying solutions to this question. Cases where an assessor has given a learner's performance an identical rating across all the scales are a minority (25%). The remainder is divided equally between cases where one or more aspects of the performance are rated *higher* than the overall level, and cases where some aspects are rated *lower*. Usually, but not always, the overall rating corresponds to the majority of ratings on the analytic scales. When a user starts an assessment, it is always the overall scale that is displayed first, but because users can skip a scale and return to it later, or can go back and change their mind before publishing an assessment, it is impossible to know whether most users make a holistic assessment first and then look at the analytic scales for confirmation, or whether they use the analytic scales to guide them towards an overall rating. In their annotations, assessors do sometimes mention a characteristic in the production to explain their overall rating. For instance, a learner rated at B2 for range, fluency, interaction and coherence was rated B1 overall, with the explanation 'He communicates with confidence. However, he does not speak in a fluent way but speaks slowly, which will "impose strain" (not imposing strain as a B2 prerequisite) on a native speaker.'

Annotations

The annotations are an important feature of the WebCEF assessment tool, as the most useful information is often not so much *which* level a rater has assigned a given sample to, but *why*. For collaborative assessment, and for providing useful feedback to learners, assessors' annotations are a valuable indication of which features have influenced their decisions. These annotations can also be retrieved from the WebCEF database, and thus constitute a mini-corpus of assessors' comments.

The platform provides a separate annotation box for each of the CEFR scales; some assessors systematically gave comments on their evaluation for each scale, while others were more selective in their annotations. A simple word count of the assessors' annotations shows that the 10 most frequently used terms (in descending order of frequency, and excluding neutral terms such as 'language' or 'speaks') are: 'fluent(ly), basic, simple, vocabulary, mistakes, complex, grammatical, pauses, appropriate, pronunciation'. As we shall see, these are a good reflection of the features that assessors appear to retain as indications of a learner's performance. All of these terms, with the notable exception of 'pronunciation', also appear in the CEFR descriptors, although only two of them – 'simple' and 'grammatical' – are among the most frequent.

Range

Range was the one scale that all assessors systematically annotated. However, it is noticeable that the annotations focus almost exclusively on the speaker's lexical range: 'makes use of a broad lexicon, always choosing the appropriate expression'; 'range of vocabulary is very limited'; 'did not have enough vocabulary to do the task very well'. There are a few comments on syntax ('Most sentence structures are simple, but with one or two more complex sentences'), and occasional remarks that concern neither lexis nor syntax ('A fairly strong accent'). A number of annotations mention the apparent consequences, either positive or negative, of lexical range: 'Can express herself without effort and there is almost no searching for lexical items'; 'Doesn't quite have enough language to get by, and there is a lot of hesitation and circumlocutions'; 'Very basic range of vocabulary, long pauses'.

Accuracy

Like the CEFR descriptors themselves, most of the annotations relating to accuracy are concerned with grammatical control (e.g. 'Good grammatical control with no noticeable errors'). They sometimes include observations on the degree of confidence ('is relatively confident using the most common grammatical structures') or the extent to which errors may interfere with understanding ('only a handful of mistakes in this sample, which do not cause any misunderstanding'; 'makes some errors which create ambiguity'). The question of intelligibility and misunderstanding will be discussed below. There are also some comments on self-correction, although it is not always clear whether this is seen as a positive or a negative characteristic ('Uses a lot of self-correction. Although simple structures are mostly correct, she has more difficulty with more complex structures'; 'Makes numerous beginner's mistakes and does not correct them'). Compared with the annotations relating to other CEFR scales, those for accuracy tend to be a little longer and to contain more specific examples, including time-stamped illustrations. Not surprisingly, the examples illustrate cases where the learner fails to achieve accuracy, but the relatively strong agreement between raters suggests that they share a common understanding of how to relate the limits of a speaker's grammatical control to a specific point on the CEFR scale. In other words, it looks as though raters are able to work upwards through the accuracy descriptors, and reliably find the cut-off point at which learners are *not* able to do the things described, so that they can situate the learner's performance at the level immediately below. It may be that this does not work so well for other scales, such as those for range or for coherence, simply because assessors are not able to find appropriate evidence of learners' inability to do things. Clearly this runs somewhat counter to the CEFR philosophy of positiveness, but identifying the limits of a performance is a common way of situating it on a scale, and is well established in assessment practices.

The descriptors for accuracy do not mention pronunciation; indeed out of more than 30 CEFR scales relevant to oral production only one, 'Phonological control' (Council of Europe, 2001: 117), relates to pronunciation issues, offering a series of very brief descriptors whose criteria are debatable (see Horner, 2010). Yet, pronunciation is the most immediately salient feature of a learner's production, to the extent that listeners can detect accentedness in portions of speech as short as 30 ms (Flege, 1984) or in a single word presented backwards (Munro *et al.*, 2003, 2010). Nearly half of the WebCEF assessments mention pronunciation at some point in the annotations. Because pronunciation does not figure in the main CEFR descriptors, assessors chose various places in which to place their comments, but most included them under 'accuracy', with remarks that are either restricted to pronunciation ('L1 influence in pronunciation quite noticeable') or which relate it to intelligibility ('In pronunciation, has a perceptible accent which might very occasionally require effort from the listener'; 'Some pronunciation/vocabulary errors could cause misunderstanding, e.g. the "warm" game, for worm – i.e. snake – game').

The criterion of intelligibility appears in several guises in the CEFR, notably in the scale for phonological control referred to above (B1: 'Pronunciation is clearly intelligible even if a foreign accent is sometimes evident'), but also in those for accuracy (B2: 'Does not make errors which cause misunderstanding') and for fluency (B1: 'Can keep going comprehensibly'). It is not clear whether the characterization of B2-level accuracy should be taken to imply that misunderstandings do occur at lower levels. If that is the case, then combining these descriptors would give a portrait of a B1 speaker who is intelligible and can keep going comprehensibly, but whose errors may cause misunderstanding, while his/her foreign accent is only 'sometimes' evident.

This somewhat improbable identikit picture of a foreign language learner illustrates the difficulty of applying these criteria without having an overview of what constitutes intelligibility (Munro, 2011), how it is related to comprehensibility (Smith & Nelson, 1985) and how it can be measured (Munro, 2008: 201–210). It also raises questions about the way in which intelligibility is influenced by the context of communication (Levis, 2005; Pickering, 2006) or by the proximity of the speaker's and listener's respective L1s (Munro et al., 2006).

Fluency

A term that occurs regularly in the annotations for fluency, but which does not figure at all in the CEFR descriptors, is 'slow(ly)'. Clearly, assessors consider that slowness is a salient characteristic that needs to be taken into account, but which they generally balance against some other feature: 'fluently but slowly', 'careful and quite slow', 'slow but quite regular', 'slow but even tempo', 'relatively slow but there are no conspicuous hesitations'. The CEFR defines fluency as 'the ability to articulate, to keep going, and to cope when one lands in a dead end' (Council of Europe, 2001: 128) and avoids any mention of 'slow' or 'fast' speech as being a factor in fluency. Undoubtedly, speech rate is not in itself a measure of fluency, and is subject to considerable individual variation. As one annotator puts it, 'It is not easy to tell, whether this is his natural tempo or due to his difficulties in producing English language in particular.' Nevertheless, the number of comments on slow speech indicates that it is a feature that assessors, and probably listeners more generally, do notice in learner speech, and a number of studies (Freed, 2000; Iwashita et al., 2008; Kormos & Dénes, 2004; Lennon, 1990; Osborne, 2011; Riggenbach, 1991) have found a good correlation between speech rate, in words or syllables per minute, and perceived fluency.

The other characteristic that is frequently mentioned in the annotations, and which does figure in the CEFR descriptors, is the presence of pauses or hesitations (see Hilton's analysis, this volume, of a parallel corpus, which leads her to conclude that clause-internal pauses may constitute a good indication of oral proficiency levels). Pauses are characterized either by their frequency ('speaks with many pauses') or by their duration ('pauses are short'), rather than by whether they are 'evident' or 'noticeable', as in the CEFR level descriptors for fluency. It is not very clear whether assessors make a distinction between 'pauses' and 'hesitations'. For some, there seems to be a difference of degree, with 'hesitation' indicating a minor interruption of the speech flow, and 'pause' a longer one. For others, 'hesitation' appears to refer to a mental state, and 'pause' to its manifestation in speech ('long pauses of hesitation').

Many annotators make a connection between fluency and lexical and/or grammatical control, both as a positive factor ('Due to her high degree of grammatical accuracy and wide range of vocabulary, she speaks in a very fluent, almost natural flow') or as a negative factor ('Minor hesitations show that he sometimes has problems choosing the appropriate word or forming a correct sentence'). One aspect of fluency that does not figure prominently is the 'false starts', 'cul de sacs' and 'dead ends' that are referred to in the CEFR. The one annotator who does mention these as a characteristic does not appear to be singling out false starts as a phenomenon, but rather to be using a formula from the CEFR to justify rating a speaker at A2 rather than B1: 'Her pauses, false starts and reformulation are very evident, so I don't think she's quite a B1.'

Interaction

The CEFR descriptors for interaction focus mostly on issues of turn-taking and maintaining conversation. Many of the assessors' annotations also mention the ability to initiate and maintain exchanges, sometimes indicating specifically how this is achieved ('A typical way of turntaking: How about you?'). However, for many assessors, interaction clearly includes other factors. Some of these have to do with the smoothness of interaction, thus partly overlapping with fluency ('a natural flow of interaction between the speakers'; 'interacts easily and naturally'; 'the pace of interaction is relatively slow'). Other remarks touch on questions of coherence, concerning transitional markers between turns ('there is some jumpiness') or referencing between participants' contributions ('is able to ask questions, reply when being asked and refer to statements previously made'), a feature which the CEFR descriptors mention only at C1 and C2 level, but which is noted here at B1 level.

Another interactive feature that appears in a number of annotations is the extent of linguistic collaboration between the participants ('Maintains and re-initiates exchanges, sometimes providing linguistic help for her partner'; 'Helps the discussion along by indicating understanding and sometimes providing a more appropriate word'). The cooperative nature of interaction is evoked in the CEFR via an allusion to Grice: 'In interactive activities the language user acts alternately as speaker and listener with one or more interlocutors so as to construct conjointly, through the negotiation of meaning following the co-operative principle, conversational discourse' (Council of Europe, 2001: 73). Because Grice's aim in proposing this principle was to see talking as a special case of more general purposive behaviour (Grice, 1975: 47), the principle itself, and its accompanying maxims, are presumably not problematic for learners. The question – apart from the possibility of intercultural variations – is to what extent they possess the linguistic means to follow the maxims: to be as informative as required, to avoid obscurity and ambiguity, to be brief and orderly. The linguistic aspects of interactive collaboration between learners, and specifically the ways in which they may help each other to construct their discourse, are not mentioned at all in the CEFR descriptors, which, as McNamara (2012) observes, assume that the interlocutor is a native speaker.

The main gradient along which assessors appear to rate interaction runs from one-sided question-and-answer sequences ('Gives mostly short answers and hands initiative back to her partner': A2) through more sustained and balanced exchanges ('Maintains and re-initiates exchanges': B1) to those where there is greater variety in turn-taking ('Is able to initiate and maintain exchanges and to interrupt appropriately where necessary': B2). Along with accuracy, interaction was the scale where agreement between raters was strongest. To a large extent assessors appear to share a common understanding of what constitutes successful interaction, although what they include under this goes beyond the questions of turn-taking, initiation and maintenance described in the CEFR scale.

Coherence

Coherence is the feature that is least frequently annotated. Most of the comments relating to coherence are a direct reflection of the CEFR descriptors themselves: 'Structures her speech using a range of basic connectors, such as "and", "or" and "so"'; 'structures his speech making use of the most common connectors'. Although the CEFR descriptors are always formulated positively (Council of Europe, 2001: 205–206), raters' annotations frequently re-use phrases from the descriptors but in a more negative context (e.g. 'Does not use very complex cohesive devices'). This is usually done in order to explain why this is the case ('There isn't much chance here to show her ability regarding coherence') or to explain what the speaker does instead ('Does not use very complex cohesive devices, but introduces appropriate linking expressions in the interaction [Really? That's weird!]'). Possibly one of the reasons why raters show relatively weak agreement in their assessment of coherence is that they diverge in their interpretation of what constitutes a 'cohesive device', particularly in the context of a non-argumentative interactive task, where cohesion may be marked by such things as prosody, gesture and co-referencing: 'Good nonverbal communication and rhythm. Elicits a lot of response.'

Expert and Non-Expert Raters

The CEFR descriptors were originally developed in a four-stage process involving analysis of teachers' discussions and the organization of workshops where teachers sorted descriptors into categories (see Council of Europe, 2001: Appendix B). The three principal levels – A, B and C – correspond roughly to the long-standing division in language teaching between elementary, intermediate and advanced levels (Little, 2007). To a large extent, then, the descriptors simply pin down what experienced language teachers already know about what their learners can do. Less experienced raters do not have this fund of prior knowledge to draw upon, and so will need to relate an individual learner's performance more directly to points mentioned in the descriptors. Some of the WebCEF groups are composed of less experienced users of this kind, typically trainee language teachers, who are familiar with the basic principles of the CEFR but have relatively little first-hand experience of teaching or assessment. The examples briefly discussed below are taken from one such group, composed of future teachers of French as a foreign language (47 in all, in three sub-groups, composed of native speakers of French and of speakers of other languages, principally Spanish, Polish, Chinese, Arabic, Russian and English), who were asked to assess productions in French by speakers of Arabic, Dutch and Italian. Comparison of multiple assessments of the same production shows more pronounced divergences than between those of practicing teachers. In some cases, the difference between the lowest and highest overall rating for the same production is as much as three CEFR levels (e.g. ranging from A1 to B2, or from A2 to C1). In cases where the overall ratings are more consensual, there can still be considerable variation in the ratings for the qualitative scales. For example, a production which the majority of users rated as B1 for overall oral production has ratings for fluency ranging from C1 to A2. The annotations that accompany these ratings for fluency, however, all say much the same thing (translated from the original French):

(4) He is very much at ease in oral production and in front of the camera. He uses hand gestures to illustrate what he is saying and not as a sign of stress. Pauses are almost non-existent. (C1)
He has a regular flow without hesitations or long pauses. His facial expression shows that he is at ease and in control of the situation. (C1)
He is at ease in communication. He manages to keep his discourse going all the time and does not seem perturbed. He is spontaneous. (B1)
Few pauses, does not hesitate to express himself at the risk of making mistakes. He is clearly at ease. (B1)

The divergences in the ratings appear to come not from a difference in how the speaker's fluency is perceived – as an impression of being comfortable and at ease – but in how to relate this perception to a specific descriptor. The annotations suggest that 'ease' in speech is perceived not as a purely linguistic phenomenon, definable in terms of pauses and false starts, but as a more general behavior that includes paralinguistic signs of fluency or disfluency:

(5) She uses appropriate tone and gesture to aid understanding
She acts out her account instead of developing it
[...] although there are several hesitations that are made noticeable by her gestures

Table 3.2 Successive assessments by the same rater (example)

Assessment	CEF scale Overall	Range	Accuracy	Fluency	Coherence
1st assessment	B1	A2	A2	B1	B2
2nd assessment	B1	B1	B1	B1	B1
3rd assessment	B1	B1	B2	C1	B1

Comparing their ratings and comments with those of other members of their group often leads assessors to revise their evaluation. When a new assessment is published, it does not replace the previous one, but is displayed above it, so it is possible to follow any adjustments that an assessor may have made to his/her evaluation. There are several examples of this in the non-expert group, including some where the same assessor has made three successive assessments. In most cases, the 'overall' rating has not been changed, but the ratings on the qualitative scales are revised to give a more contrasted view of the speaker's performance, often accompanied by progressively more detailed annotations. An example of this is shown in Table 3.2.

The successive alignment and separation of the overall and qualitative scales seems to reflect a changing strategy on how to assess a performance that is strong in fluency but weak in content. The overall comment accompanying the first assessment reads, 'This learner shows a certain fluency. However he lacks the vocabulary necessary to give a more detailed account.' In the third and final assessment, where the fluency rating has been revised two levels upwards, the following explanation is given: 'The learner seems to be quite at ease. His pronunciation is correct. I chose level B1 overall because the content remains very limited compared to a B2 learner who could have given a fuller description of the setting.' This is indeed in accordance with the CEFR descriptor for overall oral production at B2 level, 'Can give clear, detailed descriptions', but betrays a justifiable hesitation as to how different facets of a performance are to be weighed against each other, particularly in the absence of guidelines on what constitutes a 'detailed' description, and when we know relatively little about how factors such as individual variation, level of education or cultural expectations may influence the quantity of detail delivered, irrespective of proficiency level (see also Callies *et al.*, this volume, for a discussion of individual differences within learner corpora).

Conclusion

Whatever its shortcomings (Fulcher, 2004; Hulstijn, 2007), there is no doubt that the CEFR has gained widespread recognition. Although national practices vary (see EACEA, 2012: 129), it is increasingly common for learners in European educational systems to be aware of their CEFR level (or the level they are supposed to have reached), or to know that for certain purposes along their educational or professional path – to obtain a school certificate, to be accepted on an Erasmus mobility program, to qualify as a primary school teacher – a certain level is required. On the face of it, a CEFR level, with its attendant descriptors, is more meaningful and transparent than a numerical test score. But the divergences discussed above, and the fact that similar annotations may be related to different ratings, suggest that the CEFR descriptors are, as Sajavaara (2005) put it, 'deceptive in their transparency'. They thus need to be complemented by other anchor points: the sample DVDs mentioned earlier, or the development of reference level descriptions by language, and by relating proficiency levels to objective linguistic features in learner language, through projects such as CEFling[6], English Profile[7] (Hendriks, 2008), and other investigations loosely grouped in the SLATE network[8] (Bartning *et al.*, 2010). But these are long-term research projects that necessitate sifting through large amounts of data, and their results are not directly applicable to the everyday needs of language teachers and learners. For them, it is important not only to be aware that the descriptors lend themselves to divergent interpretations, but also to see how, with experimentation and experience, they can lead to a degree of consensus.

Notes

(1) See http://www.ciep.fr/publi_evalcert/dvd-productions-orales-cecrl/index.php
(2) Details of the illustrative DVDs can be found on the Council of Europe site: http://www.coe.int/t/dg4/education/elp/elp-reg/CEFR_speaking_EN.asp. The illustrations for French are included with the paper version of the CEFR, published by Didier.
(3) See http://www.helsinki.fi/project/ceftrain/
(4) The WebCEF platform was developed with funding from the European Lifelong Learning Programme. The project website (http://www.webcef.eu/) gives information on the project and on how to create an account.
(5) The CEFcult website (http://www.cefcult.eu/) provides information about the project, training materials and immediate access to the platform through self-registration.
(6) See https://www.jyu.fi/hum/laitokset/kielet/tutkimus/hankkeet/paattyneet-hankkeet/cefling/en
(7) See http://www.englishprofile.org/
(8) See http://www.slate.eu.org/

References

Alderson, C. (2007) The CEFR and the need for more research. *Modern Language Journal* 91 (4), 659–663.
Bartning, I., Martin, M. and Vedder, I. (eds) (2010) *Communicative Proficiency and Linguistic Development: Intersections between SLA and Language Testing Research*. EUROSLA Monographs Series 1. See http://eurosla.org/monographs/EMhome.html.

Baten, L., Beaven, A., Osborne, J. and Van Maele, J. (2012) WebCEF: An online collaboration tool for assessing foreign language proficiency. In P. Pumilla-Gnarini, E. Favaron, E. Pacetti, J. Bishop and L. Guerra (eds) *Handbook of Research on Didactic Strategies and Technologies for Education: Incorporating advancements* (pp. 559–570). Hershey, PA: IGI Global.

Council of Europe (2001) *Common European Framework of Reference for Languages: Learning, Teaching, Assessment*. Cambridge: Cambridge University Press.

EACEA (2012) Key data on teaching languages at school in Europe. See http://eacea.ec.europa.eu/education/eurydice/documents/key_data_series/143EN.pdf.

Figueras, N., North, B., Takala, S., Van Avermaet, P. and Verhelst, N. (2003) *Relating Language Examinations to the Common European Framework of Reference for Languages: Learning, Teaching, Assessment (CEF). Preliminary Pilot Version*. Strasbourg: Council of Europe.

Flege, J. (1984) The detection of French accent by American listeners. *Journal of the Acoustical Society of America* 76 (3), 692–707.

Freed, B. (2000) Is fluency, like beauty, in the eyes (and ears) of the beholder? In H. Riggenbach (ed.) *Perspectives on Fluency* (pp. 243–265). Ann Arbor, MI: University of Michigan Press.

Fulcher, G. (2004) Deluded by artifices? The Common European Framework and harmonization. *Language Assessment Quarterly* 1 (4), 253–266.

Grice, H.P. (1975) Logic and conversation. In P. Cole and J. Morgan (eds) *Syntax and Semantics 3: Speech acts* (pp. 41–58). New York: Academic Press.

Hendriks, H. (2008) Presenting the English Profile Programme: In search of criterial features. In *Research Notes* (vol. 33) (pp. 7–10). Cambridge: Cambridge ESOL.

Horner, D. (2010) A critical look at the CEFR 'Phonological Control' grid. In J. Mader and Z. Urkun (eds) *Putting the CEFR to Good Use - IATEFL TEA SIG/EALTA Conference Proceedings* (pp. 50–57). See http://www.ealta.eu.org/documents/resources/IATEFL_EALTA_Proceedings_2010.pdf.

Hulstijn, J. (2007) The shaky ground beneath the CEFR: quantitative and qualitative dimensions of language proficiency. *Modern Language Journal* 91 (4), 663–667.

Iwashita, N., Brown, A., McNamara, T. and O'Hagan, S. (2008) Assessed levels of second language speaking proficiency: How distinct? *Applied Linguistics* 29 (1), 24–49.

Kormos, J. and Dénes, M. (2004) Exploring measures and perceptions of fluency in the speech of second language learners. *System* 32, 145–164.

Lennon, P. (1990) Investigating fluency in EFL: A quantitative approach. *Language Learning* 40 (3), 387–417.

Levis, J. (2005) Changing contexts and shifting paradigms in pronunciation teaching. *TESOL Quarterly* 39 (3), 369–377.

Little, D. (2007) The Common European Framework of Reference for Languages: Perspectives on the making of supranational language education policy. *Modern Language Journal* 91 (4), 645–653.

McNamara, T. (2012) English as a lingua franca: The challenge for language testing. *Journal of English as a Lingua Franca* 1 (1), 199–202.

Munro, M. (2008) Foreign accent and speech intelligibility. In J. Edwards and M. Zampini (eds) *Phonology and Second Language Acquisition* (pp. 193–218). Amsterdam: Benjamins.

Munro, M. (2011) Intelligibility: Buzzword or buzzworthy? In J. Levis and K. LeVelle (eds) *Proceedings of the 2nd Pronunciation in Second Language Learning and Teaching Conference, September 2010* (pp. 7–16). Ames, IA: Iowa State University.

Munro, M., Derwing, T. and Burgess, C. (2003) The detection of foreign accent in backwards speech. In M.-J. Sole, D. Recasens and J. Romero (eds) *Proceedings of the 15th International Congress of Phonetic Sciences* (pp. 535–538). Barcelona: Universitat Autònoma de Barcelona.

Munro, M., Derwing, T. and Morton, S. (2006) The mutual intelligibility of L2 speech. *Studies in Second Language Acquisition* 28 (1), 111–131.

Munro, M., Derwing, T. and Burgess, C. (2010) Detection of non-native speaker status from content-masked speech. *Speech Communication* 52 (7–8), 626–637.

Osborne, J. (2011) Oral learner corpora and assessment of speaking skills. In A. Frankenburg-Garcia, L. Flowerdew and G. Aston (eds) *New Trends in Corpora and Language Learning* (pp. 181–197). London: Continuum.

Osborne, J., Mateusen, L., Neuhoff, A. and Valentine, C. (2009) Practical guidelines on the use of the WebCEF online assessment environment. In H. Bijnens (ed.) *WebCEF: Collaborative evaluation of oral language skills through the web* (pp. 51–68). Leuven: AVNet KU Leuven. See http://webcef.open.ac.uk/task_documents/webcef_environment.pdf.

Pickering, L. (2006) Current research on intelligibility in English as a lingua franca. *Annual Review of Applied Linguistics* 26, 219–233.

Prechtl, E. and Davidson Lund, A. (2007) Intercultural competence and assessment: Perspectives from the INCA Project. In H. Kotthoff and H. Spencer-Oatey (eds) *Handbook of Intercultural Communication* (pp. 467–490). Berlin: Mouton de Gruyter.

Riggenbach, H. (1991) Towards an understanding of fluency: A microanalysis of non-native speaker conversations. *Discourse Processes* 14, 424–441.

Sajavaara, K. (2005) The CEFR and its impact on a national language policy. *CEL/ELC Workshop on the Implementation of the Common European Framework of Reference at Higher Education Level*, Berlin. See here: http://www.celelc.org/archive/speeches/2005_FUB_workshop_Sajavaara/index.html.

Smith, L. and Nelson, C. (1985) International intelligibility of English: Directions and resources. *World Englishes* 4 (3), 333–342.

4 Using Learner Corpora for Testing and Assessing L2 Proficiency

Marcus Callies, María Belén Díez-Bedmar and Ekaterina Zaytseva

Introduction

The compilation and accessibility of computer corpora and software tools for corpus analysis has revolutionized (applied) linguistics in the last two decades. Corpora and corpus linguistic tools and methods are also increasingly used in the study of second and/or foreign language (L2) learning. Learner corpus research (LCR) is an interdisciplinary field at the crossroads of corpus linguistics, second language acquisition (SLA) research and foreign language teaching that makes use of computer learner corpora to improve the description of interlanguages and to create and develop pedagogical tools and materials that more accurately target the needs of specific learner populations (Granger, 2009). Learner corpora are also increasingly used to test and assess L2 proficiency. It seems necessary at this point to address these concepts briefly.

Language testing and assessment (LTA) as a sub-field in applied linguistics subsumes a vast field of different assessment and testing contexts in which the terms 'testing' and 'assessment' are often used interchangeably. They are linked by a core meaning that denotes 'the systematic gathering of language-related behavior in order to make inferences about language ability and capacity for language use on other occasions' (Chapelle & Plakans, 2012: 241); however, language *assessment* is often used to refer to a more varied process of data gathering and interpretation than language *testing*, which applies to assessment practices in institutional contexts (Chapelle & Plakans, 2012: 241). The present chapter deals with the ways in which learner corpora can be used in the assessment of L2 proficiency in the written mode. L2 proficiency is a construct that is considered multi-componential in nature, and its dimensions are frequently captured and operationalized by the notions of complexity, accuracy and fluency (see Housen *et al.*, 2012; Housen & Kuiken, 2009; Skehan, 1998; Wolfe-Quintero *et al.*, 1998, as well as the special issue of *Applied Linguistics* 30 (4)). Complexity, accuracy and fluency have figured as major research variables in applied linguistics, and have been used both as performance descriptors for the assessment of oral and written skills of L2 learners, and as indicators of the proficiency underlying learners' performance; they have also been used for measuring learning progress (Housen & Kuiken, 2009: 461).

LCR has so far typically focused on L2 writing at advanced levels of proficiency (broadly speaking), and has contributed significantly to the description of advanced interlanguages by specifying the areas that are still problematic even for learners at advanced stages of L2 learning (e.g. Granger, 2009). Current practices in LCR thus mirror the interest that advanced stages of acquisition and questions of near-native competence have received in SLA research in general (see Callies, 2009; Labeau & Myles, 2009; Ortega & Byrnes, 2008; Walter & Grommes, 2008). However, the ways in which the concept of 'advancedness' has been operationalized and assessed in published research differ considerably. And in fact, generally, the effects of varying levels of proficiency among subjects have received too little attention in SLA research. Thomas (1994, 2006), for instance, concludes from her review of methods used to assess L2 proficiency in published SLA research that proficiency is sometimes inadequately assessed, thereby often limiting the generalizability of results. This is particularly true of global proficiency measures, such as institutional status (a learner's position within some kind of hierarchically organized educational setting or institution), assessment on the basis of the subjective intuition of raters (e.g. Coppieters, 1987), or learners' scores on standardized tests (e.g. the 'Test Of English as a Foreign Language') where learner output is tightly constrained by the respective task(s).

Due to the practical constraints of corpus compilation, proficiency level in learner corpora has frequently been assessed globally by means of external criteria (most often the institutional status of the learners), and not by means of the actual corpus data, i.e. the texts that learners have produced (Carlsen, 2012: 165; see also Chapter 1, this volume, for an overview of measurement practices in SLA research). Recent studies show that global proficiency measures based on external criteria alone are not reliable indicators of proficiency for corpus compilation (Callies, 2013a, 2013b; Mukherjee, 2009). The field thus needs to develop and operationalize a corpus-based description of language proficiency for L2 assessment that will provide homogeneity in learner corpus compilation while accounting for inter-learner variability.

In LTA, writing proficiency has largely been assessed by evaluating written sections from language tests, and interpreting those in terms of the 'degree of task fulfilment and evidence of target language control according to criteria such as *communicative effectiveness, register, organisation, linguistic range and accuracy*' (Hawkey & Barker, 2004: 122f.; emphasis in original). Test results are then evaluated and interpreted in accordance with expectations of what learners can do at a particular level of language proficiency as specified, for example, in the *Common European Framework of Reference for Languages* (CEFR; Council of Europe, 2001, 2009). While the CEFR is highly influential in language testing and assessment, the way it defines proficiency levels using can-do statements has been criticized (see e.g. Hawkins & Filipović, 2012; Hulstijn, 2007; Weir, 2005). Its can-do statements are often impressionistic and turn out to be too global and underspecified to be of practical value to distinguish between the different proficiency levels (but see Osborne, this volume, for insight into rating practices using the CEFR on an online collaborative platform). They moreover have limited value when it comes to providing a detailed linguistic description of language proficiency as regards individual languages and learners' skills in specific registers.

Learner corpora present an option to inform, supplement and possibly advance the way proficiency is operationalized in the CEFR, and they may also be used in a more data-driven approach to the assessment of proficiency that is partially independent of human rating. In this chapter, we present two examples that describe, in complementary fashion, ways in which learner corpora can be used to increase transparency, consistency and comparability in the assessment of L2 writing proficiency. The chapter is structured as follows. In the next section we will review recent developments in the application of learner corpora in LTA, proposing a tripartite distinction of approaches. The following two sections present our example studies, and the final section concludes our chapter.

Learner Corpora and their Application in Language Testing and Assessment

Computer learner corpora are generally defined as systematic collections of authentic, continuous and contextualized language use (spoken or written) by L2 learners stored in electronic format. In a narrower sense, Granger (2008: 261) highlights the length of language samples and the context in which the language has been produced as the most important criteria for a learner corpus:

> the notion of 'continuous text' lies at the heart of corpushood. A series of decontextualized words or sentences produced by learners, while being bona fide learner production data, will never qualify as learner corpus data. In addition, it is best to restrict the term 'learner corpus' to the most open-ended types of tasks, viz. those tasks that allow learners to choose their own wording rather than being requested to produce a particular word or structure.

In other words, language samples should be representative of learners' contextualized language use. Examples of well-known learner corpora that have been used within both SLA research and LTA are the *International Corpus of Learner English* (ICLE; Granger *et al.*, 2009) and the *Cambridge Learner Corpus* (CLC; e.g. Hawkins & Filipović, 2012). Generally speaking, learner corpora bring with them a number of potential benefits, have the potential to increase transparency, consistency and comparability in the assessment of L2 proficiency, and are thus increasingly being used in LTA (Barker, 2010; Hawkins & Buttery, 2009, 2010; Hawkins & Filipović, 2012; Taylor & Barker, 2008). We will first discuss several ways in which learner corpora have been and can be applied in the field of LTA before we highlight several challenges and pitfalls of using them in the assessment of proficiency.

Three Approaches to Using Learner Corpora in LTA

In corpus linguistics, there is a general distinction between corpus-based and corpus-driven approaches.[1] The former is sometimes narrowly considered 'a methodology that avails itself of the corpus mainly to expound, test or exemplify theories and descriptions that were formulated before large corpora became available to inform language study' (Tognini-Bonelli, 2001: 65). From this point of view, a corpus is used as evidence corroborating pre-existing linguistic description, for example, as a source of examples to check a researcher's intuition or to examine the frequency of occurrence of a specific language structure within a dataset. By contrast, corpus-driven approaches make minimal prior assumptions about language structure, and are said to be more 'inductive', because the corpus itself is the data and the patterns of language use found in the corpus become the basis for defining regularities and exceptions in language. While this seemingly clear distinction is probably overstated (McEnery *et al.*, 2006: 8), 'corpus-based' is the more vague and general term of the two because it is often used in a much wider sense than the narrow definition given above, referring to any work that makes use of a corpus.

It seems important, therefore, to distinguish between different approaches to using learner corpora in LTA according to three criteria: (1) the way corpus data are actually put to use, (2) the aims and outcomes for LTA, and (3) the degree of involvement of the researcher in data retrieval, analysis and interpretation. These criteria enable us to divide applications of learner corpora in LTA into *corpus-informed*, *corpus-based* and *corpus-driven* approaches. It is important to stress that these are not strict distinctions, and that the three approaches may overlap or even merge in some practices, as we will see in the examples discussed below.

In *corpus-informed* applications, learner corpora are used as reference sources to provide test evidence: for example, corpus data are used to inform test content or to validate human raters' claims (e.g. Alderson, 1996; Barker, 2004, 2010; Granger & Thewissen, 2005; Taylor & Barker, 2008). Barker points out that

> [t]here are many ways in which learner corpora can inform various stages in the lifecycle of a language test [...]. In relation to user needs and test purpose, learner corpora show us what learners of a language *can do* at certain levels of proficiency, which can inform what is tested at a particular proficiency level, whether overall or at task or item level. (Barker, 2010: 639, emphasis in original)

The stages of evaluation and interpretation of test results can also be informed by learner corpora. Hawkey and Barker (2004) show how information gained by manual grading of writing scripts can be combined with insights obtained from a learner corpus and corpus techniques in order to suggest a number of criterial features (that is, features that can be used to distinguish between different performance levels) for differentiating between several proficiency levels that could be further incorporated into a scale for writing assessment. Granger and Thewissen (2005), Thewissen (2011) and Díez-Bedmar (2010) are examples of studies representing a separate strand of research that makes use of error-tagged corpora to provide insights into those areas that are problematic at each proficiency level. They may also be considered corpus-based, because they investigate criterial features; the next section provides an example of corpus-informed applications for LTA.

In *corpus-based* approaches, corpus data are used to explore learner language, often – but not necessarily – comparing it to the language of native speakers (NSs), in search of empirical evidence confirming or refuting a researcher's hypotheses. Recent work by Hawkins and colleagues (2010, 2012) on criterial features in L2 English exemplifies the corpus-based approach. Their work aims at identifying linguistic descriptors to make information on CEFR proficiency levels more explicit by adding 'grammatical and lexical details of English to CEFR's functional characterisation of the different levels' (Hawkins & Filipović, 2012: 5). The procedure involves comparing particular linguistic features as used by learners and native speakers in two kinds of corpora: the *Cambridge Learner Corpus*, composed of exam scripts produced by learners at different proficiency levels, and a corpus of native-speaker English, the *British National Corpus* (BNC). Depending on similarities and differences in usage patterns across corpora, linguistic features acquire the status of either positive or negative linguistic properties, respectively, and are interpreted as criterial features that are 'characteristic and indicative of L2 proficiency at each level, on the basis of which examiners make their practical assessments' (Hawkins & Filipović, 2012: 6).

Finally, *corpus-driven* approaches presuppose the least degree of involvement by the researcher, as they rely on computer techniques for data extraction and evaluation. Here, *corpus-driven* truly means *data-driven* (see Francis, 1993: 139). The questions and conclusions formulated by the researcher will be derived from what the corpus data actually reveal when subjected to statistical analysis; the researcher does not approach the data influenced by *a priori* ideas and claims. An illustration of the corpus-driven approach in L2 proficiency assessment is provided by Wulff and Gries' (2011) proposal to measure learners' accuracy through probabilistic analysis of lexico-grammatical association patterns. While such methods have not yet been widely used in LTA, this kind of approach is particularly useful for a 'text-centred' (Carlsen, 2012: 165), data-driven classification of proficiency based on linguistic descriptors, such as those that are typical of a specific register. Table 4.1 presents a comparative summary of the three approaches to using learner corpora discussed in this section.

Table 4.1 Three approaches to using learner corpora in LTA

	Approach		
	Corpus-informed	*Corpus-based*	*Corpus-driven*
Use	Corpus as reference source, provides practical information on learners' language use at certain levels of proficiency	Corpus as source of data for linguistic research, testing existing hypotheses about learner language	No preconceptions/ hypotheses prior to corpus analysis; computer techniques for data extraction and evaluation
Aims and outcomes for LTA	Evidence for test content and for validating human ratings	Evidence used to identify a set of distinct features or descriptors for differentiating proficiency levels	Evidence of proficiency based on statistical analyses (such as clustering)
Degree of involvement of researcher/test designer	High	Medium	Low
Example	CLC (Hawkey & Barker 2004)	CLC (Hawkins & Filipović 2012)	ICLE (Wulff & Gries 2011)

Challenges Associated with the Use of Learner Corpora in LTA

Notwithstanding obvious benefits, the use of learner corpora in LTA faces several challenges that should also be discussed here briefly. Their use can be problematic and might even lead to misleading generalizations if a number of criteria have not been satisfied. Generally speaking, a corpus is useful for LTA if the information it contains is reliable in terms of the language variety it represents, useful with respect to the test purposes, and in turn valid for identifying CEFR levels (or other proficiency scales). Whereas both the CLC and the most widely used learner corpus to date, the *International Corpus of Learner English*, both represent learner language, they provide two different kinds of data. The CLC is a collection of learner exam scripts across different proficiency levels, whereas the ICLE samples the writing of intermediate to advanced learners of English in the form of literary and argumentative essays. In the case of the CLC, the learner data are constrained by the task setting and possibly influenced by the test environment. Corpus-based enquiries relevant for LTA must consider how the production situation may have influenced the language contained in the corpus, and whether such language use is relevant for the analysis at hand. It is also important to consider whether the native versus non-native speaker distinction is the only variable used to identify features of L2 proficiency in the CLC, or whether other variables are at play. A related question concerns the extent to which the analyses suggested by Hawkins and colleagues are appropriate in terms of corpus comparability. Language produced in an exam situation as a response to a particular task is compared with the highly contextualized native-speaker usage represented in the BNC; language use is thus radically different from one corpus to the other, making comparisons problematic. Differences between texts produced by native speakers and L2 learners may in fact result from differences in task setting (prompts, timing, access to reference works, and so on; see Ädel, 2008), and possibly task instruction and imagined audience (see Ädel, 2006: 201–208, for a discussion of corpus comparability).

Similar questions apply to the use of the ICLE. ICLE-informed generalizations in the context of LTA are valid provided that variables such as language proficiency, register/genre, task setting, imagined audience and so on, have been sufficiently controlled and documented. In the compilation of the ICLE, learners' proficiency level was assessed globally by means of external criteria: learners were considered advanced because of their institutional status as 'university undergraduates in English (usually in their third or fourth year)' (Granger *et al.*, 2009: 11). However, the results of human rating of 20 essays per ICLE sub-corpus according to the CEFR levels (Granger *et al.*, 2009: 12) showed that the proficiency level of learners represented in the ICLE actually varies between (higher) intermediate and advanced (see also Pendar & Chapelle, 2008). While some ICLE sub-corpora seem to predominantly include learners from either the CEFR's B2 (e.g. Chinese, Japanese, Tswana and Turkish EFL learners) or C1 proficiency levels (Bulgarian, Russian and Swedish learners), others show a higher degree of intragroup variability (Czech, German and Norwegian learners) (Granger *et al.*, 2009: 12). Such individual differences often go unnoticed or tend to be disregarded in learner corpus analysis and are thus not reported in favor of (possibly skewed) average frequency counts. Recent studies confirm that global proficiency measures based on external criteria alone are not reliable indicators of proficiency for corpus compilation (Callies, 2013a, 2013b; Mukherjee, 2009). However, once such challenges have been tackled, language corpora present LTA experts with diverse possibilities for exploring learner language and L2 proficiency.

In what follows, we present two examples that describe different approaches to the use of learner corpora for assessing L2 proficiency in writing. The first example emphasizes the existence of various proficiency levels within the same institutional groups (even in a high-stakes examination situation), and the nature of 'negative linguistic properties' (Hawkins & Buttery, 2010: 4f.) at each of these levels. Employing a combination of computer-aided error analysis (CEA) and expert ratings using the CEFR proficiency levels, the study reported below examined a learner corpus of English compositions written for the English section of the University Entrance Examination at the University of Jaén, Spain (Díez-Bedmar, 2010, 2011a, 2011b, 2012). The second example outlines how a Language-for-Specific-Purposes learner corpus, the *Corpus of Academic Learner English* (CALE), which is currently being compiled for the study of academic learner writing, can be used to operationalize 'positive linguistic properties' (Hawkins & Buttery, 2010: 4f), e.g. language- and register-specific linguistic descriptors, in a text-centered, corpus-driven approach to assess writing proficiency in the academic register (Callies & Zaytseva, 2013b).

Example 4.1: Considering the students' institutional status or their proficiency level(s) in a high-stakes examination: Are we missing anything?

The description of students' written production at various proficiency levels can be made by means of objective measures, such as complexity, accuracy and fluency (e.g. Housen *et al.*, 2012; Housen & Kuiken, 2009; Ortega, 2003; Polio, 1997; Wolfe-Quintero *et al.*, 1998; the special issue of *Applied Linguistics* 30 (4)). Another possibility is to focus exclusively on the type and frequency of errors that students make when writing in the L2 by means of a CEA (Dagneaux *et al.*, 1998).

Whatever the approach, the students' institutional status has been a widely used proficiency measure to compile (learner) corpora and analyse learner writing. Institutional status has, however, proved to be problematic (Pendar & Chapelle, 2008; Granger et al., 2009; Díez-Bedmar, 2012), because the same institutional level frequently conflates students of heterogeneous proficiency levels. Analyses based on learner corpora compiled according to this variable may, therefore, not offer a clear snapshot of a particular proficiency level, but rather a picture blurred by the various proficiency levels involved.

To avoid these methodological limitations, a fruitful line of research combines the use of the CEFR to establish students' proficiency level, and the use of CEA to analyse their written production. In this way, errors that characterize each CEFR level can be identified – along the lines of Hawkins and Filipović (2012: 19) 'negative grammatical features' – and considered as criterial in the identification of CEFR levels (Department of Theoretical and Applied Linguistics, 2011; Díez-Bedmar, 2011a; Hawkey & Barker, 2004; Hawkins & Buttery, 2009, 2010; Hawkins & Filipović, 2012; Thewissen, 2011).

To further recent analyses (Díez-Bedmar 2011a, 2012), this section examines possible differences in L2 proficiency level within the same institutional learner group, and the ways in which error type and frequency vary at different proficiency levels. This analysis thus involves three steps: (1) identifying the most frequent errors in learner writing at a particular institutional level (Díez-Bedmar, 2011a); (2) showing that the same institutional status may conceal various proficiency levels (Díez-Bedmar, 2012); and (3) uncovering the possible differences regarding the type and frequency of errors in learner writing at the proficiency levels found.

The institutional status analysed here is that of secondary school leavers in Spain who take the University Admission Examination (UAE), that is, students who have finished their optional secondary school education and want to study for a degree at university. Among the sections of the UAE, only the final part of the English exam – in which students are asked to write a composition – was considered. The learner corpus analysed is composed of 302 compositions (34,403 words) that students wrote on the topic 'Where outside Spain would you like to go on a short pleasure trip? Give reasons' for the UAE in June 2008 at the University of Jaén.

To analyse the problems that this learner group had when writing in their L2 for the English section of the UAE, the learner corpus was error-tagged by means of the error taxonomy in the *Error Tagging Manual*, version 1.1. (Dagneaux et al., 1996).[2] This error taxonomy considers 43 tags distributed in seven error categories: Form (F), Grammar (G), Lexico-Grammar (X), Lexis (L), Word Redundant, Word Missing and Word Order (W), Register (R) and Style (S). In addition, the learner corpus was error-tagged for another error category, Punctuation (P), because the error-tags Punctuation Missing (PM), Punctuation Redundant (PR) and Wrong Punctuation (PX) were included in the *UCL Error Editor* (Hutchinson, 1996).

As a result of the error-tagging process applied to the 302 compositions, an overview of the students' problems was obtained. Table 4.2 presents the

Table 4.2 Top five error-tags, with percentage per total number of errors – same institutional status (based on Díez-Bedmar, 2011a)

Error-tag	Raw frequency	Percentage
LS (selection of vocabulary)	591	16.8
FS (spelling)	570	16.3
GP (pronoun use)	292	8.4
GA (article use)	262	7.5
XVCO (verbal complementation)	144	4.4

error-tags for the five most frequent errors per total number of errors in the entire group. As the table shows, problems related to the selection of vocabulary and spelling are the most frequent, followed by errors in the use of pronouns, articles and verbal complementation.

The next step consisted in the analysis of the different proficiency levels within the institutional group. Two independent experienced raters were asked to assess the compositions in the learner corpus, using the CEFR. As described in Díez-Bedmar (2012), inter-rater reliability was found to be low ($k = 0.245$). Therefore, only the 196 compositions on which there was full inter-rater agreement were considered. After collating all the data provided by the raters, four CEFR levels were found to be represented in the learner corpus. As shown in Figure 4.1, B1 (Threshold level) is the most widely represented level in the corpus (179 = 91.3% of the total sample), which is in line with the linguistic policy determining the curriculum for secondary school leavers in Spain (optional secondary education is to consolidate CEFR B1 level in English as a foreign language). Nevertheless, the learner corpus also contains compositions that the raters evaluated as A2 (Waystage level, 10 compositions), B2 (Vantage level, six compositions) and C1 (Effective operational proficiency level, one composition). Therefore, different proficiency levels (according to the CEFR reference scales) were found within a group having the same institutional status (Díez-Bedmar, 2012). Although a large

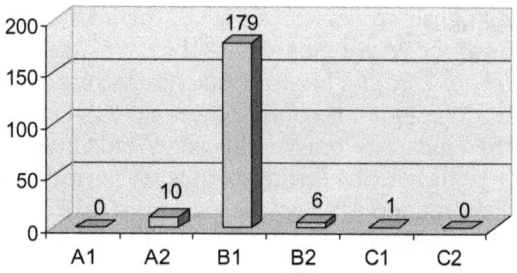

Figure 4.1 Number of compositions at each CEFR level within the same institutional status: full inter-rater agreement (based on Díez-Bedmar, 2012: 71–72)

majority of these secondary school leavers were found to perform at the same B1 proficiency level, the human raters found that 10 students lag behind the established level, while seven students outperform their classmates in EFL writing. Claiming that all students found in a group of secondary school leavers are at CEFR level B1 would therefore not faithfully reflect the reality found in this learner group.

The third step focused on the type and percentage of errors in the texts for each of the CEFR levels identified. The 196 compositions on which there had been full inter-rater agreement were divided into three sub-corpora (A2, B1 and B2).[3] For each sub-corpus, the percentage of errors for each error-tag (per total number of errors) at each CEFR level could be calculated. As shown in Table 4.3, two interesting aspects are worth noting.

First, the error-tags for vocabulary selection, spelling, article use and pronoun use show the highest means at each of the three CEFR levels. It is interesting to notice that problems related to vocabulary selection and spelling are the two most frequent error types, regardless of the level. Second, the different error types occur in differing proportions at the different levels. For instance, errors in the appropriate selection of lexical items amount to 21.5% at CEFR A2 level, dropping to 17.1% at B1, and increasing to 25.6% at B2,

Table 4.3 Error-tags that show the five highest means of errors per total number of errors at each CEFR level

CEFR level	Number of occurrences	Percent of total errors
A2		
LS (selection of vocabulary)	47	21.5
FS (spelling)	46	21
GVAUX (modal auxiliary verbs)	20	9.1
GA (article use)	17	7.8
GP (pronoun use)	14	6.4
B1		
LS (selection of vocabulary)	533	17.1
FS (spelling)	509	16.3
GP (pronoun use)	274	8.8
GA (article use)	241	7.1
XVCO (verbal complementation)	137	4.4
B2		
FS (spelling)	14	32.5
LS (selection of vocabulary)	11	25.6
GP (pronoun use)	4	9.3
GA (article use)	3	6.9
GWC (incorrect word class)	3	6.9

thus describing an inverted U (as is also the case with the errors regarding spelling). Errors in pronoun use increase across the sub-corpora, rising from 6.4% of the error total in the CEFR A2 level sub-corpus, to 8.8% (B1) and 9.3% (B2). Conversely, errors with article use decrease, from 7.8% at CEFR A2 level, to 7.7% (B1) and then to 6.9% (B2). Due to the small numbers of texts at the A2 and B2 levels in this corpus, these are only possible trends, but they give an idea of how corpus analysis may help teachers and students to identify a composition as being at CEFR A2, B1 or B2 level.

It is also important to highlight two other frequent problems in learner writing at two levels (see Table 4.3), namely the use of modal auxiliary verbs at the A2 level (the third most frequent error type in this sub-corpus) and errors in word class at the B2 level (the fifth most frequent type). These two error types would have gone unnoticed if the students' institutional status rather than proficiency level had been considered – compare the list of error types for the entire institutional group in Table 4.2. The assumption that all students at the same institutional level have the same L2 proficiency no doubt affects the choice of pedagogical materials. Tasks designed to favour remedial teaching for secondary school leavers may not have included materials on the appropriate use of modal verbs or the correct selection of word classes, as these error types did not emerge from an analysis of the whole group. Consequently, the linguistic needs of those students at the CEFR A2 and B2 levels would not have been met.

To sum up, even in this particular case we have seen that apparent or assumed homogeneity actually hides a certain heterogeneity in proficiency in written L2 production. This would be even more clearly the case for learner groups in institutions that are not so influenced by the washback effect of the high-stakes UAE examination in Spain. Tasks designed to improve the students' written language at a certain institutional status (e.g. secondary school leavers) may not fully coincide with the linguistic tasks used in the classroom to improve the students' proficiency level(s), as each CEFR level may require special attention to some aspects of the L2 that are not that problematic at other levels (e.g. pronoun use at CEFR A2 level).

In addition to further analysis of the differences found in the type and frequency of errors in learner writing when considering their institutional level versus their proficiency levels, future lines of research should include further analysis of the type and frequency of errors produced by students at the B1 level, as well as statistical analyses of the differences between the levels in the learner corpus to see if they are criterial. Analyses of larger learner corpora for Spanish learners of English are needed to verify the trends identified here. Finally, comparisons with written productions by students of English from other L1 backgrounds would also be interesting, as they would allow us to determine whether these errors point to possible criterial features for all learners of English at the A2–B2 proficiency levels, or only for students of English whose L1 is Spanish.

Example 4.2: Using the *Corpus of Academic Learner English* (CALE) to assess writing proficiency in the academic register

Our second example demonstrates how a corpus representing L2 use in a non-testing situation can be employed to assess advanced learner language produced in an academic context. We will show the potential of using a corpus to implement and operationalize a set of 'positive linguistic properties' to determine what learners can do with language at an advanced level when writing for academic purposes.

As discussed above, the construct of advanced language proficiency, although the focus of much recent research, remains difficult to pin down and, as a result, the field is still struggling to define and clarify the concept of 'advancedness' (see Callies, 2013a, for further discussion). Recently, Ortega and Byrnes (2008) have discussed four partially overlapping global measures commonly used to operationalize advancedness: institutional status, standardized tests, late-acquired linguistic features and a concept they call 'sophisticated language use in context'. In this construct, advancedness is conceptualized not only in terms of 'purely linguistic accomplishments', but also – among other things – in terms of literacy, 'choice among registers' and 'voice' (Ortega & Byrnes, 2008: 8). We intend to elaborate on the concept of advancedness in academic writing, operationalizing it by identifying linguistic descriptors that are characteristic of this register, and which we will subsequently apply to L2 assessment.

Academic writing is among the most difficult registers for language users to master (Callies *et al.*, 2013). Given the high cognitive demand posed by academic writing and the fact that exposure and use are generally limited to higher levels of education, it is worth emphasizing that even many native speakers never achieve mastery in this skill. Indeed, for native and non-native users alike, academic writing skills represent perhaps one of the most advanced levels of writing proficiency. Many of the difficulties that have been observed in academic learner writing seem to be caused by a lack of understanding of the conventions of this register, or a lack of practice, but are not necessarily a result of interference from L1 academic conventions (McCrostie, 2008: 112).

There is an increasing awareness among researchers of the need to identify linguistic descriptors or criterial features that will enable us to differentiate reliably between the proficiency levels described in the CEFR, but also to describe L2 proficiency as regards individual languages and learners' skills in specific registers. As possible candidates for criterial features, Hawkins and Filipović (2012), for example, list different clause types and verbal complementation patterns. Neff van Aertselaer and Bunce (2011) identify the use of reporting verbs as a means of expressing stance in written academic discourse, while Wulff and Gries (2011) propose the proficient use of constructions in their lexico-grammatical association patterns as a discriminating descriptor.

In our approach, we suggest making use of well-known linguistic features characteristic of academic prose (e.g. Biber & Conrad, 2009), and operationalizing them in a corpus-driven assessment of writing proficiency. The corpus that we use for that purpose is the *Corpus of Academic Learner English* (CALE), currently being compiled to represent advanced learner writing in an academic context. CALE comprises seven academic text types ('genres') produced as assignments by learners of English as a foreign language in university courses in English linguistics; our corpus may therefore be considered a Language for Specific Purposes learner corpus. The corpus is being annotated for learner variables, such as L1, age and gender, as well as text characteristics such as genre, type of course and the discipline for which the text was written (see Callies & Zaytseva, 2013a, for a more detailed description).

Our corpus-driven approach to LTA using the CALE proceeds in a number of steps. The first step is to draw up a list of characteristic features of academic prose from which a list of possible linguistic descriptor candidates is selected in terms of their keyness (i.e. how important and characteristic they are of the register) and their operationalizability (i.e. how well they can be retrieved from the corpora and subjected to statistical analysis). This selection is based on a review of the existing research literature on academic writing and of studies that have identified some of the features that remain problematic even for highly proficient L2 learners (possibly similar to what Ortega & Byrnes, 2008: 283, call 'late acquired features'). Some possible candidates include (1) specific constructions (verb–argument constructions, such as causative constructions, focus constructions, raising, or mediopassive) (Callies, 2008, 2009; Gilquin, 2012; Hawkins & Filipović, 2012; Wulff & Gries, 2011); (2) inanimate subjects (e.g. *This paper discusses...*, *The results suggest that...*) (Callies, 2013a; Dorgeloh & Wanner, 2009; Master, 1991); (3) phrases to express rhetorical functions (e.g. *by contrast, to conclude, in sum*) (Paquot, 2010; Siepmann *et al.*, 2008); (4) reporting verbs (e.g. *discuss, claim, suggest, argue*, etc.) (Callies, 2013a; Granger & Paquot, 2009); and (5) typical lexical co-occurrence patterns (e.g. *conduct, carry out, undertake* as typical verbal collocates of *experiment, analysis, research*) (Ackermann *et al.*, 2011; Durrant, 2009). This step takes into account if and how these linguistic structures are used in a specific way in the academic register. For example, reporting verbs tend to exhibit preferences for certain lexico-grammatical association patterns in academic writing (as shown, for example, by Biber & Conrad, 2009; Callies, 2013a; Granger & Paquot, 2009).

In a second step, all occurrences of a given feature are retrieved from the corpus and subjected to statistical analysis, for instance clustering techniques. These are used to identify clusters in the learner texts that exhibit the highest degree of similarity as to the occurrence and use of one or more features, while taking into account individual learner and task variables. The clusters that emerge represent gradual usage-based information on advancedness in academic writing. To illustrate, we will briefly consider the use of reporting verbs as one possible feature of written academic prose.

A close investigation of studies of the use of reporting verbs by English native speakers and L2 learners reveals several register-specific characteristics for this particular descriptor, which we take as a local measure of writing proficiency (Figure 4.2). One possible measurement is the diversity and frequency of the reporting verbs used by a writer, that is, how many different verbs are used and how often these occur. Previous learner corpus studies report that even learners demonstrating a high level of language proficiency seem to have a limited inventory of these verbs in academic writing (Callies, 2013a; Granger & Paquot, 2009). A list of the most commonly used reporting verbs can be drawn up from the research literature. These verbs will then be extracted from the corpus semi-automatically, yielding patterns of similarities and differences in the number and variety of reporting verbs used by the writers in the corpus. Depending on how diverse the use of reporting verbs is in comparison to the other texts in the corpus (and, eventually, to novice and expert academic writing produced by native speakers), individual papers will be placed into one or more clusters, as shown in Figure 4.2. Our procedure thus involves all three approaches to the use of (learner) corpora within LTA discussed above: the selection of pertinent linguistic features of academic prose is informed by corpus research on native speaker usage; the analysis of the characteristic use of these features in advanced learner writing is corpus-based; and their retrieval and classification is corpus-driven and requires the use of statistical techniques.

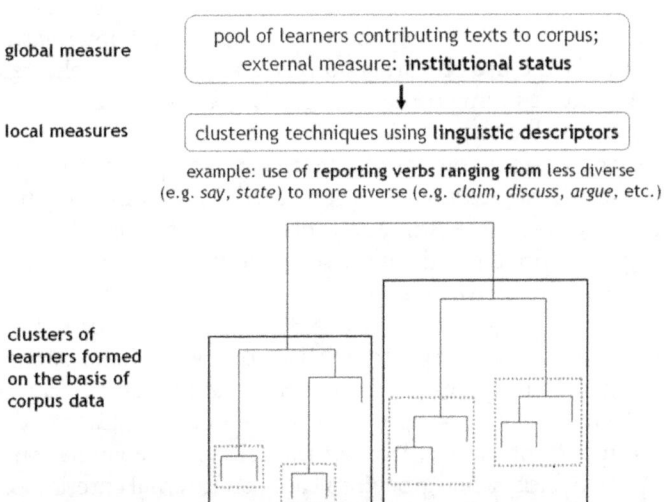

Figure 4.2 Applying linguistic descriptors and clustering techniques in the assessment of advanced writing proficiency

Multiple analyses involving a variety of descriptors will enable the researcher or the assessor to visualize learner performance as a continuum of advancedness, where an individual learner is assigned a particular level of proficiency. Depending on research or testing objectives, this procedure can be extended to allow for a comparison of the writing of learners with different L1s. Such an extension would provide information concerning the register-specific use of reporting verbs by advanced learners, which could be used to specify further the descriptors for advanced levels within the CEFR. This type of analysis has the potential to inform various stages of testing. For test development, it can provide evidence of what to measure in academic writing; for test design it can influence the development of realistic tasks. Corpus analysis of this type can also provide usage-based, empirical information relevant to the rating/evaluation process, and to the interpretation of results and the reliable identification of a proficiency level.

Conclusion

This chapter has discussed some applications of learner corpora to language testing and assessment. We have distinguished between corpus-informed, corpus-based and corpus-driven approaches as to three criteria: the ways that learner corpus data are actually put to use, the aims and outcomes for LTA, and the degree of involvement of the researcher in terms of data retrieval, analysis and interpretation. Learner corpora can serve as a highly valuable source of information on learner language use in the context of LTA, provided that a number of criteria have been met. Our chapter has presented two examples of the use of learner corpus data that were collected in test-taking and non-test-taking contexts to study both negative and positive linguistic properties that can be used to assess L2 proficiency.

The second example proposed a text-centered approach illustrating all three uses of learner corpora (corpus-based, corpus-driven and corpus-informed) to overcome the limitations of human rating in LTA, and to help in the analysis of linguistic details associated with proficiency in academic writing. The first example demonstrated that while learner corpora can be useful to abstract away from individual learners to identify a corpus-based description of a specific learner group based on institutional status or proficiency level, for the purposes of LTA it is important to remember that corpus data are often subject to a significant degree of inter-learner variability, which has important implications for learner corpus compilation, analysis and exploitation. Proficiency groupings based on external criteria alone – such as institutional status – are not reliable, as they are likely to conflate intra-group variability. In a substantial number of learner corpus studies to date, individual differences often go unnoticed or tend to be disregarded, and are not reported in favor of (possibly skewed) average frequency counts. Mukherjee (2009), who provides one of the few studies where the issue of inter-learner variability is explicitly addressed, concludes that 'the fiction of homogeneity that is often associated with the compilation of a learner corpus according to well-defined standards and design criteria may run counter to the wide range of differing individual levels of competence in the corpus' (2009: 216).

Notes

(1) See Tognini-Bonelli (2001) and McEnery et al. (2006: 8–11) for discussions of differences between corpus-based and corpus-driven approaches.
(2) Two independent raters annotated the learner corpus for errors. With the information provided by both raters, the researcher error-tagged the corpus following the Dagneaux taxonomy. So as not to bias the results due to the different degrees of leniency when tagging the learner corpus, only the errors that the two raters had highlighted were considered.
(3) CEFR level C1 was not further analysed because there was only one composition at this level.

References

Ackermann, K., Biber, D. and Gray, B. (2011) *An Academic Collocation List*. Paper presented at *Corpus Linguistics 2011*, 20–22 July 2011, Birmingham, UK.
Ädel, A. (2006) *Metadiscourse in L1 and L2 English*. Amsterdam: Benjamins.
Ädel, A. (2008) Involvement features in writing: Do time and interaction trump register awareness? In G. Gilquin, S. Papp and M.B. Diez-Bedmar (eds) *Linking Up Contrastive and Learner Corpus Research* (pp. 35–53). Amsterdam: Rodopi.
Alderson, C. (1996) Do corpora have a role in language assessment? In J. Thomas and M. Short (eds) *Using Corpora for Language Research. Studies in Honour of Geoffrey Leech* (pp. 3–14). New York: Longman.
Barker, F. (2004) Using corpora in language testing: Research and validation of language tests. *Modern English Teacher* 13 (2), 63–67.
Barker, F. (2010) How can corpora be used in language testing? In A. O'Keeffe and M. McCarthy (eds) *The Routledge Handbook of Corpus Linguistics* (pp. 633–645). New York: Routledge.
Biber, D. and Conrad, S. (2009) *Register, Genre, and Style*. Cambridge: Cambridge University Press.
Callies, M. (2008) Easy to understand but difficult to use? Raising constructions and information packaging in the advanced learner variety. In G. Gilquin, S. Papp and M.B. Diez-Bedmar (eds) *Linking Up Contrastive and Learner Corpus Research* (pp. 201–226). Amsterdam: Rodopi.
Callies, M. (2009) *Information Highlighting in Advanced Learner English. The Syntax–Pragmatics Interface in Second Language Acquisition*. Amsterdam: Benjamins.
Callies, M. (2013a) Agentivity as a determinant of lexico-syntactic variation in L2 academic writing. *International Journal of Corpus Linguistics* 18 (3), 357–390.
Callies, M. (2013b) Advancing the research agenda of Interlanguage Pragmatics: The role of learner corpora. In J. Romero-Trillo (ed.) *Yearbook of Corpus Linguistics and Pragmatics 2013: New Domains and Methodologies* (pp. 9–36). New York: Springer.
Callies, M. and Zaytseva, E. (2013a) The *Corpus of Academic Learner English* (CALE) – A new resource for the study and assessment of advanced language proficiency.

In S. Granger, G. Gilquin and F. Meunier (eds) *Twenty Years of Learner Corpus Research: Looking Back, Moving Ahead* (Corpora and Language in Use – Proceedings Vol. 1, pp. 49–59). Louvain-la-Neuve: Presses Universitaires de Louvain.

Callies, M. and Zaytseva, E. (2013b) The *Corpus of Academic Learner English* (CALE) – A new resource for the assessment of writing proficiency in the academic register. *Dutch Journal of Applied Linguistics* 2 (1), 126–132.

Callies, M., Zaytseva, E. and Present-Thomas, R. (2013) Writing assessment in higher education: Making the framework work. *Dutch Journal of Applied Linguistics* 2 (1), 1–15.

Carlsen, C. (2012) Proficiency level – a fuzzy variable in computer learner corpora. *Applied Linguistics* 33 (2), 161–183.

Chapelle, C.A. and Plakans, L. (2012) Assessment and testing: Overview. In C.A. Chapelle (ed.) *The Encyclopedia of Applied Linguistics* (pp. 241–244). New York: Blackwell.

Coppieters, R. (1987) Competence differences between native and near-native speakers. *Language* 63, 545–557.

Council of Europe (2001) *Common European Framework of Reference for Languages: Learning, teaching, assessment*. Cambridge: Cambridge University Press.

Council of Europe (2009) *Relating Language Examinations to the Common European Framework of Reference for Languages: Learning, teaching, assessment (CEFR): A manual*. Strasbourg: Language Policy Division.

Dagneaux, E., Denness, S. and Granger, S. (1998) Computer-aided error analysis. *System* 26, 163–174.

Dagneaux, E., Denness, S., Granger, S. and Meunier, F. (1996) *Error Tagging Manual. Version 1.1*. Louvain-la-Neuve: Centre for English Corpus Linguistics, Université Catholique de Louvain.

Department of Theoretical and Applied Linguistics (2011) *English Profile. Introducing the CEFR for English. Version 1.1*. Cambridge: Cambridge University Press.

Díez-Bedmar, M.B. (2010) Analysis of the written expression in English in the University Entrance Examination at the University of Jaén. Unpublished PhD dissertation, University of Jaén.

Díez-Bedmar, M.B. (2011a) Spanish pre-university students' use of English: CEA results from the University Entrance Exam. *International Journal of English Studies* 11 (2), 141–158.

Díez-Bedmar, M.B. (2011b) Learner Corpora and Testing: Analysing CEFR levels by means of Computer-aided Error Analysis. Paper presented at *Learner Corpus Research 2011*, 15–17 September 2011, Louvain-la-Neuve, Belgium.

Díez-Bedmar, M.B. (2012) The use of the Common European Framework of Reference for Languages to evaluate compositions in the English exam section of the University Entrance Examination. *Revista de Educación* 357 (1), 55–79.

Dorgeloh, H. and Wanner, A. (2009) Formulaic argumentation in scientific discourse. In R. Corrigan, E.A. Moravcsik, H. Ouali and K.M. Wheatley (eds) *Formulaic Language: Volume 2. Acquisition, Loss, Psychological Reality, and Functional Explanations* (pp. 523–544). Amsterdam: Benjamins.

Durrant, P. (2009) Investigating the viability of a collocation list for students of English for academic purposes. *English for Specific Purposes* 28, 157–169.

Francis, G. (1993) A corpus-driven approach to grammar; principles, methods and examples. In M. Baker, G. Francis and E. Tognini Bonelli (eds) *Text and Technology: In Honour of John Sinclair* (pp. 137–156). Amsterdam: Benjamins.

Gilquin, G. (2012) Lexical infelicity in causative constructions. Comparing native and learner collostructions. In J. Leino and R. von Waldenfels (eds) *Analytical Causatives*. München: Lincom.

Granger, S. (2008) Learner corpora. In A. Lüdeling and M. Kytö (eds) *Corpus Linguistics. An International Handbook*, Vol. 1 (pp. 259–275). Berlin and New York: Mouton de Gruyter.

Granger, S. (2009) The contribution of learner corpora to second language acquisition and foreign language teaching: A critical evaluation. In K. Aijmer (ed.) *Corpora and Language Teaching* (pp. 13–33). Amsterdam: Benjamins.

Granger, S. and Paquot, M. (2009) Lexical verbs in academic discourse: a corpus-driven study of learner use. In M. Charles, D. Pecorari and S. Hunston (eds) *Academic Writing. At the Interface of Corpus and Discourse* (pp. 193–214). London and New York: Continuum.

Granger, S. and Thewissen, J. (2005) *Towards a Reconciliation of a 'Can Do' and 'Can't Do' Approach to Language Assessment*. Paper presented at the 2nd Annual Conference of EALTA, Voss, Norway, 2–5 June 2005.

Granger, S., Dagneaux, E., Meunier, F. and Paquot, M. (2009) *The International Corpus of Learner English. Version 2. Handbook and CD-ROM*. Louvain-la-Neuve: Presses Universitaires de Louvain.

Hawkey, R. and Barker, F. (2004) Developing a common scale for the assessment of writing. *Assessing Writing* 9, 122–159.

Hawkins, J. and Buttery, P. (2009) Using learner language from corpora to profile levels of proficiency: Insights from the English Profile Programme. In L. Taylor and C.J. Weir (eds) *Language Testing Matters: Investigating the wider social and educational impact of assessment* (pp. 158–175). Cambridge: Cambridge University Press.

Hawkins, J. and Buttery, P. (2010) Criterial features in learner corpora: Theory and illustrations. *English Profile Journal* 1 (1), 1–23.

Hawkins, J. and Filipović, L. (2012) *Criterial Features in L2 English*. Cambridge: Cambridge University Press.

Housen, A. and Kuiken, F. (2009) Complexity, accuracy and fluency in second language acquisition. *Applied Linguistics* 30 (4), 461–473.

Housen, A., Kuiken, F. and Vedder, I. (eds) (2012) *Dimensions of L2 Performance and Proficiency. Complexity, accuracy and fluency in SLA*. Amsterdam: Benjamins

Hulstijn, J.H. (2007) The shaky ground beneath the CEFR: Quantitative and qualitative dimensions of language proficiency. *The Modern Language Journal* 91 (4), 663–667.

Hutchinson, J. (1996) *UCL Error Editor*. Louvain-la-Neuve: Centre for English Corpus Linguistics, Université Catholique de Louvain.

Labeau, E. and Myles, F. (eds) (2009) *The Advanced Learner Variety. The Case of French*. Frankfurt/Main: Peter Lang.

Master, P. (1991) Active verbs with inanimate subjects in scientific prose. *English for Specific Purposes* 10, 15–33.

McCrostie, J. (2008) Writer visibility in EFL learner academic writing: A corpus-based study. *ICAME Journal* 32, 97–114.

McEnery, T., Xiao, R. and Tono, Y. (2006) *Corpus-based Language Studies: An Advanced Resource Book*. London: Routledge.

Mukherjee, J. (2009) The grammar of conversation in advanced spoken learner English: Learner corpus data and language-pedagogical implications. In K. Aijmer (ed.) *Corpora and Language Teaching* (pp. 203–230). Amsterdam: Benjamins.

Neff van Aertselaer, J. and Bunce, C. (2011) The use of small corpora for tracing the development of academic literacies. In F. Meunier, S. De Cock, G. Gilquin and M. Paquot (eds) *A Taste for Corpora. In Honour of Sylviane Granger* (pp. 63–84). Amsterdam: Benjamins.

Ortega, L. (2003) Syntactic complexity measures and their relationship to L2 proficiency: A research synthesis of college-level L2 writing. *Applied Linguistics* 24, 492–518.

Ortega, L. and Byrnes, H. (2008) The longitudinal study of advanced L2 capacities: An introduction. In L. Ortega and H. Byrnes (eds) *The Longitudinal Study of Advanced L2 Capacities* (pp. 3–20). New York: Routledge/Taylor & Francis.

Paquot, M. (2010) *Academic Vocabulary in Learner Writing: From Extraction to Analysis*. London: Continuum.

Pendar, N. and Chapelle, C.A. (2008) Investigating the promise of learner corpora: Methodological issues. *CALICO Journal* 25, 189–206.

Polio, C. (1997) Measures of linguistic accuracy in second language writing research. *Language Learning* 47, 101–143.
Siepmann, D., Gallagher, J., Hannay, M. and Mackenzie, L. (2008) *Writing in English. A Guide for Advanced Learners*. Tübingen: Narr Francke Attempto.
Skehan, P. (1998) *A Cognitive Approach to Language Learning*. Oxford: Oxford University Press.
Taylor, L. and Barker, F. (2008) Using corpora for language assessment. In E. Shohamy and N.H. Hornberger (eds) *Encyclopedia of Language and Education* (2nd edn) Volume 7. *Language testing and assessment* (pp. 241–254). New York: Springer.
Thewissen, J. (2011) A Learner-Corpus-Based Study of Error Developmental Patterns: The impact of proficiency level. Paper presented at *Learner Corpus Research 2011*, 15–17 September 2011, Louvain-la-Neuve, Belgium.
Thomas, M. (1994) Assessment of L2 proficiency in second language acquisition research. *Language Learning* 44 (2), 307–336.
Thomas, M. (2006) Research synthesis and historiography: The case of assessment of second language proficiency. In J.M. Norris and L. Ortega (eds) *Synthesizing Research on Language Learning and Teaching* (pp. 279–298). Amsterdam: Benjamins.
Tognini-Bonelli, E. (2001) *Corpus Linguistics at Work*. Amsterdam: Benjamins.
Walter, M. and Grommes, P. (eds) (2008) *Fortgeschrittene Lernervarietäten. Korpuslinguistik und Zweitsprachenerwerbsforschung*. Tübingen: Niemeyer.
Weir, C.J. (2005) Limitations of the Common European Framework for developing comparable examinations and tests. *Language Testing* 22, 281–300.
Wolfe-Quintero, K., Inagaki, S. and Kim, H.Y. (1998) *Second Language Development in Writing: Measures of fluency, accuracy, and complexity*. Honolulu, HI: University of Hawaii Press.
Wulff, S. and Gries, S.Th. (2011) Corpus-driven methods for assessing accuracy in learner production. In P. Robinson (ed.) *Second Language Task Complexity: Researching the Cognition Hypothesis of Language Learning and Performance* (pp. 61–87). Amsterdam: Benjamins.

Part 2

Language Processing and L2 Proficiency

5 Listening Comprehension: Processing Demands and Assessment Issues

Peter Prince

Introduction

Most of the papers in this volume address issues relating to productive L2 proficiency. However, listening comprehension is a crucial language skill, and listening tests are a standard feature of most L2 certification batteries. The aim of this chapter is to present an account of assessing L2 listening comprehension in an institutional setting, namely a higher-education language course in France (for an account of L2 oral production, see Hilton, this volume). Issues relating to the type of test best suited to listening are first discussed, and the nature of listening comprehension proficiency then reviewed. Finally there is an analysis of the processing demands involved in comprehension-restitution (C-R), in which students write down what they have understood. Special reference is made to two variations of the task: summarizing a news bulletin and dictogloss. Summarizing a news bulletin consists in giving the main points in each news item. In dictogloss, the meaning of a paragraph read aloud by the teacher/examiner is reported in as much detail as possible. The performance of 10 students on these tasks, and the crucial role of word recognition, are examined in relation to a third task, the repetition of sentence fragments.

The Assessment Challenge

Listening is a difficult skill to assess because it cannot be observed directly. Listening is therefore tested by asking learners to indicate what they have understood. The test-taker's cognitive capacity is thus solicited not just for comprehension of input, but by the specific demands of providing the answers. In a classroom this can often be done orally. In a more official examination, answers generally involve some form of written production, ranging from ticking a box to writing complete sentences. Many forms of test are possible, including gap-filling, matching, multiple-choice, short answers, recall and summary. It is beyond the scope of this chapter to discuss each of these forms in detail (Buck, 2001, provides a comprehensive discussion), but one question of interest concerns the distinction between two widely used forms of test that sit at opposite extremes, namely the closed format of multiple choice and the open format of C-R.

When choosing a test, there are many factors to consider, not least ease of conception, administration and marking. These need to be weighed against the extra processing demands that the chosen test imposes on the test-taker. In multiple choice, output is restricted to ticking an answer out of several possibilities. There is thus no extra demand in terms of writing, but the test-taker has to read and consider all possible choices before answering. In C-R, no reading is involved, but test-takers have to write down, in more or less detail, what they have understood. One question, therefore, in both cases, is whether the extra processing required distorts the listening process and, if so, whether the assessment of listening that the test affords nonetheless remains valid.

Hansen and Jensen (1994: 250) cast doubt on the validity of multiple choice to test listening. They point to the heavy cognitive load it places on listeners, and argue that other capacities and knowledge, such as memory, reading skill and grammar, are being assessed on top of listening itself. This objection could also apply to C-R, as in written forms of C-R, the output phase, which can often overlap with the listening phase, is both time-consuming and cognitively demanding. As pointed out by Piolat *et al.* (2008), combining the processes involved in both comprehension and writing may lead to an overload that exceeds working memory capacity. The resulting demands on attention can be explained in terms of a multiple resources framework, such as proposed by Wickens (2002). Most relevant here is the extent to which C-R involves simultaneously allocating attention to both the perceptual/cognitive and the response stages of the task. Although these stages are seen as functionally separate, they are supported by common resources within working memory (WM) and are therefore in competition. Furthermore, depending on the input characteristics, the listening component itself may be more or less demanding. In order to cope with these demands, students tend to favor one or the other skill, either listening without writing much or writing as much as possible to the detriment of attending to the incoming input (Piolat, 2004). If such is the case, the listening process itself becomes distorted no less than in multiple choice. It appears, then, that whatever the form adopted, assessing listening involves extraneous processing demands that interfere with the demands of listening on its own. By manipulating the input, however, variations can be devised, both in multiple choice and C-R, which are less demanding. For example, the input can be repeated several times, played at a slower pace, or pauses can be inserted. Zhao (1997) found that comprehension improved when listeners were allowed to control the rate of speech. McBride (2011) found that groups trained on slow recordings fared better on a post-test than groups allowed to pause the recordings or choose the speech rate, a result she suggests is due to improved bottom-up decoding skills. Such expedients give listeners time to cope with the input as well as with any extra processing demands. Thus, even if listeners juggle between different demands, the input can be manipulated to ensure that differences in performance are revealing of different proficiency levels in the listening skill itself. However, such manipulation needs to be carefully tested to ensure that in a test situation the task remains discriminatory.

As regards multiple choice, even if one sets aside doubts about validity, a potentially more serious charge is that the task does not correspond to any real-life situation. Field (2011) suggests that task-specific strategies of the multiple choice format, such as listening for words that appear in the written items, undermine its cognitive validity (Baxter & Glaser, 1997), which is defined by Field (2011: 106) as 'the extent to which the types of behaviour elicited by a pedagogical task or a test correspond to the demands of a real-life event'. As Buck (2001: 92) points out, all test procedures are to some extent inauthentic outside of the academic context; however, if one is to train students in a skill, it can be argued that it should be a skill that can serve them beyond the single context of the exam (Canale & Swain, 1980). In this respect, C-R tasks appear to be better suited to students' real needs. For example, we often report a conversation or a news item we have heard to another person, an activity that requires understanding spoken input, storing it in memory, and retrieving it for output. This is usually done orally, but in a university context where many students will study abroad, training them in note-taking is also potentially a useful preparation for what is to come.

A second reason for using C-R tasks is the washback effect they have in the classroom. Sheerin (1987) notes that listening activities in class often turn into a form of test, and that the skill of listening itself is rarely taught. Training for a multiple-choice exam may focus on specific strategies that help to improve scores rather than on the listening process itself, whereas C-R tasks lend themselves to a teaching approach that can focus both on the sub-skills needed to decode the input (Field, 2008: 100) and on the metacognitive strategies that can improve listeners' effectiveness in reaching an understanding at text level (Goh, 2008). C-R also appears to lead to better global understanding. Schütze (2010) had one group of pupils reconstruct a text they had listened to, while another answered questions by filling in a grid. The second group successfully filled in the grid but was less able than the first to report the overall content of the text. The C-R procedure, which requires learners to focus on the full message rather than on isolated information, appears to promote better text-level understanding.

The Nature of Listening Comprehension

One theoretical framework for describing what is involved in understanding spoken input is the three-phase model developed to account for L1 listening (Anderson, 1995: 379; see also Rost, 2011, for a more detailed account of the linguistic, semantic and pragmatic processing of spoken input). The first phase, perception, involves the initial decoding of the acoustic stream into phonemes and words. These are then parsed into the thematic and grammatical roles they serve in a sentence. Finally, utilization involves constructing a personal interpretation at the sentence and text level. In this phase, listeners add their own knowledge and expectations to what they have perceived. While the temporal nature of speech means that for a given segment of input the three phases follow each other, they can overlap for different segments because listeners can be making sense of the first part of a sentence while decoding the sound stream of a later part. The model can be extended to include the two types of processing, bottom-up and top-down, which are commonly recognized to interact during any listening activity. Bottom-up processing occurs during the perceptual decoding of the input, while top-down processing involves listeners making use of their knowledge of the world, of the ongoing situation and of the language itself to reach an understanding of the input. Graham and Macaro (2008) emphasize that even before listening begins, listeners have certain expectations and goals, so a purely linear conception of listening does not do full justice to the interaction between top-down and bottom-up processes.

Field (2008: 133) cautions against the tendency to think of the information used in top-down processing as exclusively extra-linguistic or contextual, as it may also be linguistic. Collocational knowledge, for example, might allow a listener to comprehend the expression 'in broad day(light)', even if the final syllable is inaudible. Multiple sources of information are available to the listener when reaching an interpretation, and the interaction between linguistic and pragmatic information is not steady but oscillates according to circumstances. When listeners lack the linguistic knowledge that allows them to match incoming sounds to stored representations of word forms and meanings rapidly, greater reliance is placed upon top-down processing. In that case, it is largely compensatory. However, as Graham and Macaro (2008) point out, when a listener's decoding skills are good, top-down processing becomes confirmatory. In other words, contextual knowledge is used to enrich the listener's understanding of the message rather than to compensate for what has not been understood (Field, 2008: 132). What characterizes skilled listeners is not so much their ability to compensate for lack of understanding, important though that is, nor whatever pertinent top-down knowledge they can bring to bear, but the ability to understand without having to resort to compensatory strategies. This is achieved, as stressed by Field (2008: 136), by automatic and accurate decoding of the input.

Within the decoding skill, the main component is word recognition. If the individual words that make up a sentence are not recognized quickly and accurately, the comprehension process is bound to be affected. Although word recognition is driven by the phonological characteristics of the input, it is not just a matter of phoneme discrimination: the resulting interpretation will also depend on the listener's linguistic knowledge. Broersma and Cutler (2008) note that all listeners have to deal with misperceptions, noise and competition from phonologically similar words. Knowledge of vocabulary is important here, as the more words a learner knows phonologically the less risk there is of failing to recognize a word, or of activating spurious competitors. In other words, although a poor knowledge of spoken word forms may lead to a failure to activate any representation at all, it may also result in the activation of an inappropriate representation that is phonologically quite far removed from the input. In some cases, misperceptions or activation of spurious competitors may be temporary, but this still leads to a delay in recognition (Norris *et al.*, 1995). The ability to recover quickly from a misperception by using semantic information from the context is an important part of the word recognition skill (Mayo *et al.*, 1997).

If perceptual decoding and word recognition are central to understanding spoken input, a valid test should seek to measure this capacity. There is, however, more to comprehension than recognizing words. The listener must extract a propositional representation by exploiting the semantic and syntactic relationships between the words. The semantic content is not stored in memory in the same surface form as the initial input, but in propositional form (Gernsbacher, 1985). In storing semantic relationships, rather than individual words, we also select what we consider most relevant and omit inessential details. Word recognition provides the basis for making sense of the input, meaning integration and storing propositional content belong to the subsequent utilization stage. Here, the listener makes most use of inferencing skills, encyclopedic knowledge and, where necessary, compensatory strategies. To assess only word recognition in order to evaluate L2 listening proficiency would therefore be restrictive as it would deprive listeners of the opportunity to demonstrate the higher-order skills that allow them to construct a coherent representation of the document as a whole. A balanced test would seek to assess both lower- and higher-order skills (see Zoghlami, this volume, for a presentation of a competence-based framework of listening comprehension and an investigation that looks into the different listening skills measured by two norm-referenced tests of L2 proficiency in English).

The document referred to by most certification bodies when describing learners' command of an L2 is the *Common European Framework of Reference*

(CEFR), which has provided a valuable impetus to the teaching profession and allowed institutions to set attainment levels to be achieved at specific points in the learning process. However, the document is not without problems. Alderson *et al.* (2006) note a certain inconsistency and vagueness in some of the terms used. For example, the question of speed of speech in listening comprehension is absent at level B1, where learners can understand 'clear, standard speech on familiar matters' (Council of Europe, 2001: 66) but it appears at A2 (clear, slow and articulated speech) and B2 (normal speed, standard language). Furthermore, words such as 'standard', 'familiar' and 'normal' are not easy to interpret precisely (see Osborne, this volume, for a presentation of CEFR scales and a description of their use within a collaborative platform for oral proficiency assessment). More importantly, Hulstijn (2007) contends that the CEFR levels do not reflect proficiency as demonstrated by native speakers, many of whom lack the intellectual skills needed to perform at C1 or C2 levels. Conversely, L2 learners may reach C2 without having developed the online processing skills displayed by native speakers. This is because all native speakers possess a core language proficiency, covering knowledge of frequently occurring language items and the skill to process them accurately and rapidly (see Tracy-Ventura *et al.*, this volume, for a discussion of the proficiency construct in SLA studies). However, levels C1 and C2 call for higher-order cognition that covers other knowledge such as less frequent vocabulary and a wide range of cultural topics. For example, the C1 descriptor for listening comprehension stipulates that the learner 'can understand enough to follow extended speech on abstract and complex topics beyond his/her own field' (Council of Europe, 2001: 66). This goes beyond the rapid processing skills involved in understanding speech to embrace reasoning, encyclopedic knowledge and metacognition.

The extent to which higher-order cognition is assessed in a particular test will depend on the topic chosen and the task requirements, but in devising a test it is useful to bear in mind the distinction between core language proficiency and higher-order cognition that Hulstijn (2007) proposes. A C-R task such as sentence completion, in which students see and hear the first part of a sentence and then must provide the second part, presented orally, can easily be conceived to test learners' core language proficiency, that is, the rapid and accurate processing of short fragments of speech containing frequent lexical items. Summarizing a news bulletin, on the other hand, involves higher-order cognition to a greater extent, because topic knowledge and metacognitive strategies will also come into play.

Context of the Study

Several different tests are used in the four-semester listening comprehension course followed by students enrolled in Applied Foreign Languages at the University of Aix-Marseille in France. This section focuses on the listening tasks proposed in semester three: news summary and dictogloss. In the news summary task, students write down the main points of a news bulletin (BBC World). In dictogloss, they listen to a text, take notes, and reconstruct the text as accurately as possible. The input in the first task consists of authentic material taken from the radio, while the dictogloss material is adapted from a newspaper article and spoken slowly and clearly. As Gilmore (2007) demonstrates, there is no clear-cut distinction between authentic and inauthentic material in language teaching; dictogloss would be at the more literate end of a continuum between oral and written forms of expression (Tannen, 1982). As a classroom activity, used with appropriate training, dictogloss can improve students' metacognitive awareness as well as their confidence (Prince, 2013; Vasiljevic, 2010; Wilson, 2003). Nonetheless, the type of input is very different from that of a news bulletin.

The aim of the study was to examine the relationship between word recognition and task accomplishment, defined as the extent to which participants accurately reported the input in accordance with task instructions. From a previous study of eight students' listening comprehension strategies (Prince, 2012), it emerged that word recognition correlated highly with task accomplishment in dictogloss but not in news summary. With all the due precaution that needs to be taken with regard to small-scale studies, the result suggested that in a task where top-down processing plays a relatively larger role, performance need not be affected greatly by differences in word recognition skills. However, in that study, participants were of a similar proficiency level, as assessed by their scores on an in-house examination the previous year (mean = 10.2, SD = 2.9). Note that while such a score may be equated approximately to B1+, the CEFR levels are unlikely to fully capture certain individual differences that a finer-grained analysis reveals. Indeed, interviews conducted subsequently revealed different strategies and attitudes to the tasks, with some students showing more metacognitive awareness (choosing a semantic strategy of writing a coherent account), while others opted for a more error-prone phonological strategy of transcribing what they perceived. In that study, word recognition was measured by the percentage of words from the input correctly noted. While this provides an insight into students' ability to cope with the two stages of perception and written response, it is not a direct measure of word recognition itself as, on the one hand, not all the recognized words may be noted and, on the other, the concurrent demand of noting words may detract from the recognition process. A repetition task, in which response times were measured, was therefore included in order to obtain a more immediate appraisal. The news summary and dictogloss tasks not only involve the extra demand of writing but also allow for various degrees of top-down processing and strategies. Given the two different types of input involved, it was therefore of interest to see whether word recognition, as measured without the need to write, correlated with task accomplishment. Participants of differing proficiency levels were included in order to see the extent to which word recognition in the two input conditions was indeed a crucial factor related to the ability to construct an accurate interpretation. It was hypothesized that word recognition, as determined both by the number of words recognized in the repetition task and the repetition response times, would correlate highly with performance on the other tasks.

Methodology

Ten students (eight female, two male, average age 19.7 years) were chosen on the basis of their first-year results on two comprehension tasks of a similar nature (dictation and lecture summary). The average marks on these tasks ranged from 5.6 out of 20 to 17 (mean = 10.7, SD = 4.4). All participants had been studying English for eight years. As part of their university course they also studied a second foreign language: Spanish for four of them, Italian (three), Chinese (two) and Japanese (one).

The input characteristics of the three tasks are indicated in Table 5.1. Dictogloss and news summary were performed collectively in class, with the

Table 5.1 Input characteristics of three C-R tasks

	Task			
		Repetition		
Input characteristics	Dictogloss	Text 1	Text 2	Summarizing
Average number of words per item (sentence in dictogloss, fragment in repetition, news item in summary)	26.6	4.5	7.5	92
Number of times heard	2	1	1	2
Average duration of continuous input (s)	80 (1st time: complete paragraph) 14.7 (2nd time: sentence by sentence, 30 s pause between each)	3.6	1.4	18.9 (1st time: normal speed) 22.7 (2nd time: reduced tempo)
Average speed (words/minute)	108	206	131	180 (1st time) 150 (2nd time)

answers provided in writing. In the summarizing task, a 10 s pause was inserted after the first sentence of the news item to allow participants to process the most important information before listening to the rest. Note-taking was allowed, and no time limit or word limit was imposed. In the repetition task, performed individually, participants saw and heard the beginning of a text presented on a computer screen, and listened to subsequent fragments, which they repeated both as accurately and as soon as they could; two texts were used, one an extract from a radio broadcast, the other adapted from a newspaper and read relatively slowly (see Appendix 5A for example). Participants were able to anticipate the end of each fragment by watching a screen on which a cursor moved over the sound spectrum. When participants articulated poorly they were asked to repeat so as to dispel any doubt in the experimenter's mind about the classification of words as correct or incorrect. The fragment was then displayed to provide feedback and to allow participants to construct a text-level representation. Participants were asked afterwards to reflect upon their performance as well as upon the listening comprehension course itself. The entire session (fragments, repetitions and interviews) was recorded using a Dictaphone.

The word recognition score in repetition equalled the number of word forms correctly repeated, as judged by the experimenter. Morphological errors that did not alter meaning (e.g. *manager* for *managers*) were counted as correct. In dictogloss and summary, words corresponding to the meaning, although not necessarily the form, of those in the input were also scored as correct. No account was taken of spelling or morphosyntactic errors. In order to assess task accomplishment in the written tasks, two different teachers first identified the information to be reported. They then scored participants' productions independently, using a scale from 0 (information missing or inaccurate) to 5 (information complete) for each sentence (dictogloss) or main point (summary). Inter-rater reliability was 0.88. Differences were resolved through discussion.

Analysis of task performance

It should be noted that this is a small-scale study, limiting therefore the extent to which the results can be generalized. The aim, however, was to obtain a broad assessment of the contribution of word recognition to task accomplishment in two different types of task and at different proficiency levels. As such, the results clearly indicate that below a certain level of word recognition, it becomes extremely difficult to reach an understanding of the input that is accurate enough to provide a basis from which compensatory strategies can come into play effectively. While this might be expected in dictogloss, where the emphasis is on noting details, it is also the case in the news summary task.

Table 5.2 provides an overview of mean percentage scores in the three tasks, mean response time (RT) in repetition, and correlations between

Table 5.2 Scores and correlations for three tasks

Task	Scores	Task Dictogloss WR	TA	Repetition WR/TA	RT	Summary WR	TA
Dictogloss							
WR	54%	1.00					
TA	52%	0.94	1.00				
Repetition							
WR/TA	68%	0.93	0.94	1.00			
RT	530 ms	−0.89	−0.80	−0.76*	1.00		
Summary							
WR	27%	0.92	0.93	0.92	−0.72*	1.00	
TA	49%	0.89	0.89	0.86	−0.79	0.94	1.00

Note: *$p < 0.05$. All other values, $p < 0.01$ or less.

criteria and tasks. The task accomplishment (TA) score in repetition is by definition the same as the word recognition (WR) score. Task accomplishment is lowest in summarizing (49%), but only slightly lower than in dictogloss (52%). This is because more detail is required in dictogloss, whereas in summarizing only the main points are required, and these can be identified even if the level of word recognition is low.

The wider range of proficiency levels compared to Prince (2012), with standard deviations in word recognition scores almost double those of the previous study, leads to significant correlations between all tasks and criteria. This lends support to Field's (2008) assertion that rapid and accurate decoding of the input is the essential characteristic of listening proficiency. Confirmation of this comes from the RTs. Because any error in repeating the sentence fragment may lead to hesitation, RTs for only those fragments repeated without any error by all the participants were taken into account. Average RTs ranged from 303 ms to 856 ms (mean = 530.2 ms; SD = 197.2). The negative correlation between RT and WR scores indicates that participants who noted the most words correctly were also able to respond most rapidly. Here, it is not simply a matter of recognizing and writing down individual words more quickly, although that certainly plays a part in successful task accomplishment in C-R. As noted by Tracy-Ventura *et al.* (this volume), one way of assessing proficiency is through elicited imitation, which bears a strong similarity to the repetition task used here. The task taps into the ability to parse input into a meaningful chunk, which is stored in short-term phonological memory. It is noteworthy that even when fragments are accurately identified and repeated, the weaker listeners perform less efficiently, suffering a slight delay not just in word recognition per se, but in the parsing process involved in making sense of fragments of speech.

The differing scores in the word recognition component of the repetition task (ranging from 54% to 87%) can be said to reflect different levels in the core language proficiency postulated by Hulstijn (2007), that is, the knowledge and skill needed for online processing of frequent lexical items and grammatical constructions. The scores also tie in with participants' own comments. When questioned about the strategy training undertaken in class, the stronger listeners did not find it especially useful as they were able to understand without it. The weak listeners said they were not sure of enough words to be able to use any compensatory strategies effectively. The intermediate listeners, who identified around 70% of the words, said that strategy training was of great benefit to them.

Discussion

The input processing for the listening tasks discussed here fits with the perception, parsing and utilization of Anderson's (1995) three-phase model. However, while perception and parsing can be seen as similar in each of the tasks, utilization is modulated by the nature of the task requirements as perceived by the listener. Taking the term 'utilization' in a broad sense to cover not just meaning integration but the production of an overt response, the three tasks make different demands. In dictogloss, the length of the items and the need to reproduce the details tax WM capacity to the full. Unless listeners are able to chunk the input into semantic units, they may be quickly overwhelmed by this demand. Chang (2006) cautions against the use of recall tasks to assess reading comprehension as they can be a test of memory more than of comprehension. Although this certainly needs to be borne in mind, WM can also be seen as an integral part of proficiency (Robinson, 2001; Van den Noort et al., 2006). Put another way, dictogloss taps less into WM as such than into the chunking ability that makes information manageable in WM. As noted by Call (1985: 767), 'short-term memory, by using syntactic rules to chunk incoming linguistic data, plays a central role in the extraction of meaning and potential long-term retention of meaning from spoken language.' Loe (1964), cited in Ohata (2006), found that proficient students recalled sentences containing clauses better than sentences composed of a series of phrases, whereas for less proficient students it was the reverse. Because higher proficiency is demonstrated through more efficient processing, it is not easy to distinguish this from WM capacity. Miyake and Friedman (1998) suggest that WM span contributes to proficiency development because it influences learners' ability to identify informative syntactic cues in the input. Higher-proficiency learners can then make better use of these cues during listening. This ability to chunk complex sentences is also useful in summarizing, but because less detail is required, only the key semantic relationships need to be stored. This, however, means that information must be sorted and non-essential details ignored, a process abetted by inferencing skills and top-down knowledge of the topic.

For purposes of establishing a learner's core proficiency, a repetition task would appear to be well suited. In an academic context, however, it could not suffice on its own, as students would consider it too reductive, and the washback effect on classroom instruction would doubtless be negative. Furthermore, proficiency levels determined by the task may not correspond to those of the CEFR, as the task does not call for the higher-order cognition of the more advanced levels of the CEFR. When a group is more homogeneous in core language proficiency, as in Prince (2012), the differences between them will be reflected more in tasks that call for higher-order cognition, such as the news summary. In the context of a university course in Applied Foreign Languages, such a task appears appropriate. In other contexts, it is a matter for examiners to decide.

While this study has stressed the role of word recognition, it is in no way suggested that other factors do not play a part. In this respect, further research could usefully combine a larger number of participants in a single design examining both word recognition and compensatory strategies at different proficiency levels. Strategy use is known to differ considerably among listeners (Graham *et al.*, 2008), and even when word recognition is low, it may nonetheless allow some listeners to perform better than others. Thus, taking care to control for prior knowledge (Chiang & Dunkel, 1992), it would be of interest to see what minimum level of word recognition is necessary for learners of differing strategy use to achieve a certain level of task accomplishment. Although the present study does not address that question, it is likely, however, that differences in top-down processing or compensatory strategies will not be able to negate any substantial differences in word recognition. As noted by Graham *et al.* (2010), non-linguistic knowledge is not a reliable basis for making decisions (in their study, multiple choice) unless a threshold of accurate linguistic recognition has been attained. However, they also note that a high level of linguistic knowledge does not always go hand in hand with effective strategy use. Extrapolating from this, while assessment procedures should indeed allow learners to make as much use as they can of prior knowledge and strategies, it remains an inescapable fact that the more pieces of a puzzle one has, the easier it is to gain an idea of the whole picture.

Conclusion

This chapter described two forms of C-R used to assess L2 learners' listening comprehension in a French university. While the marking of written answers is longer than that of a multiple-choice test, it is suggested that the C-R format has greater cognitive validity than multiple choice. Furthermore, compared to multiple choice, such tests are relatively easy to conceive. It is nonetheless important to bear in mind the processing demands that the task imposes. In other words, the characteristics of the input – notably speed of delivery, number and length of pauses, and number of repetitions – can be carefully manipulated so that the demands of writing do not submerge the listening process itself.

It is suggested that the C-R format also has construct validity in that it does indeed measure listening comprehension, at least in its one-way, non-interactional form. Where possible, however, it is desirable to include variations of C-R (e.g. sentence completion, summary of mini-lectures) in order for both basic language proficiency and the higher-order cognition postulated by Hulstijn (2007) to be assessed. As noted by Song (2012), the quality of students' notes taken while listening to lectures, an activity combining the two, is itself a good indicator of L2 listening proficiency. The precise test format chosen will reflect examiners' choices and depend on the institutional context. Where possible, it may also be desirable to test forms of listening that involve visual input such as computerized slide-shows, increasingly prevalent in academic settings (Lynch, 2011), or video documents (Wagner, 2007).

References

Alderson, J.C., Figueras, N., Kuijper, H., Nold, G., Takala, S. and Tardieu, C. (2006) Analysing tests of reading and listening in relation to the Common European Framework of Reference: The experience of the Dutch CEFR Construct Project. *Language Assessment Quarterly* 3 (1), 3–30.
Anderson, J.R. (1995) *Cognitive Psychology and its Implications* (4th edn). New York: Freeman.
Baxter, G.P. and Glaser, R. (1997) *An Approach to Analyzing the Cognitive Complexity of Science Performance Assessments*. Los Angeles, CA: CRESST/UCLA.
Broersma, M. and Cutler, A. (2008) Phantom word activation in L2. *System* 36, 22–34.
Buck, G. (2001) *Assessing Listening*. Cambridge: Cambridge University Press.
Call, M. (1985) Auditory short-term memory, listening comprehension, and the input hypothesis. *TESOL Quarterly* 19, 765–781.
Canale, M. and Swain, M. (1980) The theoretical bases of communicative approaches to second language teaching and testing. *Applied Linguistics* 1, 1–47.
Chang, Y. (2006) On the use of the immediate recall task as a measure of second language reading comprehension. *Language Testing* 23 (4), 520–543.
Chiang, C.S. and Dunkel, P. (1992) The effect of speech modification, prior knowledge, and listening proficiency on EFL lecture learning. *TESOL Quarterly* 26 (2), 345–374.
Council of Europe (2001) *Common European Framework of Reference for Languages: Learning, teaching, assessment*. Cambridge: Cambridge University Press.
Field, J. (2008) *Listening in the Language Classroom*. Cambridge: Cambridge University Press.
Field, J. (2011) Into the mind of the academic listener. *Journal of English for Academic Purposes* 10 (2), 102–112.
Gernsbacher, M.A. (1985) Surface information loss in comprehension. *Cognitive Psychology* 17, 324–363.
Gilmore, A. (2007) Authentic materials and authenticity in foreign language learning. *Language Teaching* 40, 97–118.

Goh, C. (2008) Metacognitive instruction for second language listening development: Theory, practice and research implications. *RELC Journal* 39 (2), 88–213.

Graham, S. and Macaro, E. (2008) Strategy instruction in listening for lower-intermediate learners of French. *Language Learning* 58 (4), 747–783.

Graham, S., Santos, D. and Vanderplank, R. (2008) Listening comprehension and strategy use: A longitudinal exploration. *System* 36 (1), 52–68.

Graham, S., Santos, D. and Vanderplank, R. (2010) Strategy clusters and sources of knowledge in French L2 listening comprehension. *Innovation in Language Learning and Teaching* 4 (1), 1–20.

Hansen, C. and Jensen, C. (1994) Evaluating lecture comprehension. In J. Flowerdew (ed.) *Academic Listening: Research Perspectives* (pp. 241–268). Cambridge: Cambridge University Press.

Hulstijn, J.H. (2007) The shaky ground beneath the CEFR: Quantitative and qualitative dimensions of language proficiency. *The Modern Language Journal* 91, 663–667.

Loe, M. B., OSB (1964) Immediate memory-span in English and Chinese sentences of increasing length. MS thesis, Georgetown University.

Lynch, T. (2011) Academic listening in the 21st century: Reviewing a decade of research. *Journal of English for Academic Purposes* 10 (2), 79–88.

Mayo, L.H., Florentine, M. and Buus, S. (1997) Age of second-language acquisition and perception of speech in noise. *Journal of Speech, Language & Hearing Research* 40 (3), 686–693.

McBride, K. (2011) The effect of rate of speech and distributed practice on the development of listening comprehension. *Computer Assisted Language Learning* 24 (2), 131–154.

Miyake, A. and Friedman, N.P. (1998) Individual differences in second language proficiency: Working memory as language aptitude. In A.F. Healy and L.E. Bourne (eds) *Foreign Language Learning* (pp. 339–364). London: Lawrence Erlbaum Associates.

Norris, D., McQueen, J.M. and Cutler, A. (1995) Competition and segmentation in spoken-word recognition. *Journal of Experimental Psychology: Learning, Memory, and Cognition* 21, 1209–1228.

Ohata, K. (2006) Auditory short-term memory in L2 listening comprehension processes. *Journal of Language and Learning* 5 (1), 21–28.

Piolat, A. (2004) La prise de notes: Ecriture de l'urgence. In A. Piolat (ed.) *Ecriture: Approches en sciences cognitives* (pp. 206–229). Aix-en-Provence: Presses Universitaires de Provence.

Piolat. A., Barbier, M.-L. and Roussey, J.-Y. (2008) Fluency and cognitive effort during first- and second-language notetaking and writing by undergraduate students. *European Psychologist* 13 (2), 114–125.

Prince, P. (2012) Writing it down: Issues relating to the use of restitution tasks in listening comprehension. *TESOL Journal* 3 (1), 66–86.

Prince, P. (2013) Listening, remembering, writing: Exploring the dictogloss task. *Language Teaching Research* 17, 486–500.

Robinson, P. (2001) Individual differences, cognitive abilities, aptitude complexes, and learning conditions in second-language acquisition. *Second Language Research* 17, 368–392.

Rost, M. (2011) *Teaching and Researching Listening* (2nd edn). Harlow: Longman.

Schütze, S. (2010) Quelles alternatives aux grilles d'écoute? See Academy of Versailles education website for teachers of German, http://www.allemand.ac-versailles.fr/spip.php?article295 (accessed 12 July 2012).

Sheerin, S. (1987) Listening comprehension: Teaching or testing? *ELT Journal* 41 (2), 126–131.

Song, M.-Y. (2012) Note-taking quality and performance on an L2 academic listening test. *Language Testing* 29 (1), 67–89.

Tannen, D. (1982) The oral/literate continuum in discourse. In D. Tannen (ed.) *Spoken and Written Language: Exploring Orality and Literacy* (pp. 1–33). Norwood, NJ: Ablex.

Van den Noort, M.W.M.L., Bosch, M.P.C. and Hugdahl, K. (2006) Foreign language proficiency and working memory capacity. *European Psychologist* 11 (4), 289–296.
Vasiljevic, Z. (2010) Dictogloss as an interactive method of teaching listening comprehension. *English Language Teaching* 3 (1), 41–52.
Wagner, E. (2007) Are they watching? Test-taker viewing behavior during an L2 video listening test. *Language Learning & Technology* 11 (1), 67–86.
Wickens, C.D. (2002) Multiple resources and performance prediction. *Theoretical Issues in Ergonomics Science* 3 (2), 159–177.
Wilson, M. (2003) Discovery listening – improving perceptual processing. *ELT Journal* 57 (4), 179–185.
Zhao, Y. (1997) The effects of listeners' control of speech rate on second language comprehension. *Applied Linguistics* 18 (1), 49–68.

Appendix 5A

Dictogloss text

The Swiss bank UBS has set out a new pay system for its top executives in which senior bankers could be fined if they underperform in years of big losses. Proclaiming the end of the era of huge bonuses in the financial sector, Peter Kurer, the bank's chairman, said the new system would eradicate the culture of rewarding excessive risk taking. The proposed cultural shift would see rewards for 'those who deliver good results over several years without assuming unnecessarily high risk', he added. His comments came as the US bank Goldman Sachs said its top executives, who last year received an average of $2.4 million, would get no bonus this year. UBS said the rewards for its traders would be slashed after it accepted a 6 billion Swiss franc rescue from the authorities.

Repetition (text 1)

I've always been intrigued / by what stories do to the brain / and how storytelling / has an automatic appeal. / Now why do we always like stories? / And this fascinates me / as I think about how the brain works. / My suggestion, and I'll go to the conclusion first, / is that stories give a significance to life. / If I said to you a mountain / had a certain height / then it wouldn't be very meaningful to you, / probably wouldn't be very interesting to you / and I think it's just this sheer issue / of facts standing alone / that would make trivial pursuits / or pub quizzes / not necessarily that exciting.

Example of news item

Scientists in Canada say deep sea trawling in the Atlantic Ocean has driven some fish species to the brink of extinction in little more than a generation. Research published in the magazine Nature says five deep water species are in catastrophic decline. Here's our science correspondent, Rowland

Pearse. 'Trouble started for deep sea species when fisheries on the continental shelf round the Atlantic collapsed in the 1960s and 70s. Trawlers started moving into deeper waters, hauling in catches from down to 1800 metres depth. Species like the round nosed and onion eyed grenadier and the blue hake were soon being served up on dinner tables around the world. Untouched before the late 70s, their populations had crashed by up to 98% by the mid 90s and by 2003 the round nosed grenadier was 99.7% wiped out. By international conservation standards these species should be listed as critically in danger, the authors of the report say.'

6 A Psycholinguistic Measurement of Second Language Proficiency: The Coefficient of Variation[1]

Carrie A. Ankerstein

This chapter will focus on a central feature of second language (L2) proficiency, namely lexical access, from a psycholinguistic perspective. Lexical access is the retrieval of a lexical item (word) in the mental lexicon, including its phonological, syntactic, pragmatic and semantic features (Harley, 2010). It is a basic component of language comprehension: in order for longer texts or utterances to be understood, the individual lexical items that make up these messages have to be decoded and integrated into higher-level sentences or phrases. Fast lexical access is undoubtedly part of higher-level L2 language proficiency. (See Tracy-Ventura et al., this volume, for a discussion of the problems encountered in the defining and measuring of proficiency in SLA studies.)

This chapter is particularly concerned with automaticity of lexical access in second language acquisition and use. A process is automatic if it is fast, obligatory, ballistic (unstoppable) and unconscious (Harley, 2010; Segalowitz, 2010). For example, in their native language, adults automatically access the lexical item 'dog' when shown a picture of this four-legged mammal, and they are unlikely to be aware of how this activation process takes place. Attentional processing, in contrast, is slower, non-obligatory and explicit, requiring more complex cognitive effort. Adult L2 learners may use attentional processes to access lexical items in the L2: consciously applying mnemonic devices, checking rules or translating into the first language (L1) before the meaning of the L2 lexical item is activated. The automaticity or directness of lexical access in an L2 is likely to vary as a function of language proficiency (Segalowitz, 2010). For example, as L2 learners acquire new vocabulary, they may initially use translation or rule-checking routes to access L2 lexical items. With more L2 experience and as proficiency improves, the L2 learner may at some point be able to bypass extraneous routes and use direct concept to L2 lexical item association, thus showing a qualitative change in L2 processing. Automatic word recognition means that attentional resources can be devoted to higher-order meaning construction: 'Text comprehension is highly demanding and requires high amounts of cognitive control. If subtasks, such as word meaning retrieval, do not take place "automatically" [in a L2], they may therefore call for attentional capacity to the detriment of the higher-order comprehension task' (Fukkink *et al.*, 2005: 54).

Lexical access is often tested in psycholinguistic experiments with protocols such as the timed lexical decision task. In timed lexical decision tasks, participants are asked to make 'word' or 'nonword' responses to a series of word ('nectar') and nonword ('plind') stimuli. These studies generally compare speed and accuracy measures for word and nonword responses, in which speed is often used as an indicator of automatic versus attentional processing. Participants are generally faster and more accurate for word responses, in contrast to responses for nonword stimuli (Harley, 2010).

Using a lexical decision task, Segalowitz and Segalowitz (1993) demonstrated how L2 learners can go from initial indirect access to direct access for lexical processing after training. They argued that it is not necessarily the case that response speed is the only indicator of automaticity. As the L2 learner goes from less skilled performance at Time 1 to more skilled at Time 2, word recognition becomes faster. There are two possibilities to explain the difference in word recognition speed at Time 1 and Time 2: (1) the processing route is completed more quickly, which Segalowitz and Segalowitz call a 'speed-up' or 'facilitatory' effect; or (2) the processing route has changed qualitatively, i.e. some aspects of processing have been minimized or eliminated, and processing has become more automatic.

As a process becomes more automatic, it is not only completed faster but there is also a disproportionate change in variability due to the elimination of inefficient processes; Segalowitz and Segalowitz (1993: 374) argued that 'there is not an across-the-board reduction in speed of operation, but rather [...] a change in the number and relative variability of the components contributing to the overall variability'. They suggested that the coefficient of variation (CV) for response times (standard deviation divided by mean response time) can be used to distinguish between processing efficiency (speed-up effects) and automatization. For example, if an individual is simply twice as fast at Time 2 compared to Time 1, then the standard deviation for response times (RT) at Time 2 should be half what it was at Time 1, which means that the CV for Times 1 and 2 should be the same. However, if the individual is using a qualitatively different processing route – for example, a route that is more efficient and less noisy (more direct) – then not only may the individual be faster, but his/her RTs will be less variable (standard deviations will be smaller), resulting in a lower CV at Time 2 compared with Time 1. Thus the CV controls for general differences in response speed, and can be used to explore potential qualitative differences in language processing (see also Harrington, 2006, 2007; Hulstijn et al., 2009; Phillips et al., 2004). From this point of view, automatic (direct access) processing is not only faster than attentional (indirect access) processing, it is less noisy, more stable and therefore less variable. The more automatic L2 lexical processing is, the more 'proficient' the use of the language will be, approaching the efficiency of word recognition processes in L1 use.

Most studies using analysis of CVs in L2 lexical processing have focused on the longitudinal process of automatization within subjects following training sessions, using the correlation between RT and CV as an indicator of automatization of processing (Akamatsu, 2008; Fukkink et al., 2005; Harrington, 2007; Hulstijn et al., 2009; Segalowitz & Segalowitz, 1993). For example, Fukkink et al. (2005) explored training effects on word recognition in a group of Dutch school children (Experiment 1). The school children, aged 13–14 years and with about 3.5 years of English L2 instruction, completed a lexical decision task for 100 English words and 90 pseudowords before and after two 40-minute training sessions, administered within the same week, aimed at creating form-meaning associations for a subset of 40 words. Fukkink et al. found that the children were faster and more accurate in their responses for all words – trained and control words – following training; however, the effect was significantly greater for the trained words in comparison to the control words. In addition, CVs were lower following the training session for all words, but again significantly more so for the trained words, confirming their hypothesis that 'training leads to more automatic word recognition performance, as reflected by a reduction in CV_{RT}' (Fukkink et al., 2005: 58). The exploration of within-subject longitudinal change in the processes underlying lexical access is important for development of theories and models of second language acquisition, but few studies have investigated whether L2 speakers can attain a native-like state for lexical access.

The current study investigated whether higher-proficiency L2 speakers – that is, university students of English – process lexical items differently from L1 speakers in a semantically primed visual lexical decision task, contrasting not only RTs and error rates (ERs), but also the CV between participant groups. Semantic priming refers to the facilitation of responses to a stimulus as a result of exposure to a previously presented semantically related stimulus. For example, participants in such experiments are faster to respond to 'salt' having previously seen the related word 'pepper' (whereas an unrelated word such as 'letter' will not provoke this facilitating effect). Following the logic of Segalowitz and Segalowitz (1993), if university-level L2 speakers of English have achieved native-like lexical access, a qualitative difference in lexical activation between the L1 and L2 groups would not be expected, and this would be indicated by similar CVs for the two groups; a difference in the CV would indicate that the learners have not achieved native-like levels of automaticity in word recognition. In the current study, CVs for L1 and L2 groups were compared, as well as RT and ER data, to investigate both qualitative and quantitative aspects of possible differences in performance on a primed lexical decision task.

An additional research question was whether there are qualitative and quantitative differences in performance for words of different frequency values. Word frequency plays an important role in word recognition. Responses to higher-frequency words are generally faster and more accurate than to lower-frequency words (Harley, 2010). Balota (1994) suggested that L1 speakers of a language process high- and low-frequency words differently, which predicts a difference in the CV for high- and low-frequency words in lexical decision tasks performed by L1 speakers (Akamatsu, 2008; Harrington, 2007). Priming effects have also been shown to be stronger for lower-frequency targets in contrast to higher-frequency targets (Kinoshita, 1995). Kinoshita argued that because lower-frequency words are processed less 'fluently' than higher-frequency words, they benefit more from the pre-activation boost due to priming.

The present semantic priming experiment was designed to discourage strategic (attentional) processes – such as post-lexical checking or expectancy strategies – by using phonotactically legal pseudowords, a low proportion of related targets (8%), a continuous list presentation paradigm (in which a response is given for prime and target stimuli) and a neutral relatedness condition. In the neutral condition, the target followed the neutral prime word 'BLANK'. The neutral condition was introduced in order to check for strategic priming, and more specifically for the expectancy strategy. It is hypothesized that RTs for unrelated stimuli will be longer than for related stimuli. This may be due to an automatic priming effect as a result of the relation between the related prime and target or due to strategies. For example, participants may notice that some stimuli are related and therefore generate expectancies for possible targets based on the prime word. When the expected target is shown, responses are fast (the expectancy is confirmed); when the target is not an expected word, responses are slower, due to the mismatch between target and expectancy. Thus, an RT effect due to an expectancy strategy could be confounded with an RT effect for actual automatic priming, since both cases will give rise to faster responses in the related condition than in the unrelated condition. The neutral condition, on the other hand, would not be affected by the expectancy strategy, since participants would not be able to form expectations for the neutral prime word 'BLANK'. The neutral condition is therefore a good baseline condition for 'default' RTs for targets. If RTs for the neutral condition are faster than for the unrelated condition, this can be interpreted as evidence of an expectancy-based effect – the neutral condition producing no expectancies (and therefore no effect on RTs, as it does in the case of mismatched expectancies). If RTs for the neutral and unrelated conditions are similar, this would indicate that longer RTs observed for the unrelated condition are not due to some sort of strategy use (cf. Shelton & Martin, 1992).

CVs were analyzed in addition to traditional RT and ER measurements to investigate whether there are qualitative (measured by CV) and quantitative (measured by RT and ER) differences in lexical processing between L1 and L2 speakers. This included a comparison of responses for high- and low-frequency words, an investigation of semantic priming effects, and of the interaction between frequency and semantic relatedness effects in both participant groups. Thus the main research questions were as follows:

- *Research question 1*: Is word recognition quantitatively and qualitatively different as a function of word frequency for L1 and university-level L2 speakers of English?
- *Research question 2*: Are there quantitative and qualitative differences in semantic priming for L1 and university-level L2 speakers?
- *Research question 3*: Is semantic priming stronger for low-frequency targets compared to high-frequency targets for both groups?

Experiment

Participants

Thirty L1 speakers of British English (9 males, 21 females) aged between 18 and 30 years (mean age = 21.2 years) were recruited via email distribution lists from the University of Sheffield, England. Thirty L2 speakers of English (7 males, 23 females) aged between 19 and 33 years (mean = 23.8 years) were recruited from Saarland University, Germany. All non-native speakers were native speakers of German, had started learning English in school at the age of 10 years, and had studied or used English up to university level.

Stimuli

Stimuli consisted of 90 targets that appeared with related, unrelated and neutral prime words. Related prime-target pairs were semantically related by synonym, antonym, category coordinate or 'other', where 'other' included relationships such as part-whole (e.g. tongue-mouth) or subordinate-superordinate (e.g. spring-season) relations. The unrelated pairs were made by semi-randomly pairing the primes from the related condition to non-semantically or phonologically linked targets (e.g. tongue-season). In the neutral condition, the target followed a neutral prime (e.g. BLANK-season).

Half of the targets were high frequency (mean = 1297.2, SD = 833.1) and half were low frequency (mean = 20.5, SD = 14.8). Frequency ratings were taken from the Thorndike–Lorge written frequency ratings per 18 million words (Fearnley, 1997). The targets were matched for syllable length and imageability ratings according to the MRC Psycholinguistic Database (Fearnley, 1997). Targets were presented in counterbalanced lists so that each participant saw every target item once. The targets were distributed evenly across lists with 30 pairs each in the related, unrelated and neutral conditions.

Stimuli also included filler items. These included 30 real word filler items, 15 neutral word ('BLANK') filler items and 135 nonwords. The nonwords were taken in part from the ARC Nonword Database (Rastle et al., 2002). Polysyllabic pseudowords were created by randomly combining syllables from common nouns. All nonwords were phonotactically legal for English speakers. For some filler trials, 'BLANK' was followed by a nonword so that participants would not be biased for a 'word' response following 'BLANK'.

Apparatus and procedure

Participants were tested individually in a quiet room. The stimuli were presented in lower-case Times New Roman, font size 28, in the center of a laptop screen. Stimuli were presented in black against a light gray background. The laptop recorded RTs in milliseconds (ms) to the nearest tenth of a millisecond. The experiment was run using DMDX 3.2.6.4 (Forster & Forster, 2003).

The lexical decision task was a continuous list presentation paradigm, in which responses are made to prime and target stimuli. Participants were presented with a single stimulus and asked to judge whether the stimulus was a word or nonword as quickly and as accurately as possible. Participants responded via mouse button press with labelled buttons: left button 'word' and right button 'nonword'. There were 20 practice trials before the experiment to ensure participants understood the task. Each stimulus remained onscreen until a response was made. The interstimulus interval was set to 500 ms. Participants had 2000 ms in which to respond to the stimulus, after which the computer started the next trial. There was a total of 360 items, and there were two breaks, which came after 120 items.

Data analysis

Correct responses were analyzed and no responses reached the time-out value of 2000 ms. RT, ER and CV data were entered into separate repeated-measures analysis of variance (ANOVAs) with Condition (related, unrelated, neutral) and Frequency (high, low) as within-subjects variables and Group (L1, L2) as a between-subjects variable.

Response times

There was a significant effect of Frequency ($F[1, 58] = 283.172, p < 0.0005$), indicating that RTs for high-frequency targets (mean = 534.8 ms) were significantly faster than for low-frequency targets (mean = 652.3 ms). There was a significant interaction effect of Frequency and Group ($F[1, 58] = 14.644$, $p < 0.0005$). Both groups were significantly faster for high-frequency targets (L1 group: $t[29] = 10.258, p < 0.0005$; L2 group: $t[29] = 13.519, p < 0.0005$), but the effect was stronger for the L2 group.

There was a significant effect of Condition ($F[2, 116] = 16.777, p < 0.0005$), indicating that RTs varied across the three conditions. Post hoc tests showed that this was due to the significantly faster RTs for the related condition as compared to the unrelated condition ($t[59] = 3.445, p < 0.01$) and the neutral condition ($t[59] = 5.598, p < 0.0005$). RTs for the unrelated condition were faster than for the neutral condition ($t[59] = 2.916, p < 0.01$) (Bonferroni corrected p-value for multiple comparisons = 0.02). There was no significant interaction effect between Condition and Group ($F[2, 116] = 0.169, p = 0.845$).

There was a significant interaction between Condition and Frequency ($F[2, 116] = 5.864, p < 0.01$), indicating different priming effects for high- and low-frequency targets. Post hoc tests showed that RTs for the high-frequency related condition were significantly faster than for the high-frequency neutral condition ($t[59] = 3.281, p < 0.008$), and that RTs for the high-frequency unrelated condition were faster than for the high-frequency neutral condition ($t[59] = 3.226, p < 0.008$). There was no significant difference for the high-frequency related and unrelated comparison ($t[59] = 0.343, p = 0.733$). RTs for the low-frequency related condition were significantly faster than the low-frequency unrelated condition ($t[59] = 3.926, p < 0.0005$) and the low-frequency neutral condition ($t[59] = 5.045, p < 0.0005$), indicating a priming effect for the low-frequency targets. There was no significant difference for RTs in the low-frequency unrelated and neutral comparison ($t[59] = 0.955, p = 0.344$). (Bonferroni corrected p-value = 0.008). There was no significant interaction between Condition, Frequency and Group, ($F[2, 116] = 0.019, p = 0.981$). Mean RTs as a function of Condition and Frequency and Group are shown in Table 6.1.

There was a significant main effect of Group ($F[1, 58] = 16.673$, $p < 0.0005$), indicating that L1 speaker RTs (mean = 552.1 ms) were significantly faster than L2 speaker RTs (mean = 635.0 ms).

Table 6.1 Mean RTs (ms) for target words as a function of Condition × Frequency × Group (standard deviations given in brackets)

Group	High frequency			Low frequency		
	Related	Unrelated	Neutral	Related	Unrelated	Neutral
L1	501.3	501.3	517.5	569.8	607.2	615.7
	(72.9)	(66.1)	(72.9)	(54.1)	(84.9)	(97.4)
L2	557.0	553.4	578.1	677.7	715.4	728.3
	(81.2)	(65.5)	(96.8)	(111.5)	(127.9)	(125.7)

Error rate data

There was a significant effect of Frequency ($F[1, 58] = 151.468, p < 0.0005$) on ERs, with ERs for high-frequency targets (mean = 0.4%) significantly lower than for low-frequency targets (mean = 12.9%). There was a significant interaction effect of Frequency and Group ($F[1, 58] = 67.830, p < 0.0005$), both groups being significantly more accurate for high-frequency targets (L1 group: $t[29] = 5.163, p < 0.0005$; L2 group: $t[29] = 11.155, p < 0.0005$), but the effect was stronger for the L2 group.

There was a significant effect of Condition ($F[2, 116] = 4.866, p < 0.01$) on ERs. Post hoc tests showed that this was due to significantly lower ERs for the related condition, as compared to the unrelated condition ($t[59] = 2.478, p < 0.02$), and the neutral condition ($t[59] = 3.190, p < 0.01$). ERs for the unrelated and neutral conditions were not significantly different ($t[59] = 0.139, p = 0.890$). There was no significant interaction effect for ERs between Condition and Group ($F[2, 116] = 0.801, p = 0.451$) (Bonferroni corrected p-value = 0.02).

There was a significant interaction for ERs between Condition and Frequency ($F[2, 116] = 4.715, p < 0.02$), indicating different ERs for high- and low-frequency targets across conditions. Post hoc tests showed that the comparison of ERs for low-frequency related targets and low-frequency unrelated targets approached significance ($t[59] = 2.607, p = 0.012$), due to lower ERs for related low-frequency targets; there was a significant difference for low-frequency related and neutral targets ($t[59] = 3.010, p < 0.008$), indicating a priming effect for low-frequency targets. All other comparisons were not significant at a Bonferroni corrected p-level of >0.008. There was no significant interaction between Condition, Frequency and Group, ($F[2, 116] = 0.648, p = 0.525$). Mean ERs as a function of Condition, Frequency and Group are shown in Table 6.2.

There was a significant main effect of Group ($F[1, 58] = 61.415, p < 0.0005$), indicating that L1 speaker ERs (mean = 2.7%) were significantly lower than L2 speaker ERs (mean = 10.7%).

Table 6.2 Mean ERs (%) for target words as a function of Condition × Frequency × Group (standard deviations given in brackets)

Group	High frequency			Low frequency		
	Related	Unrelated	Neutral	Related	Unrelated	Neutral
L1	0.6	0.4	0.8	2.4	6.9	4.8
	(1.8)	(1.5)	(2.8)	(3.5)	(6.8)	(7.0)
L2	0.2	0.0	0.6	17.7	22.1	23.4
	(1.1)	(0.0)	(0.7)	(14.7)	(11.6)	(14.3)

Table 6.3 Mean CV ($SD_{RT}/mean_{RT}$) for target words as a function of Condition × Frequency × Group (standard deviations given in brackets)

Group	High frequency			Low frequency		
	Related	Unrelated	Neutral	Related	Unrelated	Neutral
L1	0.21 (0.06)	0.19 (0.06)	0.24 (0.10)	0.26 (0.08)	0.27 (0.10)	0.24 (0.06)
L2	0.20 (0.08)	0.18 (0.09)	0.22 (0.09)	0.27 (0.09)	0.27 (0.09)	0.25 (0.08)

Coefficient of variation

There was a significant effect of Frequency ($F[1, 58] = 31.841$, $p < 0.0005$), indicating that CVs for high-frequency targets (mean = 0.21) were significantly lower than for low-frequency targets (mean = 0.26). There was no significant interaction effect between Frequency and Group ($F[1, 58] = 0.571$, $p = 0.453$).

There was no significant effect of Condition ($F[2, 116] = 0.870$, $p = 0.422$), indicating that CVs across the conditions were similar. There was no significant interaction between Condition and Group ($F[2, 116] = 0.240$, $p = 0.787$).

There was a significant interaction between Condition and Frequency ($F[2, 116] = 5.855$, $p < 0.01$). Post hoc tests showed that the CVs for the high-frequency unrelated (mean = 0.18) and neutral (mean = 0.23) conditions were significantly different ($t[59] = 4.147$, $p < 0.008$). All other comparisons were not significant at a Bonferroni corrected p-level of >0.008. Mean CVs as a function of Condition, Frequency and Group are shown in Table 6.3.

There was no significant main effect of Group ($F[1, 58] = 0.024$, $p = 0.877$), indicating that the CVs for L1 speakers (mean = 0.23) and for L2 speaker (mean = 0.23) were similar.

Discussion and Conclusions

The findings will be discussed according to the three research questions set out in the first section of this chapter.

Research question 1

Are there quantitative (as measured by RT and ER) and qualitative (as reflected in the CV) differences in word recognition as a function of word frequency for L1 and university-level L2 speakers? It was hypothesized that word recognition would differ as a function of word frequency at least for L1 speakers. The results reported here show this to be the case. Responses within the L1 group for high-frequency words were faster, with a mean difference of 90.0 ms, and more accurate, with a mean difference of 4.1%, than for low-frequency words. A similar effect was observed for the L2 group, although the effect within the L2 group yielded greater discrepancies for high- and low-frequency words for RTs, with a mean difference of 144.3 ms, and ERs, with a mean difference of 20.8%. These differences in speed and accuracy may indicate that some of the low-frequency words may not have been recognized as English words (i.e. treated as nonwords) by the L2 group.

A comparison of CVs showed that they were lower for high-frequency words than low-frequency words, with no between-group differences, indicating more automatic responses for high-frequency words. The mean CV across both groups for high-frequency words was 0.21, within the automatic range of 0.20–0.22 cited by Harrington (2007); the mean CV for low-frequency words was significantly higher at 0.26. These findings are compatible with Balota's (1994) claim that L1 speakers process high- and low-frequency words differently, at least in a lexical decision task. The current data show that this is also the case for university-level L2 speakers for the set of words used.

Research question 2

Are there quantitative and qualitative differences in semantic priming for L1 and university-level L2 speakers? L2 speakers were generally slower and less accurate in their responses when compared to L1 speakers. However, with respect to priming effects, both groups were similar in showing significant priming in speed and accuracy, and both groups had similar CV values, indicating similarities in the cognitive fluency of lexical processing. There was no significant difference for CV values across the relatedness conditions. However, this needs to be explored further, because some unexpected differences for the CV in certain conditions were found that are difficult to account for, namely the difference in the CV for high-frequency targets in the neutral and unrelated conditions. The CV was highest for the unrelated condition, which could indicate more attentional processing in this condition, perhaps due to expectancy-based strategies. Participants could have generated expectancies in the unrelated condition and when these were not met, they could have responded with non-automatic, executive processes, such as inhibition of lexical and semantic representations activated by the unrelated prime, resulting in longer RTs and higher CVs. The inhibition process is unnecessary in the neutral condition, in which expectancies would be difficult to generate, and in the related condition, expectancies would facilitate activation and responses. However, the semantic priming found for low-frequency targets appears to be automatic given similar CVs across the related, unrelated and neutral conditions.

Research question 3

Is semantic priming stronger for low-frequency targets compared to high-frequency targets for both groups? It was also expected that the priming effect would differ as a function of word frequency, following Kinoshita's (1995) argument that low-frequency word targets receive a greater 'boost' from primes in contrast to high-frequency words, for which word recognition is already fast. This hypothesis was indeed confirmed in both participant groups. For both L1 and university-level L2 speakers, the effect of semantic priming on response speed and accuracy was greater for low-frequency word targets compared to high-frequency targets.

Overall, the results suggest that L1 and university-level L2 speakers of English appear to use qualitatively similar processes for word recognition, despite quantitative differences in general speed and accuracy. The results thus support qualitatively similar automatic lexical access in these two groups of English speakers. The current study complements other research in L2 word processing such as studies that have investigated longitudinal qualitative changes in word recognition (see Hulstijn et al., 2009, for a review), and studies that explore the structure of the L2 lexicon such as Frenck-Mestre and Prince (1997), who argued for autonomy of the L2 lexicon in proficient L2 speakers.

The current chapter has focused on proficiency as being related to automaticity of processing lexical items in the L2 using the CV of response times as an index of 'cognitive fluency' (Segalowitz, 2010: 76). Lexical access in university-level L2 speakers of English was found to be native-like, as indicated by the CV of RTs, which was statistically similar to that found for a L1 speaker group. This finding is important for several reasons. On a practical level, automatic lexical access is a key component of comprehension, so once L2 learners are able to automatically access L2 words in their mental lexicon, they will be able to comprehend texts better. On another level, perhaps more relevant to language acquisition researchers, it offers some insight into how native-like non-native language processing can be, a question posed by Clahsen and Felser (2006). They listed four factors that have been proposed to explain the differences between L1 and L2 processing. These include the influence of the L1, a lack of knowledge of the L2, maturational changes, and differences in cognitive resources (Clahsen & Felser, 2006). The current study sheds light on cognitive resources used in L1 and L2 processing, which relate to automatic and attentional processing, and shows that lexical access can be native-like (i.e. automatic) in an L2 as well.

The analysis of CVs offers a practical and relatively simple method to assess automaticity of language processing. Future research using L2 speakers of different certified proficiency levels will be necessary to assess more fully the usefulness of the CV as an index of processing efficiency, and significant correlations between proficiency certification and automaticity of processing should be expected. If further research confirms the CV as a valid measurement of processing efficiency, it may prove to be a useful tool for researchers – and even language teachers (Fukkink *et al.*, 2005, tested participants in the classroom) – to evaluate a number of linguistic skills such as audio and visual word recognition, translation (see Bairstow *et al.*, this volume, for an example of an innovative timed translation task), and grammatical parsing.

Acknowledgments

The design of the priming experiment and collection of native speaker data was done while the author was a postdoctoral research assistant at the Human Communication Sciences Department, University of Sheffield as part of a project supervised by Rosemary Varley, and funded by an ESRC Professorial Fellowship awarded to Rosemary Varley. A preliminary report of the data presented here appeared in Ankerstein (2011). The author would also like to thank the editors and the anonymous reviewer(s) for their helpful comments on earlier versions of the chapter.

Note

(1) This is sometimes also called the coefficient of *variance* (see Harrington, 2007) or coefficient of *variability* (see Segalowitz & Segalowitz, 1993). Segalowitz's (2010) convention for the plural form of coefficients of variation 'CVs' will be used throughout.

References

Akamatsu, N. (2008) The effects of training on automatization of word recognition in English as a foreign language. *Applied Psycholinguistics* 29, 175–193.
Ankerstein, C.A. (2011) Qualitatively similar automatic semantic priming in native and non-native speakers. *Proceedings of the 4th ISCA Workshop ExLing*, 11–14.
Balota, D.A. (1994) Visual word recognition: the journey from features to meaning. In M.A. Gernsbacher (ed.) *Handbook of Psycholinguistics* (pp. 303–358). San Diego, CA: Academic Press.
Clahsen, H. and Felser, C. (2006) How native-like is non-native processing? *Trends in Cognitive Science* 10 (12), 555–570.
Fearnley, S. (1997) MRC psycholinguistic database search program. *Behavior Research Methods, Instruments & Computers* 29 (2), 291–295.
Forster, K.I. and Forster, J.C. (2003) A Windows display program with millisecond accuracy. *Behavior Research Methods Instruments & Computers* 35 (1), 116–124.
Frenck-Mestre, C. and Prince, P. (1997) Second language autonomy. *Journal of Memory and Language* 37, 481–501.
Fukkink, R.G., Hulstijn, J. and Simis, A. (2005) Does training in second-language word recognition skills affect reading comprehension? An experimental study. *The Modern Language Journal* 89 (1), 54–75.
Harley, T.A. (2010) *The Psychology of Language: From data to theory*. Hove: Psychology Press.
Harrington, M. (2006) The lexical decision task as a measure of L2 proficiency. *EUROSLA Yearbook* 6, 147–168.

Harrington, M. (2007) The coefficient of variance as an index of L2 lexical processing skill. *University of Queensland Working Papers in Linguistics* 1, 1–21.

Hulstijn, J.H., Van Gelderen, A. and Schoonen, R. (2009) Automatization in second language acquisition: What does the coefficient of variation tell us? *Applied Psycholinguistics* 30, 555–582.

Kinoshita, S. (1995) The word frequency effect in recognition memory versus repetition priming. *Memory & Cognition* 23, 569–580.

Phillips, N.A., Segalowitz, N., O'Brien, I. and Yamasaki, N. (2004) Semantic priming in a first and second language: Evidence from reaction time variability and event-related brain potentials. *Journal of Neurolinguistics* 17, 237–262.

Rastle, K., Harrington, J. and Coltheart, M. (2002) 358,534 nonwords: The ARC Nonword Database. *Quarterly Journal of Experimental Psychology* 55 (4), 1339–1362.

Segalowitz, N. (2010) *The Cognitive Bases of Second Language Fluency*. New York, NY: Routledge.

Segalowitz, N. and Segalowitz, S.J. (1993) Skilled performance, practice, and the differentiation of speed-up from automatization effects: Evidence from second language word recognition. *Applied Psycholinguistics* 14, 369–385.

Shelton, J.R. and Martin, R.C. (1992) How semantic is automatic semantic priming? *Journal of Experimental Psychology: Learning, Memory and Cognition* 18 (6), 1191–1210.

7 Evaluating the Workings of Bilingual Memory with a Translation Recognition Task

Dominique Bairstow, Jean-Marc Lavaur, Jannika Laxén and Xavier Aparicio

Introduction

Bilingual memory connects two language systems, in which various elements may converge or differ. For example, written forms may be completely different (in languages that do not share the same writing system), or similar (in related languages using the same orthographic system, such as Dutch and German); in the same way, some phonological systems will share certain sounds, but not others. If a certain degree of knowledge of two languages is achieved, then quick links between these languages can be established within memory. An example of this would be the ability to switch easily between two languages, changing languages during a conversation, for instance, while maintaining the contents (original meaning) of the message. This skill seems to imply some sort of connection between the two language systems. Research into the bilingual mental lexicon has established that translation equivalents are more quickly and easily linked together, possibly through shared semantic features connected to the word form in each language (which can, however, differ slightly from one language to the other; de Groot, 1992; Laxén & Lavaur, 2010; van Hell & de Groot, 1998).

As is the case for the mental lexicon (a vast database containing not only all the words known by a person, but also lexical characteristics such as orthography, phonology and semantics; Dijkstra, 2005) in general, the bilingual mental lexicon can be considered as being in endless reconstruction, even for a true bilingual (completely proficient in two languages), because new words belonging to either the first language (L1) or the second language (L2) can be learnt at any moment, and other words can be momentarily forgotten. This flexible quality of the mental lexicon enables additional links to be created within memory, while others weaken, or even disappear. The mental lexicon will change gradually and constantly over time, with more abrupt changes during the first stages of L2 learning when new words aggregate around a pre-existing organization, the semantic base (the conceptual network linked to the L1 lexicon).

This chapter sets out to use a translation recognition task as a means of evaluating the types and strength of the links that exist between the two languages in the learners' mental lexicon, following the BIA+ (Bilingual Interactive Activation; Dijkstra & van Heuven, 2002) model of bilingual lexical processing. These links could be modulated by the proficiency of the bilinguals in their languages, as well as by more formal aspects of languages, such as cognate words (translation equivalents with the same, or very close, spelling). Indeed, it is assumed in the current chapter that bilingualism is not a 'fixed state' in itself. More precisely, we believe that it would be nearly impossible to find two bilinguals that have exactly the same proficiency level in each of their languages, but also the same ability to match words from each language. This assertion can be extended to include all L2 learners, because individuals cannot be expected to have the same level of proficiency in their native tongue and, of course, can be in varying stages of advancement while learning a L2 (see Gertken *et al.*, this volume, for a thorough discussion of the concept of language dominance and its link to the concept of language proficiency). In this chapter, bilingual proficiency is related to the act of frequently and efficiently activating both language systems in order to estimate the comparability of certain terms across languages.

The translation recognition task used in this research study (in which a subject has to say if two words presented simultaneously are translation equivalents or not) is designed to measure the ease with which the participants can access both languages through the formal and semantic relations that exist between different words in the two languages. The test is not solely designed to evaluate language dominance in bilinguals, but can be applied to participants with any level in a given L2, ranging from beginners to very fluent speakers (as was the case in the pilot study presented here).

Experiments in cognitive psychology are often long and demanding for the participants, so one of the goals of this research project is to create a functional and concise test to evaluate bilingual ability (not specific to bilinguals, but involving the lexicon of two languages), which can be administered before an experiment. As pointed out by Leclercq and Edmonds (this volume) and by Tracy-Ventura *et al.* (this volume), there is indeed a need for independent, valid, reliable and practical measures of language proficiency to improve the reliability of second language acquisition (SLA) and bilingualism research. After a short review of findings in cognitive research, we will present the results of the pilot version of a test probing memory for French L1 and English L2 words, followed by a discussion concerning the variables that need to be taken into account in future research evaluating bilingual proficiency.

Models of bilingual memory

Words from both languages can be linked together via semantic memory (which holds the meanings of the words from both languages, as well as other information that is not related to any particular language). This part of our memory is indeed considered to be common (at least in part) to both languages in most of the latest theoretical models (de Groot, 1992; Dijkstra & van Heuven, 2002; Eddington & Tokowicz, 2013; Kroll & Stewart, 1994; van Hell & de Groot, 1998). The connection between words, made on the basis of semantic equivalence, can be observed in many situations and is not the sole prerogative of translators and interpreters, even though they generally develop a capacity for easily and almost instantly linking them. Moreover, even for those who do not seem to have mastered the L2 at all, more or less strong links can still be created. Examples of this are the English words LOVE or HELLO, which are often quite easily recognizable for French speakers, independently of their English level, and can be easily associated with their translation equivalents in the dominant language. In other words, the capacity to link two languages within memory can develop quite quickly, beginning with the very first contacts with the L2. Yet, studies mostly evaluate proficiency in each language separately and the linking of the two languages is often overlooked. This is why we need to understand how multiple relationships between languages are established and how they promote many complex activities (such as reading or speaking in different languages successively or near-simultaneously), without requiring excessive effort.

A short review of various models of bilingual memory will allow for a better understanding of its organization and working principles. Historically, experimental research on bilingualism began by focusing on the potential difficulties that can be encountered when switching from one language to another (evidenced by slower lexical processing rhythms; Macnamara & Kushnir, 1971). Over the years, various models have tried to explain the organization of bilingual memory using one or more systems. From the point of view of cognitive psychology, the first steps taken in the direction of language studies were initiated by Weinreich (1953) and Kolers (1963), who postulated three types of organization for bilingual memory: *coordinate, subordinate* and *compound* storage.

The *coordinate* model proposes two memory systems, one for each language, thereby limiting interlingual interference. However, creating links (i.e. connecting words from each language) between the two languages might be difficult if they were either learnt separately or in very different contexts. The *subordinate* model predicts an asymmetry between the two languages (one being better known than the other), and an access to meaning almost exclusively via the dominant L1, with the L2 dependent on the rules of organization of the L1. This dependence on the L1 is thought to be particularly important during the acquisition of new L2 words, making this model particularly relevant to the first stages of language learning. Finally, the *compound* model hypothesizes equal ability in both languages, and access to meaning can happen independently from the language of the word (words are linked by concept mediation). Nevertheless, there may be some chance of interference between the two languages, in particular when similar word forms exist in both languages, but with different meanings (e.g. the French word FOUR, meaning *oven*, and the English number FOUR; Laxén et al., 2011). Weinreich's model of bilingual memory influenced SLA research right up until the end of the 1980s. With the benefit of hindsight, we can see that beyond the level achieved in each language, it is the very nature of the relationships between the two language systems within the bilingual brain (bilingual proficiency) that was really of the highest concern.

More recently, Kroll and Stewart (1994) proposed a 'hierarchical' model taking into account the evolution of bilingual memory, based on experimental results that clearly indicate asymmetries in the way each of the two languages is processed. They claim that switching from L1 to L2 follows a semantic route, whereas switching from L2 to L1 takes a formal (or lexical) path, before activating meaning. The speed with which actual meaning is accessed would therefore be faster or slower, depending on the language (L1 or L2) that initiated the chain of processing (either through a semantic or a lexical route, respectively). Moreover, words themselves, as well as their characteristics, can also modulate the links between languages, both on a lexical and a semantic level. This notion is developed in the extension of the hierarchical model proposed by Eddington and Tokowicz (2013), which takes into account the possibility of multiple translations of a word in another language. In this way, context availability (the ease with which a word can be used in one or more contexts), accuracy of word definitions, or even the word's subjective frequency (familiarity), are all good predictors of the level of difficulty involved in moving from one language to another, in individual word processing (van Hell & de Groot, 1998).

De Groot and her colleagues integrated these various principles into a distributed model of bilingual lexical memory (de Groot, 1992; van Hell & de Groot, 1998), which predicts different degrees of semantic overlap between words, that influence the speed with which they can be matched on the basis of their shared meaning from one language to the other. According to this model, some words share numerous elements of meaning with their potential translation equivalents in another language (with interlingual nodes, each representing a part of the associated meaning), but they may also possess specific features linked to one language only (the intralingual nodes). This point of view is compatible with the theory of distributed meaning representations, both within and across languages (Masson, 1995). This model also enables one to understand how a word is linked to many of its possible translations in another language, and more particularly with its dominant translation (Boada *et al.*, 2013; Eddington & Tokowicz, 2013; Laxén & Lavaur, 2010; Prior *et al.*, 2013).

Other recent models specifically dedicated to visual and auditory word recognition look more carefully at the facilitation or interference effects between languages observed in the very first stages of lexical processing. One of these – which inspired the study presented here – is the Bilingual Interactive Activation or BIA+ model (Dijkstra & van Heuven, 2002). These types of model postulate that once a lexical form has been detected by the word identification system, a decision system will take into account the demands of the task (instructions given to the participants or their expectations as to what they have been asked to do: translate, categorize or decide to which language a word belongs, for example), and modulate semantic activity within memory accordingly. Because the pilot version of this test uses a visual presentation of word pairs, our study will principally use predictions derived from the BIA+ model.

While very different in their conception and predictions, all these various models are dedicated to understanding the complex cognitive mechanisms involved when two languages are being processed within a single time frame, and their respective level of activation must be modulated. An example of this would be language switching in a particular situation or context, where one of the two languages must be deactivated or inhibited, while the other must achieve a high enough level of activation to fulfil a specific task. Hence, Weinreich (1953) was on the right path: proficient real-time use of an L2 implies being able to inhibit automatic L1 processes in order to activate concepts directly from L2 forms (in reception) or L2 forms directly from concepts (in production).

Some observations

One of the first elements revealed by previous research is that a good ability in each of the two languages (measured with self-evaluations or word translation tasks, for instance) does not necessarily imply a facility for linking them together or for switching from one language to the other. In other words, the evaluation tests proposed in experiments engaging bilingual memory/processing are not necessarily good predictors of a given participant's performance. This is particularly true if the task that needs to be completed implies the simultaneous processing of several languages, with the aim of gaining direct information concerning the workings of bilingual memory. Obviously, a low proficiency level in one of the two languages (or even in both languages, as the fluency level in the native or dominant language can also be variable from one participant to the other) will affect the concomitant processing of the two languages when they are presented simultaneously (one on a visual channel and one on an auditory channel, for example). On the other hand, a high proficiency level in both languages will not automatically ensure satisfactory processing, if the person is not in the habit of linking his/her two languages in different contexts and situations, or used to switching frequently from one language to the other.

Indeed, some people only use their L2 in a very specific context (workplace, family sphere, school, etc.) detached from the context in which the L1 is used. In this way, it often happens that each language is used in such an individual manner that they are never, or hardly ever, in contact with one another, preventing strong links being created between words belonging to the two languages within memory. This brings to light the fact that testing the way languages are linked in an individual's brain is very important as it can have strong effects on how the following task will be executed. Unlike many tasks that test only one language (e.g. the lexical decision task discussed by Ankerstein, this volume), we used a 'translation recognition task', which directly compares the two languages being tested.

Pilot Study: Testing the Bilingual Lexicon

Working from these different observations, we created a translation recognition test that presents words belonging to two different languages on the same screen. The idea is to measure the participant's ability to create satisfactory links between translation equivalents or, on the contrary, to dissociate the words from each other on the basis of their form (orthography, phonology) and/or their meaning (identifying semantic 'false friends', for example). Even if it is probably complementary to other tests evaluating certain aspects of the bilingual memory, the task we are presenting here calls upon specific abilities that go beyond the simple everyday practice of languages and that may provide us with indications as to the architecture of bilingual memory, especially as regards the way links are progressively created in the course of SLA. Indeed, in most cases, lexical tasks evaluate each one of a bilingual's languages individually, rarely examining the relationships between the two in bilingual memory. In addition, the test presented here was designed as a useful tool for language evaluation methods for participants in the context of research in cognitive psychology (Lavaur & Bairstow, 2011; Wei & Moyer, 2008). Our goal was to evaluate both the ease with which a participant goes from a formal or 'lexical' level (written or spoken word forms) to a conceptual or 'semantic' level (associated meanings), and his or her capacity to establish semantic links while language switching.

The aim of this pilot study is to investigate which factors influence the links between languages in bilingual memory, and to then integrate them into a test designed to be a sensitive measure of these factors.

The translation recognition task

In its simplest version, the translation recognition task consists of presenting two written words in different languages (here, one in French and one in English) on a computer screen in a near-simultaneous manner. The words belong to two different languages, and the participants have to decide whether or not they are translation equivalents: for the word pair MOON–LUNE, the expected answer is 'yes', whereas for the word pair RIVER–LUNE the response should be 'no'. This task has two major advantages. First, because the languages are tested two at a time, a person who knows three, four or more languages could be tested on all his/her known languages, in all possible combinations. The second point of interest is that all types of word can be tested, including words that have more than one translation in the other language (the English word NEW can be translated into either NEUF or NOUVEAU in French, for instance). Several recent studies using language recognition tasks and comparing several test languages have taken such words into account (Laxén & Lavaur, 2010, for French and English; Boada *et al.*, 2013, for Spanish and Catalan; Eddington & Tokowicz, 2013, for German and English; Laxén *et al.*, 2011, for French and Spanish; and finally Prior *et al.*, 2013, for English and Spanish).

The order in which the languages appear on the screen can have an effect on the participants' performance, because the first language presented will influence the ensuing processing. Another advantage of this test is that words from each language can be presented in turn to measure the influence of the order of language presentation on the screen. It is also possible to ignore the subject's dominant language altogether and to evaluate, for example, the strength of the links between the L2 and the L3 (which are assumed to be weaker than those connecting each of these languages to the dominant L1; see Aparicio & Lavaur, 2013). Therefore, a benefit of this test is that it can be applied to a wide population, independently of the fluency level in each of the languages tested.

A certain number of results from experiments using similar translation recognition tasks (Boada *et al.*, 2013; de Groot & Comijs, 1995; de Groot, 1992; Eddington & Tokowicz, 2013; Laxén & Lavaur, 2010; Laxén *et al.*, 2011; Prior *et al.*, 2013) have found strong effects related to the words' lexical forms (in orthographically similar languages, cognates trigger shorter response times, and interlexical homographs induce longer responses), as well as to their semantic composition (level of concreteness, number and dominance of translations, semantic distance between the different translations of a same word). It is therefore necessary to pay careful attention to the characteristics of the target words (and the relationships between them) when designing the test.

In the visual version of the test, the words' orthographic and semantic codes stored in memory are necessarily involved. More precisely, this means that the participants first have to detect the forms that are presented (which happens automatically through the identification system, according to the predictions of BIA+), then gain access to their respective meanings and match them as being translations or not (via a second decision system that takes into account the task demands and participants' expectations, and influences the decision threshold). This type of test therefore forces the participant to switch from one language to the other and to estimate the semantic relationship between the two words, since deciding if the two different language forms presented refer to the same concept (as translation equivalents) presupposes that potential interferences (due to the form of the words, for example) are resolved. Consequently, in this test, it is not the actual meaning of words that is directly or implicitly asked for, but rather the capacity to link the two words on a semantic level. If the participant does not have access to the meanings of these words, linking the words on a semantic level will not be possible (and they will not be able to answer either 'yes' or 'no', depending on the relationship between the words presented on the screen).

Method

The first step in the construction of this test was to address, one by one, the different factors that can have an influence on word recognition in any given language. We began with the *familiarity* of the words in each of the two languages: this is the language user's subjectively perceived frequency of contact with each word in one particular language through reading or speaking. Word familiarity explains certain test performances beyond the more classic written lexical frequency (the objectively determined number of occurrences of a word in a specific corpus). A word with a high written frequency rating may not seem so frequent to a person who does not have much written contact with the language in question. This is why the translation equivalents in our test were classified according to their level of familiarity (high, low), as estimated by a panel of judges using a seven-point Lickert scale. Words were taken from English (Balota et al., 1999; Davis, 2005) and French databases (Desrochers & Bergeron, 2000; Desrochers & Thompson, 2009), and the familiarity scores were generally found to correlate with objective frequency lists (see Desrochers & Saint-Aubin, 2008). The word pairs used in our test (whether they were translation equivalents or not) were matched for familiarity in both languages (see Appendix 7A for examples of word pairs).

A second criterion that influenced the design of the test stimuli was the order of the languages for each screen, and therefore the direction in which the translations are presented (L1 then L2, or L2 then L1). From a methodological point of view, this order of presentation enables us to manipulate the conditions in which the languages are presented. In addition, from a theoretical point of view, this is also important, as access to semantic memory is predicted to depend on the initial language. Bilingual memory models have hypothesized that access to semantic memory is facilitated when the dominant language is presented first (Kroll & Stewart, 1994). Therefore, the language order of the word pairs in our test was counterbalanced (L1–L2, L2–L1) so that any given word pair was presented to different participants in both translation directions (LUNE–MOON for one participant, MOON–LUNE for another).

Another important methodological factor is the predictable nature of the order in which the languages will appear within the word pairs on the screen. In this test, either the order is predictable and the participant knows that s/he will see the first word in the L1 (or in the L2), or unpredictable, in which case the presentation order is randomized (the random list). This is of utmost importance, because what we are testing with the random list is the participant's ability to switch from one language to another in a spontaneous manner (with no possibility to anticipate).

Controls

In this version of the test we also confirmed that the word pairs presented on the screen had few orthographic and phonological overlaps. These overlaps were estimated by using two indicators: IPO (*Indice de Proximité Orthographique*, an orthographic overlap index – examining the number of shared letters in the same position in translation equivalents) and IPS (*Indice de Proximité Syllabique*, a phonological overlap index – examining the number of syllables shared), and kept to the lowest possible in each case (Laxén *et al.*, 2008; Font & Lavaur, 2004), such as in the word pair BOOK–LIVRE, for instance, for which no letter and no syllable is common to both words. Because word length has an influence on recognition time, all the words presented contain a number of letters ranging from three to seven. Moreover, the difference in word length for the words in a given word pair was a maximum of two letters (for example, RABBIT–LAPIN). Finally, we controlled for the fact that each word tested had only one translation, or one predominant translation, and that when each word was tested with a word other than its translation (the 'no' condition), the two words did not share any evident semantic links (control based on the data from Laxén & Lavaur, 2010).

Participants

Twenty-five participants (75% female; mean age = 25.6 years) whose dominant language is French (L1) were randomly selected among students at a French University (in order to obtain varying levels in their L2, which was English) to be tested in our pilot study. The participants were not separated into groups depending on their self-assessed L2 level at the outset, as the aim of this test is to be able to assign participants into different language level groups without knowing their L2 level beforehand. Before the test, each participant filled in a personal data questionnaire, including a self-evaluation scale assessing four communication skills (oral and written, comprehension and production) in the foreign language (English). Again, a seven-point Likert scale was used (1 = very low ability; 7 = very strong ability) to rate different aspects of their knowledge of the non-dominant language. Although self-report is perhaps not the most reliable form of proficiency assessment, the method was chosen for two reasons. First, despite criticism, this technique has been shown to be a useful measure, provided that it is linked to other evaluations (such as questions targeting personal history of language use, translation tests or word recognition tasks, among others; Lavaur & Bairstow, 2011). Second, the purpose of this task was to provide a quick measure of bilingual ability before running the translation task.

The questionnaire also included questions concerning participants' age of acquisition and time spent using their non-dominant language.

Materials

The test was made up of three blocks of 56 word pairs, giving a total of 168 French–English items. Within each block, half of the word pairs (28) were composed of high-familiarity words, and half (28) of low-familiarity words. Again, half of these pairs were translation equivalents (BOOK–LIVRE, for instance), and the other half were non-equivalents (HOUSE–LUNE; see Table 7.1 for the overall test structure). These different types of word pairs were presented randomly within each block, so the participants could not anticipate either the degree of familiarity or the translation equivalency between the words.

Procedure

In the pilot test, the word lists were presented via PowerPoint® in three different blocks, with the same language presentation order within each block (L1–L2, L2–L1 or Random). Each word pair was presented for a fixed duration of 1400 ms (duration determined by response data from previous experiments, see Laxén & Lavaur, 2010; Laxén et al., 2011); a presentation time limit allows for faster data collection than if the participant is free to take as much time as desired. Moreover, this paradigm also enabled us to measure response times (not used in this first exploratory phase of the test,

Table 7.1 Composition of each block of word pairs, as a function of level of familiarity and translation status

Translation	High familiarity (F+)	Low familiarity (F–)	Total
Equivalents	14	14	28
Non-equivalents	14	14	28
Total	28	28	56

but included in the current running version with E-prime® software), following our previous research (Laxén & Lavaur, 2010; Laxén et al., 2011). The words were presented on-screen, one above the other, with the second word appearing immediately after the first. The aim of the task was for the participant to decide, before the appearance of the next word pair, whether the two words were translation equivalents or not (oral yes/no answer). Answers were evaluated for accuracy (1 = correct; 0 = incorrect), but omissions (no response in the time imparted) were also taken into account. At the end of each block, a PAUSE slide appeared on the screen and the presentation stopped. The next block began when the participant decided to start up again by clicking the mouse.

Results

The level in L2 was globally estimated by combining the scores (mean) on the four self-assessment scales measuring language skills (oral and written, production and comprehension). In order to determine whether our online task can relate to tasks traditionally employed to evaluate language levels (in our case, self-report), a Bravais–Pearson correlation test was applied to the self-evaluation in L2 scores and the accuracy score on the translation recognition test, yielding a positive correlation score, $r(24) = 0.52$, $p < 0.001$. Based on this result, the subjective evaluations do seem to be good predictors of the translation performance within our sample. Figure 7.1 plots individual scores on the combined self-assessment questionnaires with accuracy scores on the translation recognition task (which have been divided by ten for the sole purpose of keeping proportions adequate for comparison with the self-evaluation scores).

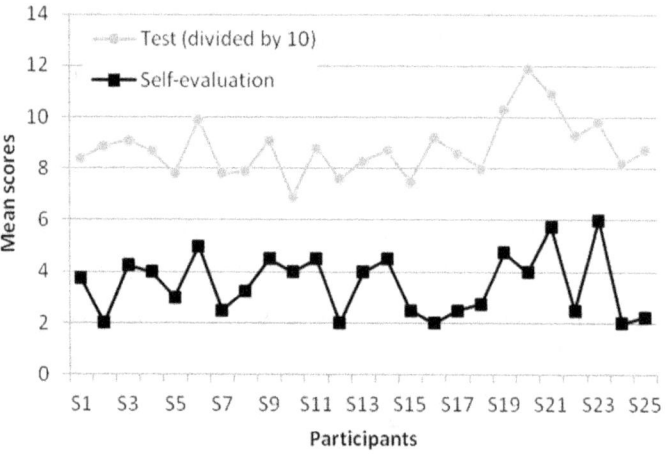

Figure 7.1 Mean scores for each participant obtained on the L2 self-evaluation scales and the translation recognition test (divided by 10)

It must be noted that although the scores that the participants attributed to themselves during L2 self-evaluation (bottom curve of the graph) are lower than the ones obtained with the test (upper curve), the two tests do not in fact measure the same thing: while the self-evaluation was designed to reflect (albeit subjectively) the student's idea of his/her proficiency in L2, the translation recognition test takes into account both languages (and therefore the supposedly high level in L1), as it measures the capacity to link words belonging to each of these languages (bilingual proficiency). This is important because it explains, at least in part, some of the difference between the two scores, which is partially due to a difference in the number of languages that were tested (one at a time in self-evaluation, two at a time in translation recognition).

A multivariate analysis of variance (MANOVA) was carried out to investigate the effect of word familiarity and the order of language presentation on performance to the translation recognition task. A significant interaction between language order (direction of translation) and familiarity was obtained, $F[2, 48] = 133.28$, η^2 partial $= 0.847$, as well as a significant simple effect of familiarity, $F[1, 24] = 1712.92$, η^2 partial $= 0.986$, with a globally higher score for high-familiarity words than for low-familiarity ones.

The simple effect of familiarity on each of the three blocks was analyzed, and revealed significant effects of familiarity on each of the three different orders of presentation (L1–L2: $F[1, 48] = 197.26$, η^2 partial $= 0.804$; L2–L1: $F[1, 48] = 1270.33$, η^2 partial $= 0.964$; Random: $F[1, 48] = 1059.89$, η^2 partial $= 0.957$), indicating in each case a higher number of correct answers for high-familiarity as opposed to low-familiarity pairs (Figure 7.2).

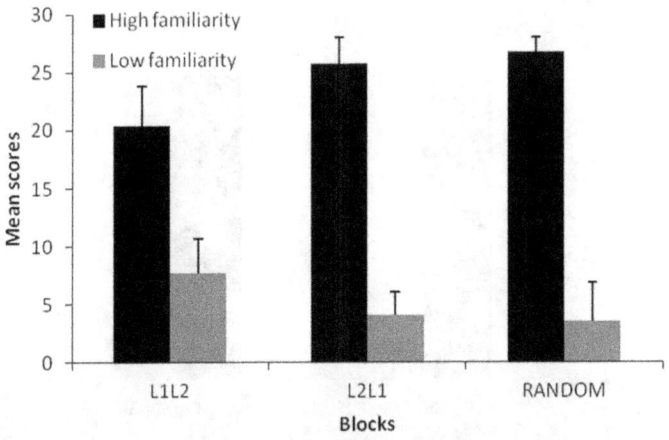

Figure 7.2 Mean scores (and error bars) as a function of the familiarity of the word pairs and the order in which the languages appear on the screen in each block

Next, a MANOVA was carried out on the mean scores, which indicated a significant interaction between the familiarity level of the words and the translation status of the pairs (equivalents or not), $F[1, 24] = 34.04$, η^2 partial = 0.586. A simple significant effect of familiarity, $F[1, 24] = 1712.92$, η^2 partial = 0.986, indicates that high-familiarity word pairs are more easily recognized as translations than low-familiarity word pairs (Figure 7.3). This familiarity effect is also found when the word pairs are not translation equivalents.

Furthermore, a significant effect of translation status was found, $F[1, 24] = 19.56$, η^2 partial = 0.449, showing a higher number of correct answers when the participants have to reject non-equivalents ('no' answer), than when the participants must accept translation equivalents ('yes' answer). This result may seem surprising, but it indicates that an absence of links between two words can be spotted easily, even for weaker proficiency levels in L2. However, analysis of this effect indicates that the translation status effect is only significant for low-familiarity word pairs, $F[1, 24] = 33.78$, η^2 partial = 0.585. We can deduce from this that it is easier to reject low-familiarity words (non-equivalents) than it is to accept low-familiarity translation equivalents.

Neither the order in which the pairs were presented (L1–L2 versus L2–L1), nor the predictability of the presentation (L1–L2 or L2–L1 versus Random) was found to be significant. It is possible that the way in which the two words are presented on the screen (near-simultaneous presentation) reduced the effects generally found in relation to the order of the languages on the screen (Kroll & Stewart, 1994; see Discussion section).

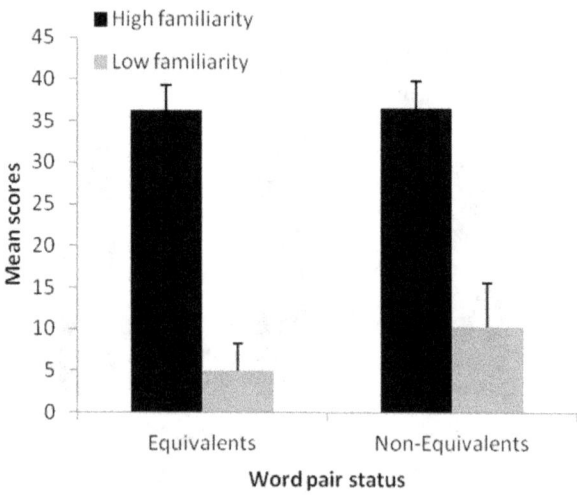

Figure 7.3 Mean scores (and error bars) as a function of familiarity and status

Discussion: Extending the Translation Recognition Test

In this pilot version of the written translation recognition test, we strictly controlled the degree of orthographic similarity between the words of each pair, and the passage from the words' form (lexical level) to their meaning (semantic level) was not taken into account. However, we know that the lexical level can play a role in the translation recognition task, as a source of interference or facilitation, depending on the lexical proximity between words but also on the strength of the link between lexical and semantic levels (see Boada *et al.*, 2013). This was confirmed in a recent study (Laxén *et al.*, 2011), in which a facilitating effect was found for cognates, which are translation equivalents that share their orthographic and phonological forms (e.g. TAXI in both French and English). That same project yielded other results showing that numerous errors were made for L1–L2 word pairs that share the same form but have different meanings (also called interlexical homographs, such as the word COIN, referring to *money* in English, but meaning *corner* in French). We are currently incorporating this new factor (phonological and orthographic similarity, equivalence of meaning/non-equivalence) in a second version of the test, in order to estimate the role played by the words' lexical characteristics and their translation equivalents (degree of lexical similarity) in the way in which they will be processed (for data concerning response times with cognate and non-cognate words using the same task, see Boada *et al.*, 2013).

The fact that no effect of language presentation order (translation direction) was found on the mean scores can probably be attributed to the procedure that we used, as we cannot be sure that the top word was actually read first (both words appeared near-simultaneously). The next version of the test will include three different procedures for presenting the words: (1) simultaneous presentation (with the second word on the bottom line of the screen; see de Groot, 1992; Laxén & Lavaur, 2010); (2) deferred presentation of the second word (leaving time for the top word to be read first; Laxén & Lavaur, 2010); or (3) a priming recognition task (the first word appearing very briefly, but long enough to be recognized, then disappearing before the second word appears). This last presentation format was successfully used by Eddington and Tokowicz (2013) in order to compare the way in which all the translations of a word were processed (multiple translation effect). The authors propose to incorporate this new factor into Kroll and Stewart's (1994) latest revised version of their hierarchical model, taking into account the lexical ambiguity of words and their translations. By varying the presentation format, we will be able to test the hypothesis according to which the longer the period between the words' appearance on the screen, the stronger the effects of the order of presentation should be (influenced by asymmetry in the proficiency level for each language). Moreover, this should also induce a higher sensitivity to language switching in the participants' responses (for electrophysiological measures of the access to semantic memory through three different languages, see Aparicio *et al.*, 2012) as well as an effect on the associated response times (Eddington & Tokowicz, 2013).

Finally, another possible extension of the translation recognition test would consist of an audiovisual presentation of the translation equivalents (spoken word first, followed by a written word – equivalent or not – in another language) in order to examine the variables that are linked to phonology in both languages. In this case, the situation could be related to the activity induced when watching a subtitled film and for which words pronounced (in the dialogues) are voluntarily or not linked to written words in another language (in the subtitles), although the linguistic context is much wider, and other non-linguistic elements (pictures, sounds, etc.) are also present (Bairstow, 2012; Bairstow & Lavaur, 2012; Lavaur & Bairstow, 2011).

Conclusion

In conclusion, throughout this chapter we have tried to clarify the link between the level achieved in two different languages (one dominant and the other in the process of being learnt) with a bilingual proficiency that enables one to create links within memory between two languages, and more particularly between translation equivalents. Our first results indicate that this ability is positively correlated with the participants' self-reported L2 level, while taking into account factors such as familiarity and the order in which the languages appear on the screen.

The familiarity effect found in our results supports the validity of this type of test, because the participants in this pilot version tend to mostly have a relatively low level in their L2 (none of the participants were fluent in L2, and the personal data questionnaires revealed that they generally had next to no contact with the L2 outside the classroom). This lower level of knowledge of the L2 could partly explain the better performance for the high-familiarity words in comparison to the low-familiarity ones, even though this assertion may be moderated by Hulstijn's (2012) call for caution concerning the use of global questionnaires for proficiency self-assessment. In this way, it is possible that participants with a stronger knowledge of the L2 would provide more correct answers to low-familiarity word pairs and thus achieve higher scores of accuracy, although this will need to be tested. Therefore, the outcome of the test is probably dependent on the participants' language level, which cannot be simply classified as either low or high, but can include any level in between. This dependency should allow even better discrimination of the different levels when words of average familiarity level are included in the test, in association with the other aforementioned factors.

However, fairly strong variations were found between the two measures (translation recognition and self-assessment), which seems to indicate that it is not only the level achieved in each of the two languages that underpins the way in which semantic bilingual memory functions.

Introducing new variables in order to extend this test of bilingual proficiency, using factors linked to word forms (cognates and interlexical homographs), and to the complexity and ambiguity of the semantic links (words with only one or with multiple translations, which can differ in meaning or not) should give us a better view of what happens when going from the lexical level to the semantic level. Indeed, much interference or facilitation can take place when passing from one level to the other, which will influence how certain tasks that directly involve semantic memory are completed. Moreover, bilingual semantic memory is also called upon when activities demand quick switching from one language to the other, during both oral and written exchanges (Aparicio & Lavaur, 2013).

Our future research looking into the precise nature and strength of connections between L1 and L2 words should enable us to establish important differences in the ways in which the two languages are processed, whether they are presented individually, one after the other, or simultaneously. We feel that the translation recognition task would be most useful for measuring an individual's progression in each of the languages (vocabulary acquisition in L1 and in L2), as well as the evolution of their capacity to link the two languages efficiently, as one must do in many bilingual situations. The more words participants learn in each language, the higher the chances to identify them as translation equivalents or not in the test. We also feel that the translation recognition task could be usefully implemented as a measuring instrument in SLA research, as it would provide researchers with an indicator of participants' flexibility and ease in handling different languages.

References

Aparicio, X. and Lavaur, J-M. (2013) Recognising words in three languages: Effects of language dominance and language switching. *International Journal of Multilingualism* 11 (2), 164–181. DOI: 10.1080/14790718.2013.783583.

Aparicio, X., Midgley, K., Holcomb, P., Pu, H., Lavaur, J.-M. and Grainger, J. (2012) Language effects in trilinguals: An ERP study. *Frontiers in Language Science* 3, 402. DOI: 10.3389/fpsyg.2012.00402.

Bairstow, D. (2012) Le rôle des sous-titres dans la compréhension et la mémorisation de films. PhD dissertation, Université Montpellier 3.

Bairstow, D. and Lavaur, J.-M. (2012) Audiovisual information processing by monolinguals and bilinguals: Effects of intralingual and interlingual subtitles. In A. Remael, P. Orero and M. Carroll (eds) *Audiovisual Translation and Media Accessibility at the Crossroads: Media for all 3* (pp. 273–293). Amsterdam: Rodopi.

Balota, D.A., Cortese, M.J. and Pilotti, M. (1999) Item-level analyses of lexical decision performance: Results from a mega-study. *Oral Communication at the 40th Annual Meeting of the Psychonomics Society*. Los Angeles, CA: Psychonomic Society.

Boada, R., Sánchez-Casas, R., Gavilan, J.M., Garcìa-Albea, J.E. and Tokowicz, N. (2013) Effect of multiple translations and cognate status on translation recognition performance of balanced bilinguals. *Bilingualism, Language and Cognition* 16 (1), 183–197.

Davis, C.J. (2005) N-Watch: A program for deriving neighborhood size and other psycholinguistic statistics. *Behavior Research Methods* 37, 65–70.

de Groot, A.M.B. (1992) Determinants of word translation. *Journal of Experimental Psychology: Learning, Memory, and Cognition* 18 (5), 1001–1018.

de Groot, A.M.B. and Comijs, H. (1995) Translation recognition and translation production: Comparing a new and old tool in the study of bilingualism. *Language Learning* 45 (3), 467–509.

Desrochers, A. and Bergeron, M. (2000) Valeurs de fréquence subjective et d'imagerie pour un échantillon de 1916 substantifs de la langue française. *Revue Canadienne de Psychologie Expérimentale* 54 (4), 274–325.

Desrochers, A. and Saint-Aubin, J. (2008) Sources de matériel en français pour l'élaboration d'épreuves de compétences en lecture et en écriture. *Canadian Journal of Education* 31 (2), 305–326.

Desrochers, A. and Thompson, G.L. (2009) Subjective frequency and imageability ratings for 3,600 French nouns. *Behavior Research Methods* 41, 546–557.

Dijkstra, T. (2005) Bilingual visual word recognition and lexical access. In J.F. Kroll and A. de Groot (eds) *Handbook of Bilingualism: Psycholinguistic Approaches* (pp. 179–200). Cambridge: Cambridge University Press.

Dijkstra, T. and van Heuven, W.J.B. (2002) The architecture of the bilingual word recognition system: From identification to decision. *Bilingualism: Language and Cognition* 5 (3), 175–197.

Eddington, C.M. and Tokowicz, N. (2013) Examining English–German translation ambiguity using primed translation recognition. *Bilingualism: Language and Cognition* 16 (2), 442–457.

Font, N. and Lavaur, J-M. (2004) Effets de la fréquence du voisinage orthographique interlangue lors de la reconnaissance visuelle de mots chez les bilingues. *L'année psychologique* 104 (3), 377–405.

Hulstijn, J.H. (2012) The construct of language proficiency in the study of bilingualism from a cognitive perspective. *Bilingualism: Language and Cognition* 15 (2), 422–433.

Kolers, P.A. (1963) Interlingual word associations. *Journal of Verbal Learning and Verbal Behavior* 2, 291–300.

Kroll, J.F. and Stewart, E. (1994) Category interference in translation and picture naming: Evidence for asymmetric connections between bilingual memory representations. *Journal of Memory and Language* 33, 149–174.

Lavaur, J.-M. and Bairstow, D. (2011) Languages on the screen: Is film comprehension related to the viewer's fluency level and to the languages in the subtitles? *International Journal of Psychology* 46 (6), 455–462.

Laxén, J. and Lavaur, J.-M. (2010) The role of semantics in translation recognition: Effects of number of translations, dominance of translations, and semantic relatedness of multiple translations. *Bilingualism, Language and Cognition* 13 (2), 157–183.

Laxén, J., Aparicio, X. and Lavaur, J.-M. (2008, September) *Base lexicale trilingue ESF. Mesure du partage orthographique et du recouvrement sémantique interlangue*. Oral presentation at the Société Française de Psychologie Symposium, Bordeaux, France.

Laxén, J., Lavaur, J.-M. and Aparicio, X. (2011) Reconnaissance en traduction et homographie interlangue. *Psychologie Française* 56 (3), 161–172.

Macnamara, J. and Kushnir, S. L. (1971) Linguistic independence of bilinguals: The input switch. *Journal of Verbal Learning and Verbal Behavior* 10, 480–487.

Masson, M.E.J. (1995) A distributed memory model of semantic priming. *Journal of Experimental Psychology: Learning, Memory, and Cognition* 21, 3–23.

Prior, A., Kroll, J.-F.and MacWhinney, B. (2013) Translation ambiguity but not word class predicts translation performance. *Bilingualism: Language and Cognition* 16 (2), 458–474.

van Hell, J.G. and de Groot, A.M.B. (1998) Conceptual representation in bilingual memory: Effects of concreteness and cognate status in word association. *Bilingualism: Language and Cognition* 1 (3), 193–211.

Wei, L. and Moyer, M. (2008) *The Blackwell Guide to Research Methods in Bilingualism and Multilingualism*. Malden: Blackwell Publishing.

Weinreich, U. (1953) *Languages in Contact: Findings and Problems*. New York, NY: Linguistic Circle.

Appendix 7A

Table 7.1A Examples of word pairs, matched for familiarity, as a function of order in which the languages appear, level of familiarity and translation status

	Presentation order		
Status	*L1L2*	*L2L1*	*Random*
Equivalent			
F+	TRAVAIL (6.52)–WORK (6.67)	WEEK (6.17)–SEMAINE (6.44)	TWO (6.37)–DEUX (5.62)
	PORTE (6.11)–DOOR (6.07)	SCHOOL (6.07)–ECOLE (6.12)	BOISSON (5.46)–DRINK (6.13)
	PETIT (5.97)–SMALL (6.20)	MEAL (6.13)–REPAS (5.90)	MUR (5.24)–WALL (5.67)
F–	FILON (1.91)–LODE (1.83)	FANG (2.80)–CROC (2.31)	FLEAU (2.66)–BANE (2.13)
	TAMIS (2.19)–SIEVE (2.09)	REED (2.77)–ROSEAU (2.36)	GLEN (2.27)–VALLON (2.0)
	ORME (2.55)–ELM (2.87)	SEER (2.53)–DEVIN (2.47)	PAWN (2.6)–PION (2.52)
Non-equivalent			
F+	PEIGNE (5.25)–MOUTH (5.77)	NAME (6.34)–SOLEIL (6.13)	NOON (5.87)–PAUVRE (5.58)
	MONDE (6.03)–PEN (6.17)	SEE (6.13)–RUE (6.08)	NEZ (5.58)–VILLE (5.61)
	PEAU (5.43)–HELL (5.63)	WEEK (6.17)–LAIT (6.36)	PRICE (5.85)–BIERE (6.01)
F–	HARGNE (2.33) – WICKER (2.33)	MAW (1.67)–LUBIE (1.5)	STORK (2.27)–FRICHE (2.25)
	PANAIS (1.84)–SPRIG (1.72)	SOOT (2.1)–APLOMB (2.39)	FIOLE (2.13)–BELFRY (2.11)
	FANION (2.02)–HUTCH (2.03)	PLOUGH (2.52) – GOUDRON (2.83)	KNEAD (2.57)–NATTE (2.43)

Note: F+ = high familiarity; F– = low familiarity. Familiarity scores are given in parentheses.

Part 3
Focused Assessment Instruments

8 'Repeat as Much as You Can': Elicited Imitation as a Measure of Oral Proficiency in L2 French

Nicole Tracy-Ventura, Kevin McManus, John M. Norris and Lourdes Ortega

Introduction

Various second language (L2) proficiency measures are used in second language acquisition (SLA) research, ranging from self-report ratings (see Gertken *et al.*, this volume) to standardized tests (see reviews by Thomas, 1994, 2006; Tremblay, 2011; and also discussion by Hulstijn, 2011, 2012). Researchers' purposes for measuring L2 proficiency are diverse, and often proficiency itself is just a secondary variable in SLA research programs that investigate some other central variable construct (e.g. development of grammatical subsystems, effects of interactional feedback, learners' vocabulary size). In this chapter we describe the development of an elicited imitation (EI) test used to measure French L2 oral proficiency. This test is the newest addition in a series of EIs that are already available in five different L2s: Chinese, English, German, Japanese and Spanish (Ortega *et al.*, 1999; Wu & Ortega, 2013; Zhou & Wu, 2009). We argue that EI offers a useful tool for systemic yet practical assessment of L2 proficiency for a variety of SLA research purposes. Among the benefits of this particular proficiency measure are that it is quick to administer, and that, with parallel versions in multiple languages, it allows for crosslinguistic SLA comparisons and accumulation of interpretable findings across a variety of L2s other than English.

Background

Problems in defining and measuring proficiency in SLA studies

Attempts at defining the construct of language proficiency have been made for many decades now (e.g. Oller, 1976). In a series of recent articles, Hulstijn (2011, 2012) has proposed definitions of first language (L1) and L2 proficiency based on the distinction between two kinds of language ability, which he calls basic (BLC) and higher (HLC) language cognition. While BLC is restricted to the processing of oral language (listening and speaking) in utterances containing high-frequency lexical, grammatical, phonotactic and prosodic elements, HLC is unrestricted in these respects. That is, HLC includes the processing of written language (reading and writing; i.e. involving literacy skills) in sentences that may contain low-frequency lexical or grammatical elements (Hulstijn, 2012: 429). In other words, BLC is what is shared relatively uniformly among adult native speakers, regardless of background characteristics. In contrast, HLC is where native speakers show variation due to differences in educational level, occupation, free-time activities and so on. Applying these constructs to non-native speakers, Hulstijn claims that L2 learners can also acquire HLC just as native speakers can (e.g. through education), but 'it remains an open question to what extent postpuberty L2 learners can fully acquire BLC in their L2' (2011: 242; see also Leclercq & Edmonds, this volume, for a presentation of Hulstijn's definition of language proficiency). With this in mind, it seems that when SLA researchers' interests lie in measuring general proficiency – what we consider BLC – then the focus should be on the assessment of oral language using tests that are literacy-independent and that focus on operations involving high-frequency elements during the integrative use of oral language, while recruiting in real time all interrelated basic linguistic levels of lexicon, grammar, phonotactics and prosody.

Furthermore, SLA researchers' interests and purposes for measuring proficiency are often quite different from those in the field of language testing, where many language tests originate (see Zoghlami, this volume, for a review of two such standardized tests). In SLA, proficiency is more often included as a secondary variable, or not included at all, in many research designs. Yet, some scholars have claimed that proficiency is a major lurking variable and should be included in all of our studies (Norris, 2010). Norris and Ortega (2012) single out several research-related purposes for the measurement and reporting of L2 proficiency, including 'to justify the sampling of participants into a study or to assign participants to distinct groups' and to 'aid readers of research when deciding the extent to which findings can be generalized to other samples and populations' (2012: 580).

Surveys of proficiency assessment methods used in SLA research by Thomas (1994, 2006) and Tremblay (2011) have continued to demonstrate the need to establish higher proficiency measurement standards and more consistency in assessing and reporting proficiency for research, rather than educational assessment purposes. For example, in Tremblay's (2011) survey of studies published from 2000 to 2008 in three refereed journals (*Studies in Second Language Acquisition, Second Language Research* and the *Journal of French Language Studies*), only 36.8% of published reports included an independent measure of learners' proficiency. By far the most popular way of estimating proficiency was using classroom level or years of instruction, a result also found in Thomas's (2006) synthesis of L2 studies published in *Applied Linguistics, Language Learning, Second Language Research,* and *Studies in Second Language Acquisition*, and confirmed by Callies *et al.* (this volume), in their chapter on the use of learner corpora to test L2 proficiency.

In French SLA studies, in particular, the problem is noteworthy. Tremblay (2011) reported that out of her total corpus of 144 SLA studies, 25 focused on L2 French but only two of those included an independent measure of learners' proficiency (they used oral interview and accent ratings, respectively). Other studies of L2 French appearing in different journals and a few recent doctoral dissertations have made use of additional independent proficiency measures, such as (1) accuracy on a written personal narrative (e.g. Bardovi-Harlig & Bergström; 1996); (2) the C-test or Cloze test (e.g. Daller *et al.*, 2003; McManus, 2011; Tremblay, 2011); (3) a grammaticality judgement with correction (Ayoun, 2004); and (4) X-lex (a measure of vocabulary size, e.g. Rogers, 2009). Many of these proficiency estimates are literacy-dependent (e.g. C-test, Cloze). In and of itself, this is not necessarily a weakness, depending on the purposes of the research and provided that the populations investigated are literate. However, the heavy literacy requirement of these proficiency assessment tools means that they allow for the intervention of explicitly learned (declarative) knowledge more than non-literacy dependent (i.e. oral) assessments would, as the latter more often tap into implicit acquired knowledge (Ellis, 2005). In terms of Hulstijn's (2011, 2012) distinction, in other words, literacy-dependent assessment tools may be inadvertently measuring forms of HLC while providing questionable evidence of learners' capacities for BLC in the L2, precisely the dimension that Hulstijn considers most relevant for the study of SLA issues. One type of assessment that is not literacy-dependent, and is arguably a measure of BLC that taps more implicit language competencies, is elicited imitation.

Elicited imitation in SLA research

EI is a technique that requires participants to listen to a stimulus and then repeat it as exactly as possible. Most of the time the repetition is done orally, but examples of written imitation also exist (see Vinther, 2002, for discussion). EI has a long tradition of use in the fields of first language acquisition (e.g. Lust *et al.*, 1996; Slobin & Welch, 1973) and bilingualism (Radloff, 1991), and it has also been used in SLA at least since the 1980s (e.g. Hameyer, 1980; Savignon, 1982). Typically, numerous stimuli are included, ranging in number of syllables and featuring a variety of grammatical structures. The theoretical rationale behind EI as a measure of language capacity is that learners can only accurately imitate sentences they have comprehended and parsed through their developing grammars (Bley-Vroman & Chaudron, 1994).

The use of EI is not without controversy. One main argument against EI relates to the issue of 'parroting', that is, whether the participant has in fact comprehended the stimulus or has just imitated a string of sounds (Vinther, 2002). Consideration of the role of working memory is important in this debate. If the stimulus is short enough, it could be stored in working memory and repeated without actual comprehension. In contrast, a stimulus that is long enough to exceed working memory capacity would be only accurately repeated if the learner has grammatically parsed and decoded the message and formed a mental representation of it. What length exceeds an individual's working memory capacity, of course, is contingent on the proficiency level of the given language user. Attention to the length of the stimuli, therefore, is one way that researchers have tried to get around this issue, and the EI stimuli typically range in length (measured in syllables, words or characters) and are presented for repetition in order of increasing length, so as to offer appropriate levels of difficulty across a wide range of proficiencies. Indeed, sentence length has proven to be a strong predictor of item difficulty in EI performance. Graham *et al.* (2010) reported that sentence length accounted for 73% of the variance in item difficulty in their EI test, compared to lexical frequency, which explained only 8%. Similar results were also found in Hendrickson *et al.* (2010) and Ortega *et al.* (2002).

Within SLA, a recent burgeoning of interest in using EI is related to the need to measure implicit language knowledge (Erlam, 2006; Verhagen, 2011), although the measurement of oral proficiency through EI tests has also been of interest since earlier years (Naiman, 1974). Recently, a group of researchers at Brigham Young University has investigated the potential of EI as an adaptive language proficiency test (Christenson *et al.*, 2010; Hendrickson *et al.*, 2010) and one that could allow for automatic scoring (Cook *et al.*, 2011; Graham *et al.*, 2008). The particular line of EI research that fuelled the present study has focused on the use of EI in crosslinguistic studies. It began when Ortega *et al.* (1999) developed parallel forms of the same EI test in four languages – English, German, Japanese and Spanish – in order to investigate the relationship between syntactic complexity measures and L2 proficiency across these four foreign languages. They compared EI scores to Simulated Oral Proficiency Interview ratings, TOEFL scores and self-assessments, and found that the EI data yielded high reliability, good discrimination and concurrent validity when used with the four university-level samples of foreign language learners in that initial study. The Spanish EI test was then employed in dissertation studies by Ortega (2000) and by Bowden (2007) with similar success. Most recently, a parallel L2 Chinese EI test was created and pilot-tested by Zhou and Wu (2009). It was also found to exhibit good reliability and validity when subsequently used with two different large samples of foreign and heritage language learners in their respective doctoral dissertations (Wu, 2011; Zhou, 2011).

Elicited imitation in L2 French research

While the popularity of EI is increasing in SLA, its use in French L2 research is scarce. To the best of our knowledge, three such studies have employed EI to date. Burger and Chrétien (2001) used an EI task to measure changes in oral production after two semesters of a French content-based class. Their test consisted of 14 sentences, which together formed a coherent text. Each sentence ranged from 12 to 15 syllables and was scored globally as either 0 or 1 for exact repetition. In contrast, the EI used in Erlam and Loewen (2010) included both grammatical and ungrammatical sentences targeting primarily noun–adjective agreement, the focus of a recast treatment. This EI also differed in that after hearing each statement, learners had to give their opinion about the statement before beginning the repetition (see also Erlam, 2006). Differences in French language competence among L1 French and L1 English children from two different age groups (grades 3 and 5) was the focus of an early study by Markman *et al.* (1975), who administered a 44-item EI test including both grammatical and ungrammatical sentences. Their results showed clear differences for both the L1 and the age grouping variables, with the French group performing significantly better than the English group and the grade 5 group outperforming the grade 3 group.

The three studies just reviewed are suggestive of the potential of an EI to measure L2 French proficiency, be it to gauge longitudinal proficiency gains resulting from a particular curricular or instructional intervention (Burger & Chrétien, 2001; Erlam & Loewen, 2010) or to ascertain global grammatical competence differences resulting from home language background or age (Markman *et al.*, 1975). Interestingly, all three research teams designed their French EI tasks in ways that departed from the traditional EI design involving straightforward repetition of grammatical sentences ordered in increasing syllable length and containing a variety of structures and forms. Whether and how the different design formats featured across studies may affect the reliability and validity of any EI test (for example, including both grammatical and ungrammatical sentences for repetition, or inserting a comprehension question between hearing the stimulus and issuing the repetition) is currently unknown and in need of future research. Nonetheless, given the growing crosslinguistic evidence in support of the EI test developed by

Ortega et al. (1999, 2002), we thought it worthwhile to continue in that tradition and adapt that instrument for L2 French. One of the main benefits of adding a comparable French version is that it will allow for crosslinguistic SLA comparisons and accumulation of interpretable findings across L2s.

Consequently, the first two authors set out to develop the parallel EI test for L2 French with the purpose of employing it as a measure of L2 proficiency in the context of a larger funded investigation into the linguistic benefits of study abroad for UK university students of L2 French (see McManus et al., this volume, for a second study that resulted from this same project). In order to determine whether the French EI test was a reasonable, useful measure of proficiency, the following main research question was posed in the present study:

> Will learners' scores on the French EI exhibit any meaningful relationship to other indices of language proficiency collected for the larger study, namely: (a) the lexical diversity they demonstrate in productive oral and written tasks; (b) their vocabulary knowledge as measured by a vocabulary test; (c) their speech rate on an oral retell of a picture-based narrative; and (d) university end-of-year marks?

Methodology

Participants

The participants were 29 French-degree students who were all recruited from the same curricular level: they had just finished their second year of university in Britain. Their L1 backgrounds varied, including 25 native English speakers, two heritage French speakers (English+French), one native Spanish speaker and one native Finnish speaker. A background questionnaire was administered to gather information about participants' age, length of time studying French, age of first exposure to French, institutional level, other languages studied and how often they use French outside the classroom. Information about participants' end-of-year marks was also collected. The participants' mean age was 21 years (range 20–24), and the sample included 26 females and three males, which is representative of a similar gender imbalance in the French language courses and study abroad program at this university. Mean length of French study was 11 years (range 9–15 years), and mean age of first exposure was 9.5 years. More than half of the participants (55%, 16) reported studying an additional language at the university (five Italian, five German, five Spanish, one Chinese). A group of 10 native French speakers who were taking part in an ERASMUS university exchange program at the same English university were also recruited to take the EI as an L1 baseline.

The EI test and other instruments

The EI instrument included 30 test sentences ranging from 7 to 19 syllables (see Appendix 8A), with the sentence stimuli presented in order from lowest to highest number of syllables. A native French speaker created all the sentences, using the English sentences from Ortega et al. (1999) as a model. A second French speaker checked them for syllable length and naturalness. As with the other EI L2 versions, a variety of grammatical structures were targeted, frequent vocabulary was used, and all sentences were grammatical. A native French speaker was digitally recorded reading the sentences at a normal rate, and the free program Audacity[1] was used to make the test audio. The phrase 'repeat as much as you can' was reiterated several times during the recorded instructions as a way to encourage learners to attempt every test sentence. Two additional recording features were implemented following Bowden (2007): (1) a 2 s pause was inserted after each target sentence and before the cue – a 0.5 s beep – signalling when the repetition should begin; (2) the length of the response time was based on the time it took the native speaker to speak the sentence plus extra time depending on the number of syllables. The resulting final EI test takes 9 min 15 s to complete, and this administration time includes 2 min of instructions and practice sentences given in English (also following those used in Bowden, 2007).[2] Given the short overall administration time, it is unlikely that fatigue played any factor in examinee performance on early- or late-appearing items.

In addition to the EI, as part of the larger study design, participants completed a range of language assessments on the same day. These included a general oral interview, an oral retelling of a picture-based narrative, a written argumentative essay and a vocabulary recognition task. The oral interview was conducted in French and focused on questions relating to learners' reasons for studying languages and expectations for their upcoming year abroad in France. The oral retelling was based on a picture story about a young girl and her cat (Langley, 2000; see McManus, 2011). Learners were given time to preview all the pictures before starting their retell in French. The written argumentative essay was computer-based and timed; learners were given a prompt on gay rights and had three minutes to plan their response before being given 15 min to write approximately 200 words. Vocabulary recognition was measured via the Swansea Levels 'X-Lex' test (Meara & Milton, 2003).[3] This is a yes/no test where learners see a word and have to decide whether they recognize it as a real French word or not. They see 120 words total, where 100 are real words and 20 are false words, and the real words come from different frequency bands.

Procedure

All participants signed an informed consent document before the start of data collection. The order in which the data collection tasks (e.g. EI test, narrative, etc.) were administered was randomized for each participant. The total time to complete all assessments took approximately 1 hour. Learners were welcome to take breaks between tasks although no breaks were requested. During data collection a member of the research team was seated with each participant the whole time. The EI audio was presented via a laptop, and learners' responses were digitally recorded. Participants were instructed not to pause the audio at any time, and the researcher ensured these procedures were followed.

Analysis of EI and other data

Learners' repetitions on the EI were scored based on a five-point scoring rubric (0–4) developed by Ortega *et al.* (1999) and used also in all previous studies that have employed the EI parallel versions in the five L2s. The maximum score possible for the test is 120 (30 × 4). The scoring rubric is presented in Table 8.1 with illustrations taken from the present data, and a complete version is provided in Appendix 8B.

Two raters (the second author and a native French speaker) coded half the EI data together, and disagreements were discussed until both coders agreed on the score. They then proceeded to code the other half of the data independently. The inter-rater reliability for this part was 94% exact agreement, and the disagreements were solved once again through discussion. Following this procedure, each individual test took between 10 and 15 min to score.

The oral interview data were transcribed according to CHAT conventions (CHILDES, MacWhinney, 2000) and the written argumentative essay data were converted into CHAT as well. Both sets of data were analyzed for lexical diversity using D (an index developed by Malvern & Richards, 2000, that accounts for text length while estimating lexical diversity for an individual), as calculated via the CLAN program (MacWhinney, 2000). The X-lex program (Meara & Milton, 2003) automatically computes a learner's final score at the end of the test. Two scores are given by the program: the raw score and the adjusted score. The adjusted score will be lower if any false words were erroneously identified as words by the testee; this was the score used in the current study. The picture-based narrative was used to estimate learners' rate of speech, operationalized as the number of pruned syllables produced per minute (see Lennon, 1990). Using pruned syllables means that any repetitions, false starts or L1 use were removed prior to analysis.

Results

In light of the overall aim, which was to test the reliability as well as the validity of this new French EI test following Ortega *et al.* (1999), we first

Table 8.1 Elicited imitation scoring rubric with French examples

		Examples	
Score	Description	Item	Repetition
4	Perfect repetition		
3	Accurate content repetition with some (un-)grammatical changes	Item 9. *Il prend une longue douche tous les matins.* ('He has a long shower every morning')	*Il prend <u>les</u> longues douches tous les matins* ('He has long showers every morning')
2	Changes in content or changes in form that affect content	Item 26. *Pourriez-vous s'il vous plaît me passer le livre qui est sur la table?* ('Would you pass me the book that is on the table please?')	<u>Pouvez-vous</u> me passer le livre qui est sur la table? ('Can you pass me the book that is on the table?')
1	Repetition of half or less of the stimulus	Item 6. *Je ne sais pas s'il sait très bien conduire.* ('I don't know if he can drive that well')	*Je ne sais pas... conduire* ('I don't know.... to drive')
0	Silence, only one word repeated, or unintelligible repetition	Item 3. *Les rues sont larges dans cette ville.* ('The streets are wide in this city')	bla bla bla *dans la ville* ('blah blah blah in the city')

Note: Changes made by the non-native speaker are underlined.

address the main research question via a Pearson product–moment correlation analysis that examines the relationship among learners' scores on the EI, D values for the oral interview and writing, X-lex score, rate of speech, and university end-of-year marks. We would expect strong and positive correlations among some of these variables – namely the speaking-related measures – if the EI test yields scores that can be used as a shortcut for the measurement of the participants' French L2 speaking proficiency in the larger study. Similarly, we would expect lower relationships with the non-speaking measures (i.e. if the construct being measured is primarily speaking proficiency). We then augment the main findings by inspecting the likely sources of difficulty that can account for the EI repetition patterns observed in the data. Finally, we report on the internal consistency of the EI test scores we obtained with this sample and compare it to the reliabilities reported for the parallel EI tests developed for L2s besides French.

Relationship between EI scores and other variables

The distribution of scores from the 29 French as a foreign language university students is displayed in Figure 8.1. The mean was 62.90 (out of 120 maximum possible score) with a standard deviation of 17.97. The range was 36–97. Because four of our participants were of an L1 background other than English only, we inspected their scores separately in order to ascertain whether their EI performance might have been in some way different from that of the L1 English participants. The participant who received the highest score (97) was one of the heritage French speakers. The native Spanish speaker received the second-highest score (96). The other French heritage speaker received a score of 74, and the Finnish native speaker received a score of 77. The mean of the native English speaking group ($n = 25$) was 59.2 (SD = 15.97, range 36–85), which is slightly lower but statistically not significantly different from the mean for the full sample. The mean for the native French speakers ($n = 10$) was 118.40 with a standard deviation of 1.65 (range 115–120). Thus, the performance by the L1 baseline is clearly at ceiling, as expected.

To test whether there was a relationship between the EI scores and other external criterion measures, a Pearson product–moment correlation was conducted using the EI scores and five additional variables: university end-of-year marks, the X-Lex adjusted score, D as measured on both the oral interview and the written argumentative essay, and speech rate on the picture-based narrative. As shown in Table 8.2, statistically significant and relatively large positive correlations were found between the EI scores and end-of-year marks ($r = 0.78$), the EI scores and D in the oral interview data ($r = 0.62$), and the EI scores and speech rate on the oral picture-based narrative ($r = 0.67$).

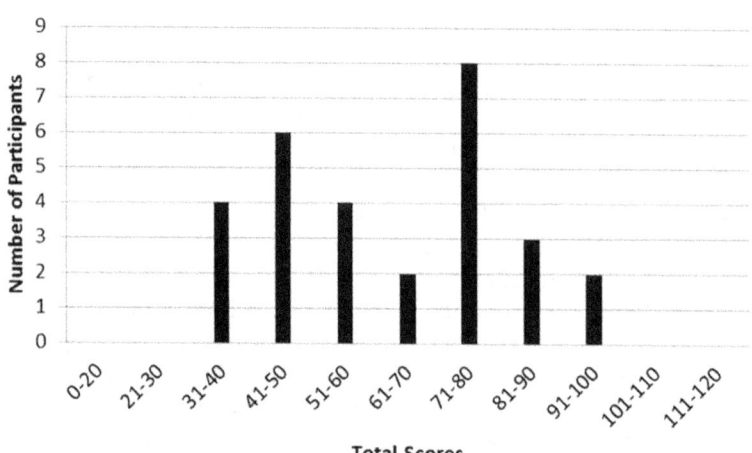

Figure 8.1 Score distribution for participants ($n = 29$)

Table 8.2 Correlation table

Measures	EI	Marks	X-lex	D Wrt	D Spk	Speech rate
EI	1.00					
Marks	0.78**	1.00				
X-lex	0.12	0.13	1.00			
D Wrt	0.32	0.25	−0.03	1.00		
D Spk	0.62**	0.47	−0.09	0.03	1.00	
Speech Rate	0.67**	0.43	−0.29	0.11	0.66**	1.00

Note: EI = elicited imitation scores; X-lex = adjusted scores for Meara and Milton's (2003) test; D Wrt = lexical diversity in written essays; D Spk = lexical diversity in oral interviews; Speech rate = number of pruned syllables per minute. **$p < 0.01$.

Sources of item difficulty

An item analysis was also conducted to investigate item difficulty, expressed as the mean score for each item across participants. The results are shown in Figure 8.2. As a reminder, each item was scored using a range from 0 to 4, with perfect repetition receiving a score of 4. A wide range of item difficulties was found, as reflected in the lowest and highest mean scores of 1.07 (item 29) to 3.97 (item 1). The most difficult items appear at the top of the graph (see Appendix 8A to read the full test sentence). The longest sentences (as counted by syllables) are the items closest in test sequence number to 30. With this in mind, the results suggest that syllable count is not the sole predictor of item difficulty.

Factors other than length seem to have appropriately taxed participants' proficiency-dependent ability to repeat the items and must be taken into account. For example, items 27 and 29 both have 18 syllables and thus both must be considered 'long' items. Yet, the difference in their mean scores is quite large (2.76 and 1.07, respectively). In this case, considerable differences in syntactic complexity can be found: item 27 is monoclausal (whereas item 29 contains two clauses) and contains fewer morphemes (9 versus 14 morphemes for item 29). Thus, the source of difficulty for item 29 may originate in morphosyntactic complexity rather than syllable length. Additionally, other aspects such as the interaction between phonology and syntax, as well as prosody and register, may also play a role. For example, item 18, which is the second most difficult item in Figure 8.2 (with a mean score of 1.14), elicited a 0 score from approximately one-third (10/29) of the participants. Of those learners who did attempt it, most scored 1, due, in part, to meaning changes and, in part, failure to repeat the whole stimulus. A change in meaning occurred because learners

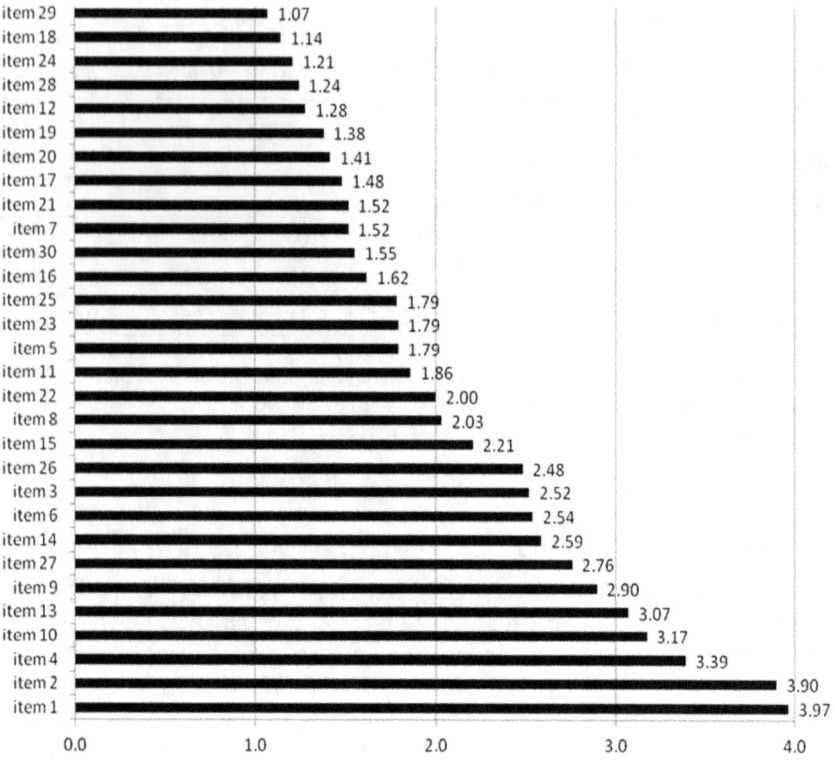

Figure 8.2 Average repetition score by item (4 = perfect repetition) across participants

incorrectly overgeneralized the negator 'ne'; the stimulus *elle ne commande que...* ('she only orders') was repeated as *elle ne commande pas* ('she does not order'). While both *ne V pas* and *ne V que* share distributional properties of negation, only *ne V pas* is a negative construction (Hawkins & Towell, 2010). Item 5 also proved challenging (mean score of 1.79) because of the initial question form *Qu'as-tu dit* ('What did you say'), which learners tended to repeat as *Qu'est-ce que tu dis* ('What do you say'), a form that is arguably more familiar to instructed learners. None of the learners received a perfect repetition score of 4 on this item, in contrast to the native speakers who all scored 4 on this item and all of the other items just discussed (27, 29 and 18).

In sum, the qualitative inspection of sources of difficulty in the EI French test provides evidence for precisely the type of differentiation that stimuli in an EI test are expected to produce, as a way to distinguish lower and higher abilities in L2 oral proficiency. Our qualitative analysis suggests that such differentiation arises from the increasing item length but also in part from specific loci for structural complexity featured in the items.

Reliability of EI scores

A test of internal consistency (Cronbach's alpha) was conducted and found to be quite high ($\alpha = 0.92$), demonstrating impressive reliability by typical measurement standards. This finding is similar to the parallel versions of this EI described in Ortega et al. (1999) and Zhou and Wu (2009), as shown in Table 8.3.

It can be argued that the high reliability comes from three factors. First, a polytomous scoring system is used (from 0 to 4 per item) rather than dichotomous (0–1), allowing for considerable fine-tuning in how performances are scored, and thus creating more variability, which is good for boosting reliability in general. Second, the scoring scale also likely supports consistent scoring by raters because at least three of the five points on the scale are quite low inference: 0 = no repetition, 1 = fragments, 4 = perfect repetition of both form and meaning. The only two score points that are more difficult to negotiate and at times engender gray areas for coding are 2 and 3 (see Appendix 8B). Third, by design, the test includes 30 items covering a wide range of difficulties suitable for the goals of both challenging and supporting test-takers with a range of proficiencies. Namely, some of the very short first stimuli are likely to be easy for even low proficiencies and some of the longest stimuli are likely to be difficult for even high proficiencies. In addition, as we have shown in the qualitative analysis, varying linguistic challenges are posed independently of syllable length by various grammatical differences across items.

Discussion

The results of the current study suggest that the French EI reported here is a reasonably valid and reliable measure of oral proficiency for use in SLA research. A strong positive correlation was found between the EI scores and (1) D in the oral interview; (2) end-of-year university marks; and

Table 8.3 Comparison of reliability analysis by EI test language

EI test language	Cronbach's alpha
English*	0.93
German*	0.96
Japanese*	0.95
Spanish*	0.97
Chinese[†]	0.97
French[§]	0.92

Note: *Reported by Ortega et al. (2002); [†]reported by Zhou and Wu (2009); [§]this study.

(3) speech rate on the oral picture-based narrative. The correlation of EI with D in speaking (rather than writing) performance is logical, as both tap into a similar aspect of proficiency and communication mode that demands integrative speaking and listening skills. Likewise, the university end-of-year marks in the present study were an average of major exams focusing on listening, speaking and writing, and thus these students were assessed in their language program, to a large extent, on their ability to do listening and speaking tasks in French. A correlation between EI and speech rate on the oral picture-based narrative is expected considering the history of research in language testing demonstrating this relationship (e.g. Iwashita *et al.*, 2008).

Furthermore, our interpretation that this EI is a valid and reliable measure of oral proficiency receives some support from the fact that, in the current study, D does not correlate between writing and speaking (note also that the third highest correlation was found between D in speaking and speech rate in the picture-based narrative, further triangulating this interpretation). This pattern is suggestive of Hulstijn's (2011, 2012) idea of a BLC and a HLC, with the EI performance, the oral picture-based narrative and the oral interview performance more clearly drawing from BLC; it may also suggest that different language use is happening in the two modes; or it may be that the mode differences are widened by genre differences between an interview and an essay. In any case, that D for speaking correlates well with EI and with speech rate serves as one source of criterion-related validity evidence for the EI; that these three scores are the highest predictors of marks is likely a good indication that EI taps into something that is close to the kind of proficiency development that we would want to predict in the instructed setting we are investigating in our main study.

The measure of vocabulary recognition, X-lex, does not correlate well with any of the other variables. This finding is most likely due to a truncated range of values; all of the learners scored more or less at the same band. This result could provide a good argument against using this lexical test measure as an indication of individual proficiency development, unless that development is investigated across major time and concomitant learning intervals.

As a reminder, the range of EI scores went from 36 to 97 (out of a total possible score of 120), thus spanning individual performances between 30% and 81% repetition success. This great variability is noteworthy, given that all 29 learners came from the same institutional level: the end of the second year in this university curriculum. This finding therefore makes a strong case against using mere institutional level as a measure of proficiency, a practice that remains widespread in SLA research (Callies *et al.*, this volume; Thomas, 2006). Where more nuanced distinctions among learners may be needed, a measure like the EI would seem to be particularly useful.

For SLA researchers working in the field of L2 French, in particular, and for those interested in crosslinguistic SLA research more generally, our item analyses uncovered interesting, possibly language-specific sources of difficulty for our French as a foreign language sample (see McManus *et al.*, this volume, for an implementation of this particular EI within a study on the acquisition of the French subjunctive). Beyond the linguistic examples we have detailed in the Results section, we imagine that a comparison of items across different language versions of this particular EI might uncover more language-specific sources of difficulty, including those that may be uniquely French. This would be a fruitful area of future research, particularly for those interested in crosslinguistic SLA. Additionally, this type of analysis could be a way to investigate the effect that language cognates might have on specific item scores. For example, German speakers of English and Portuguese speakers of Spanish may be at an advantage on certain EI test items if cognates are used (e.g. Van der Slik, 2010).

Conclusion

We would like to acknowledge some limitations of the current study. First, because all participants came from the same institutional level, our investigation of the predictive validity of this EI test is limited; in the future we hope to employ the EI with a much wider range of proficiencies spanning all curricular levels. Additional investigations would also look into distinct populations of learners, comparing for example heritage and non-heritage learners (see Wu, 2011; Wu & Ortega, 2013; Zhou, 2011), school and university learners, and so on. Overall, a larger n-size and a wide range of proficiencies would be necessary to produce conclusive evidence of the validity of the French EI and of its utility as a tool for measuring L2 French proficiency for the many research purposes demanded in SLA, from recruitment, to assignment to treatments or groups, to contextualization and interpretation of any findings about L2 acquisition (Norris & Ortega, 2012). Assuming a larger sample tapping wider-ranging proficiencies and other salient learner variables, it would be interesting to conduct a cluster analysis on the data and look for natural subgroups that could serve as examples of proficiency level or other factorial differences.

These limitations notwithstanding, the results of the present study highlight the benefits of this parallel EI version. First and foremost, the French EI seems to be a reasonably valid and reliable measure of oral proficiency, demonstrating substantial concurrent validity with lexical diversity in oral interviews, with speech rate on an oral picture-based narrative, and with end-of-year university course marks largely derived from speaking and listening performance. Second, and equally important for research use purposes, it is quick to administer and score. Third, the test itself is inexpensive, although some kind of recording device is necessary. Free recording software is available online (e.g. Audacity) making the possession of a separate digital recorder unnecessary. Fourth, based on the present suggestive – if tentative – results, the French EI could be used in conjunction with Tremblay's (2011) French Cloze test to investigate whether differences appear in assessment of learner proficiency based on mode, oral or written, type of knowledge, implicit or explicit (Ellis, 2005), or type of competence along the BLC and HLC distinction (Hulstijn, 2011, 2012). Some research is already under way by Gaillard (2014; Gaillard *et al.*, 2011), albeit with a considerably different EI design. Comparing EI tests with differing designs to other types of proficiency tests would prove useful in adding to the debate on defining the construct of proficiency. Last, but not least, the existence of parallel versions of our EI test in five other languages (Chinese, English, German, Japanese and Spanish)[4] allows for crosslinguistic comparisons that have been limited in SLA until now, but which may open new research venues for crosslinguistic SLA programs in the future.

Acknowledgments

This work was funded by the Economic and Social Research Council, UK (RES-062-23-2996). We are extremely grateful to our colleagues on the LANG-SNAP project for their valuable contribution to this research: Rosamond Mitchell, Laurence Richard, and Patricia Romero de Mills. We would also like to thank two anonymous reviewers for their helpful suggestions.

Notes

(1) See http://audacity.sourceforge.net/
(2) This French EI test will be available for download via IRIS (http://www.iris-database.org)
(3) See http://www.lognostics.co.uk/tools/index.htm
(4) A Korean version of the same EI test has recently been developed and piloted by Kim *et al.* (under review).

References

Ayoun, D. (2004) The effectiveness of written recasts in the second language acquisition of aspectual distinctions in French: A follow-up study. *The Modern Language Journal* 88, 31–55.

Bardovi-Harlig, K. and Bergström, A. (1996) Acquisition of tense and aspect in second language and foreign language learning: Learner narratives in ESL and FFL. *The Canadian Modern Language Review* 52, 308–329.

Bley-Vroman, R. and Chaudron, C. (1994) Elicited imitation as a measure of second-language competence. In E.E. Tarone, S.M. Gass and A.D. Cohen (eds) *Research Methodology in Second-Language Acquisition* (pp. 245–261). Hillsdale, NJ: Lawrence Erlbaum.

Bowden, H.W. (2007) Proficiency and second-language neurocognition: A study of Spanish as a first and second language. Unpublished PhD thesis, Georgetown University, Washington, DC.

Burger, S. and Chrétien, M. (2001) The development of oral production in content-based second language courses at the University of Ottawa. *The Canadian Modern Language Review* 58, 84–102.

Christensen, C., Hendrickson, R. and Lonsdale, D. (2010) Principled construction of elicited imitation tests. Paper presented at the *Language Resources and Evaluation Conference*, Malta, 17–23 May 2010.

Cook, K., McGhee, J. and Lonsdale, D. (2011) Elicited imitation as prediction of OPI scores. In *Proceedings of the Sixth Workshop on Innovative Use of NLP for Building Educational Applications* (pp. 30–37). Portland, OR: Association for Computational Linguistics.

Daller, H., van Hout, R. and Daller-Treffers, J. (2003) Lexical richness in the spontaneous speech of bilinguals. *Applied Linguistics* 24, 197–222.

Ellis, R. (2005) Measuring implicit and explicit knowledge of a second language: A psychometric study. *Studies in Second Language Acquisition* 27, 141–172

Erlam, R. (2006) Elicited imitation as a measure of L2 implicit knowledge: An empirical validation study. *Applied Linguistics* 27, 464–491.

Erlam, R. and Loewen, S. (2010) Implicit and explicit recasts in L2 oral French interaction. *The Canadian Modern Language Review* 66, 887–916.

Gaillard, S. (2014) Implementing an elicited imitation task as a component of a language placement test in French at the university level. Unpublished PhD thesis, University of Illinois Urbana-Champaign.

Gaillard, S., Yi, Y.-S. and Tremblay, A. (2011) Implementing an elicited imitation task as a component of a language placement test in French at the university level. Poster presented at the *Midwest Association of Language Testers and Technology for Second Language Learning Conference*, Aimes, IA, 16–17 September 2011.

Graham, C.R., Lonsdale, D., Kennington, C., Johnson, A. and McGhee, J. (2008) Elicited imitation as an oral proficiency measure with ASR scoring. In *Proceedings of the 6th International Conference on Language Resources and Evaluation* (pp. 1604–1610). Paris: European Language Resources Association.

Graham, C.R., McGhee, J. and Millard, B. (2010) The role of lexical choice in elicited imitation item difficulty. In M.T. Prior, Y. Watanabe and S. Lee (eds) *Selected Proceedings of the 2008 Second Language Research Forum* (pp. 57–72). Somerville, MA: Cascadilla Proceedings Project.

Hameyer, K. (1980) Testing oral proficiency via elicited imitation. *Revue de Phonetique Appliquée* 53 (1), 11–24.

Hawkins, R. and Towell, R. (2010) *French Grammar and Usage*. London: Hodder Education.

Hendrickson, R., Aitken, M., McGhee, J. and Johnson, A. (2010) What makes an item difficult? A syntactic, lexical, and morphological study of elicited imitation test items. In M.T. Prior, Y. Watanabe and S. Lee (eds) *Selected Proceedings of the 2008 Second Language Research Forum* (pp. 48–56). Somerville, MA: Cascadilla Proceedings Project.

Hulstijn, J.H. (2011) Language proficiency in native and nonnative speakers: An agenda for research and suggestions for second-language assessment. *Language Assessment Quarterly* 8, 229–249.

Hulstijn, J.H. (2012) The construct of language proficiency in the study of bilingualism from a cognitive perspective. *Bilingualism: Language and Cognition* 15, 422–433.

Iwashita, N., Brown, A., McNamara, T. and O'Hagan, S. (2008) Assessed levels of second language speaking proficiency: How distinct? *Applied Linguistics* 29 (1), 24–49.

Kim, Y., Tracy-Ventura, N. and Jung, Y. (under review) A proposal for improving proficiency assessment in SLA research: An elicited imitation test. *Studies in Second Language Acquisition*.

Langley, J. (2000) *Missing*. London: Frances Lincoln.

Lennon, P. (1990) Investigating fluency in EFL: A quantitative approach. *Language Learning* 40, 387–417.

Lust, B., Flynn, S. and Foley, C. (1996) What children know about what they say: Elicited imitation as a research method for assessing children's syntax. In D. McDaniel, C. McKee and H.S. Cairns (eds) *Methods for Assessing Children's Syntax* (pp. 55–76). Cambridge, MA: MIT Press.

MacWhinney, B. (2000) *The CHILDES Project: Tools for Analyzing Talk* (3rd edn). Mahwah, NJ: Lawrence Erlbaum.

Malvern, D.D. and Richards, B.J. (2000) Validation of a new measure of lexical diversity. In M. Beers, B. van den Bogaerde, G. Bol, J. de Jong and C. Rooijmans (eds) *From Sound to Sentence: Studies on first language acquisition* (pp. 81–96). Amsterdam: Benjamins.

Markman, B., Spilka, I. and Tucker, G. (1975) The use of elicited imitation in search of an interim French grammar. *Language Learning* 75, 31–41.

McManus, K. (2011) The development of aspect in a second language. Unpublished PhD thesis, Newcastle University.

Meara, P. and Milton, J. (2003) *X_Lex The Swansea Levels Test*. Newbury: Express.

Naiman, N. (1974) The use of elicited imitation in second language acquisition research. *Working Papers on Bilingualism* 2, 1–37.

Norris, J.M. (2010) Understanding instructed SLA: Constructs, contexts, and consequences. Plenary address delivered at the *20th Annual Conference of the European Second Language Association*, Università di Modena e Reggio Emilia Reggio Emilia, Italy, 1–4 September 2010.

Norris, J.M. and Ortega, L. (2012) Assessing learner knowledge. In S.M. Gass and A. Mackey (eds) *The Routledge Handbook of Second Language Acquisition* (pp. 573–589). New York, NY: Routledge.

Oller, J. (1976) Evidence for a general language proficiency factor: An expectancy grammar. *Die Neuren Sprachen* 2, 165–174.

Ortega, L. (2000) Understanding syntactic complexity: The measurement of change in the syntax of instructed L2 Spanish learners. Unpublished PhD thesis, University of Hawaii at Manoa.

Ortega, L., Iwashita, N., Rabie, S. and Norris, J.M. (1999) *A Multilanguage Comparison of Measures of Syntactic Complexity* [Funded Project]. Honolulu, HI: University of Hawaii, National Foreign Language Resource Center.

Ortega, L., Iwashita, N., Norris, J.M. and Rabie, S. (2002) An investigation of elicited imitation tasks in crosslinguistic SLA research. Paper presented at the *Second Language Research Forum*, Toronto, Canada, 3–6 October 2002.

Radloff, C.F. (1991) *Sentence Repetition Testing for Studies of Community Bilingualism*. Arlington, TX: Summer Institute of Linguistics and The University of Texas at Arlington.

Rogers, V. (2009) Syntactic development in the second language acquisition of French by instructed English learners. Unpublished PhD thesis, Newcastle University.

Savignon, S. (1982) Dictation as a measure of communicative competence in French as a second language. *Language Learning* 32 (1), 33–51.

Slobin, D.I. and Welsh, C.A. (1973) Elicited imitation as a research tool in developmental psycholinguistics. In C. Ferguson and D.I. Slobin (eds) *Studies of Child Language Development* (pp. 485–497). New York: Holt, Rinehart & Winston (Reprinted from 1968 *Working Paper No 10, Language Behavior Research Laboratory*, University of California, Berkeley.)

Thomas, M. (1994) Assessment of L2 proficiency in second language acquisition research. *Language Learning* 44, 307–336.

Thomas, M. (2006) Research synthesis and historiography: The case of assessment of second language proficiency. In J. Norris and L. Ortega (eds) *Synthesizing Research on Language Learning and Teaching* (pp. 279–298). Amsterdam: Benjamins.

Tremblay, A. (2011) Proficiency assessment standards in second language acquisition research: 'Clozing' the gap. *Studies in Second Language Acquisition* 33, 339–372.

Van der Slik, F.W.P. (2010) Acquisition of Dutch as a second language: The explanative power of cognate and genetic linguistic distance measures for 11 West-European first languages. *Studies in Second Language Acquisition* 32, 401–432.
Verhagen, J. (2011) Verb placement in second language acquisition: Experimental evidence for the different behavior of auxiliary and lexical verbs. *Applied Psycholinguistics* 32, 821–858.
Vinther, T. (2002) Elicited imitation: A brief review. *International Journal of Applied Linguistics* 12, 54–73.
Wu, S.-L. (2011) Learning to express motion events in L2 Chinese: A cognitive linguistic perspective. Unpublished PhD thesis, University of Hawaii at Manoa, Honolulu, HI.
Wu, S.-L. and Ortega, L. (2013) Measuring global oral proficiency in SLA research: A new elicited imitation test of L2 Chinese. *Foreign Language Annals* 46, 680–704.
Zhou, Y. (2011) Willingness to communicate in learning Mandarin as a foreign and heritage language. Unpublished PhD thesis, University of Hawaii at Manoa, Honolulu, HI.
Zhou, Y. and Wu, S.-L. (2009) Can elicited imitation be used for the measurement of oral proficiency in L2 Chinese? A pilot study. Unpublished manuscript, University of Hawaii at Manoa, Honolulu, HI.

Appendix 8A

Elicited Imitation – Newly developed French stimuli, literal English translation, and parallel English stimuli from Ortega et al. (1999)

Syllable numbers for the English version in parentheses

1. *Je dois aller au coiffeur.* ('I have to go to the hairdresser's')
   I have to get a haircut (7 syllables)
2. *Le livre rouge est sur la table.* ('The red book is on the table')
   The red book is on the table (8 syllables)
3. *Les rues sont larges dans cette ville.* ('The streets are wide in this city')
   The streets in this city are wide (8)
4. *Il prend une longue douche tous les matins.* ('He has a long shower every morning')
   He takes a shower every morning (9)
5. *Qu'as-tu dit que tu vas faire aujourd'hui?* ('What did you say that you are going to do today?')
   What did you say you were doing today? (10)
6. *Je ne sais pas s'il sait très bien conduire.* ('I don't know if he can drive all that well')
   I doubt that he knows how to drive that well (10)
7. *Après le repas, j'ai fait une paisible sieste.* ('After dinner I had a peaceful nap')
   After dinner I had a long, peaceful nap (11)
8. *Il est possible qu'il se mette à pleuvoir demain.* ('It is possible that it might rain tomorrow')
   It is possible that it will rain tomorrow (12)

9. *J'adore les films, surtout ceux qui finissent bien.* ('I love films, especially those that have happy endings')
   I enjoy movies which have a happy ending (12)
10. *Les maisons sont très jolies mais inaccessibles.* ('The houses are very nice, but inaccessible')
    The houses are very nice but too expensive (12)
11. *Le petit garçon, dont le chaton est mort, est triste.* ('The little boy whose kitten died is sad')
    The little boy whose kitten died yesterday is sad (13)
12. *Le restaurant est censé servir de très bons plats.* ('The restaurant is supposed to serve very good food')
    That restaurant is supposed to have very good food (13)
13. *Je veux une maison où mes animaux peuvent habiter.* ('I want a home where my pets can live')
    I want a nice, big house in which my animals can live (14)
14. *Tu aimes bien écouter de la musique country, n'est-ce pas?* ('You like listening to country music, don't you?')
    You really enjoy listening to country music, don't you (14)
15. *Elle a fini de peindre les murs de son appartement.* ('She finished painting the walls in her flat')
    She just finished painting the inside of her apartment (14)
16. *Traverse la rue au feu rouge et puis continue juste tout droit.* ('Cross the street at the red light and then just continue straight on')
    Cross the street at the light and then just continue straight ahead (15)
17. *La personne que je vois a un sens de l'humour fabuleux.* ('The person I'm dating has a great sense of humour')
    The person I'm dating has a wonderful sense of humour (15)
18. *Elle ne commande que de la viande et ne mange aucun légume.* ('She only orders meat and never eats vegetables')
    She only orders meat dishes and never eats vegetables (15/16)
19. *J'aimerais que le prix des maisons de ville soit accessible.* ('I would like town houses to be more accessible')
    I wish the price of town houses would become affordable (15)
20. *J'espère que le printemps arrivera plus tôt que l'an dernier.* ('I hope spring arrives sooner than last year')
    I hope it will get warmer sooner this year than it did last year (16)
21. *Un de mes meilleurs amis s'occupe des enfants de mon voisin.* ('One of my best friends looks after my neighbour's children')
    A good friend of mine always takes care of my neighbour's three children (16)
22. *Le chat noir que tu as nourri a été chassé par le chien.* ('The black cat that you fed was chased by the dog')
    The black cat that you fed yesterday was the one chased by the dog (16)

23. *Avant de pouvoir sortir, il doit finir de ranger sa chambre.* ('Before going out, he has to finish tidying his room')
Before he can go outside, he has to finish cleaning his room (16)
24. *Je me suis bien amusé lors de notre sortie à l'opéra* ('I had a great time when we went to the opera')
The most fun I've ever had was when we went to the opera (16)
25. *Le voleur que la police a arrêté était très grand et mince.* ('The thief that the police arrested was very tall and thin')
The terrible thief whom the police caught was very tall and thin (17)
26. *Pourriez-vous s'il vous plaît me passer le livre qui est sur la table?* ('Would you please pass me the book that is on the table?')
Would you be so kind as to hand me the book which is on the table? (17)
27. *Le nombre de fumeurs de cigares augmente chaque année.* ('The number of cigar smokers goes up each year')
The number of people who smoke cigars is increasing every year (17/18)
28. *Je ne sais pas si le train de 11h30 a déjà quitté la gare.* ('I don't know if the 11.30 train has already left the station')
I don't know if the 11:30 train has left the station yet (18)
29. *L'examen n'était pas aussi difficile que ce que vous m'aviez dit.* ('The exam was not as difficult as you had said')
The exam wasn't nearly as difficult as you told me it would be (18)
30. *Il y a énormément d'individus qui ne mangent rien du tout le matin.* ('There are a lot of people who do not eat anything in the mornings')
There are a lot of people who don't eat anything at all in the morning (19)

Appendix 8B

Scoring guidelines for French elicited imitation task (rubric from Ortega et al., 1999)

SCORE 0

Criteria	Examples
• Nothing (silence).	
• Garbled (unintelligible, usually transcribed as XXX).	
• Minimal repetition, then item abandoned: – only one word repeated – only one content word plus function word(s) – only one content word plus function word(s) plus extraneous words that were not in the original stimulus – only function word(s) repeated.	– *le voleur bla bla bla la commerce* (item 25) ('the thief blah blah blah the shop') – *suive la rue jusqu'au feu rouge* (item 16) ('follow the street until the red light') – *bla bla bla dans la ville* (item 2) ('blah blah blah in the city')

Note: with only, just, yet (meaningful adverbs), score 1.

SCORE 1

Criteria	Examples
• When only about half of idea units are represented in the string but a lot of important information in the original stimulus is left out.	– *je ne sais pas... conduire* (item 6) ('I don't know... drive') – *J'adore **la** film...* (item 9) ('I love the movie') – *quitter la gare* (item 28) ('leave the station') – *XXX dans ce ville* (item 3) ('XXX in this city')
• When barely half of lexical words get repeated and meaningful content results that is unrelated (or opposed) to stimulus, frequently with hesitation markers.	– *bla bla bla tu vas faire aujourd'hui* (item 5) ('blah blah blah you are going to do today') – *Le petit garçon dans le château est très triste* (item 13) ('The little boy in the castle is very sad')

(Continued)

SCORE 1 (Continued)

• Or when string does not in itself constitute a self-standing sentence with some (target-like or non-target-like) meaning (this may happen more often with shorter items, where if only two of three content words are repeated and no grammatical relation between them is attempted, then score 1).	*Je sais passe s'il a un très bien conduire* (item 6) ('I know happen if he has a very good drive')
• Also when half of a long stimulus is left out, and the sentence produced is incomplete.	

SCORE 2

Criteria	Examples
• When content of string preserves at least more than half of the idea units in the original stimulus; string is meaningful, and the meaning is close or related to original, but it departs from it in some slight changes in content, which makes content inexact, incomplete or ambiguous.	– *J'adore les films, surtout **les** qui finissent bien* (item 9) ('I love movies, especially them that finish well') – *J'aimerais que **les** prix **de** maison **est plus** accessible* (item 10) ('I would love the house prices is more accessible') – ***Les voleurs** étaient très grand et mince* (item 25) ('The thieves were very tall and thin') – *Je ne sais pas si le train de **11h00** a déjà quitté la gare.* (item 28) ('I don't know if the 11 o'clock train has already left the station') – ***La maison** est très jolie mais **accessible*** (item 12) ('The house is very pretty but accessible')
• Cases of extra marking or more marked morphology should be considered as meaning change. For example, a present tense repeated as past or as future should be scored as meaning change (score 2).	– *Je veux une maison ou **les** animaux **peut** habiter* (item 13) ('I want a house or the pets is able to live')
• Similarly, singular/plural differences between stimulus and repeated string change the meaning, not only the grammar (score 2).	– ***La rue** sont larges dans **le** ville* (item 3) ('The street are wide in the city') – *Il prend **les longues douches** tous les matins* (item 4) ('He has long showers every morning')

(Continued)

SCORE 2 (Continued)

Criteria	Examples
• Changes of person (il for elle) change the meaning, so score 2	– *Avant de pouvoir sortir, **elle** doit finir de ranger sa chambre.* (item 16) ('Before going out, she has to finish tidying his room')

SCORE 3

Criteria	Examples
• Original, complete meaning is preserved as in the stimulus. Strings which are quite ungrammatical can get a 3 score, as long as exact meaning is preserved. Synonymous substitutions are acceptable.	– *Pourriez-vous me passer le livre qui est sur la table?* (item 26) ('Would you pass me the book which is on the table?') – *Je dois aller à coiffeur* (item 1) ('I have to go to hairdresser's') – *J'espère que le printemps arrivera plus tôt que **l'année dernière*** (item 20) ('I hope that spring will arrive sooner than last year')
• Changes in grammar that do not affect meaning should be scored as 3. For instance, failure to supply past tense (had > have) and missing articles should be considered grammar change only (score 3).	– *J'espère que le printemps **arrive** plus tôt que l'an dernier* (item 20) ('I hope that spring arrives sooner than last year')
• Ambiguous changes in grammar that COULD be interpreted as meaning changes from a NS perspective should be scored as 2. That is, as a general principle in case of doubt about whether meaning has changed or not, score 2.	

SCORE 4

Criteria	Examples
• Exact repetition: string matches stimulus exactly. Both form and meaning are correct without exception or doubt.	
• Missing liaison acceptable	– *Je **dois aller** au coiffeur* (item 1) ('I have to go to the hairdresser's')

9 Exploring the Acquisition of the French Subjunctive: Local Syntactic Context or Oral Proficiency?

Kevin McManus, Nicole Tracy-Ventura, Rosamond Mitchell, Laurence Richard and Patricia Romero de Mills

Introduction

Indicators of advanced/high-level proficiency in a second language (L2) are an increasingly active focus of L2 acquisition research (e.g. Bartning & Schlyter, 2004; Bartning, 2009; Bartning *et al.*, 2009, 2012), primarily because uncovering what they are has clear implications for understanding L2 developmental processes and proficiency assessment. In particular, in order to design reliable assessments that can distinguish learners of different proficiencies, we need to know which language features are acquired early, late, and so on, to be able to build that knowledge into our designs. Areas of relatively late acquisition in L2 French morphosyntax include tense, aspect and mood (Bartning & Schlyter, 2004; Howard, 2005). To date, however, although the acquisition of tense and aspect in advanced-level French has received a great deal of attention (e.g. Ayoun, 2005; Howard, 2005; Labeau, 2005; McManus, 2013), much less research has focused on the acquisition of mood (i.e. the subjunctive). Yet, in other Romance languages, such as Spanish, a large body of research on the acquisition of mood already exists (e.g. Collentine, 2010; Gudmestad, 2012; Isabelli & Nishida, 2005). One possible explanation for this imbalance across different L2 Romance languages could reside in the problematic nature of measuring and coding the French subjunctive compared to its Spanish equivalent. Spanish has a specific morpheme that is consistently supplied for marking mood (Butt & Benjamin, 2000), whereas French does not. For some French verbs there are morphological and phonological distinctions between indicative and subjunctive forms (e.g. *faire* 'do': *il fait*-INDIC versus *il fasse*-SUBJ), but this is not consistent (e.g. *jouer* 'play': *il joue*-INDIC versus *il joue*-SUBJ). In Spanish, however, the presence of a subjunctive morpheme is clearly identifiable (e.g. *jugar* 'play': *juega*-INDIC versus *juegue*-SUBJ).

In terms of acquisition, second language acquisition (SLA) researchers have suggested that the subjunctive is late-acquired because 'learners need to be at a point in their development where they reliably produce subordinate clauses' (Collentine, 2010: 41) because, as Bartning (forthcoming: 24) argues, 'complex syntax has to be acquired as a prerequisite'. Such claims are based on observations that the subjunctive largely occurs in subordination, but previous research has suggested that learners' knowledge and use of the subjunctive is not only an issue of subordination, but also influenced by local syntactic context (e.g. whether the main clause – the subjunctive trigger – is affirmative or negative) as well as semantics (e.g. whether the main clause expresses doubt or emotion). In fact, Bartning (forthcoming) suggests that certain uses of the subjunctive emerge earlier than others (e.g. affirmative before negative constructions). However, no research has yet examined how differences in the main clause's local syntax influence learners' use of this form and, importantly, how L2 proficiency contributes to its use. If productive subjunctive use is characterized by the interfacing of different types of knowledge – such as knowledge of form (i.e. subjunctive inflections), complex syntax, and semantics, then performance differences between learners at different proficiency levels would be expected. Further research is required to understand the factors at play in learners' acquisition, knowledge and use of the subjunctive. In the present study, we explore the subjunctive's 'late acquisition' by investigating how differences in (1) oral L2 proficiency and (2) local syntactic context (affirmative, adverbial and negative constructions) account for learners' use and knowledge of the subjunctive.

Mood in French

Modality refers to the status of propositions, including 'the speaker's assumptions or assessment of possibilities and, in most cases, it indicates the speaker's confidence (or lack of confidence) in the truth of the proposition expressed' (Coates, 1980: 18). In French, mood is expressed in two main ways: morphosyntax and prosody (Bassano & Mendes-Maillochon, 1994). In terms of morphosyntax, the subjunctive is claimed to be the typical and specific marker of mood in traditional accounts of standard

French (Frontier, 1997; Hawkins & Towell, 2010; Judge & Healey, 1983; Lang & Perez, 1996; L'Huillier, 1999). Rowlett (2007) notes, however, that historical prescriptivism, as ordered by the *Académie française*, has strongly influenced subjunctive use. For instance, whilst concessive conjunctions (e.g. *bien que* 'although') were previously compatible with either indicative or subjunctive forms, the *Académie* ordered they should only be used with subjunctive forms (Rowlett, 2007). As a consequence, Rowlett recommends a cautious approach to the relevance behind certain triggers selecting subjunctive over indicative forms.

As previously mentioned, modern French lacks a consistently supplied subjunctive morpheme; with certain verbs there is no overt morphophonological distinction between the present indicative and present subjunctive. With the exception of the first and second person plural, the present subjunctive is identical to the present indicative for regular verbs ending in *–er* (e.g. *regarder* 'watch'). However, with irregular verbs (e.g. *avoir* 'have') and verbs ending in *–ir* (e.g. *finir* 'finish') and *–re* (e.g. *prendre* 'take'), an identifiable present subjunctive verbal inflection distinct from the present indicative is supplied. The sentences in examples (1)–(4) illustrate these differences.

(1) Regular *–er* verbs: *regarder* ('watch')
    Present indicative: *je regarde*
    Present subjunctive: *je regarde*
(2) *–ir* verbs: *finir* ('finish')
    Present indicative: *je finis*
    Present subjunctive: *je finisse*
(3) *–re* verbs: *prendre* ('take')
    Present indicative: *je prends*
    Present subjunctive: *je prenne*
(4) Irregular verbs: *faire* ('do')
    Present indicative: *je fais*
    Present subjunctive: *je fasse*

Although identification of the subjunctive can be problematic, it is also noted that it is infrequent in spontaneous speech (Bartning, forthcoming; Howard, 2008; O'Connor DiVito, 1997; Poplack, 1992, 2001). In a corpus study based on 53,265 clauses of spoken and written native-speaker French from a variety of different genres (e.g. conversations, interviews, magazines, novels), O'Connor DiVito (1997) found that only 2% ($n = 342$) of 16,236 spoken clauses and 3% ($n = 1034$) of 37,029 written clauses contained a subjunctive form. These percentages fall to 1% ($n = 233$) and 2% ($n = 789$), respectively, when only clearly identifiable subjunctive forms are counted (e.g. *fasse, finisse*). Furthermore, she notes person and verb type restrictions on the use of the subjunctive. The verbs *être* ('be'), *avoir* ('have'), *pouvoir* ('be able to'), *faire* ('do') and regular *–er* verbs (e.g. *regarder* 'watch') account for 78% of all subjunctive forms in the corpus, whilst 'many other verbs frequently occurring in the French language (e.g. *savoir* 'know' and *aller* 'go') are rarely found in the subjunctive in any genre' (O'Connor DiVito, 1997: 51). In fact, O'Connor DiVito reports that in this corpus, '53% of all subjunctives are accounted for by only four oral forms' (1997: 51):

(5) /swa/   *sois, soit, soient*
    /E/   *aie, aies, ait, aient*
    /pɥis/ *puisse, puisses, puissent*
    /fas/   *fasse, fasses, fassent*

In terms of use, the subjunctive is mainly used in subordinate clauses, but it is also found in independent clauses and some fixed expressions (L'Huillier, 1999). The sentences in example (6) illustrate the main uses of the subjunctive as described in several standard accounts of modern French (e.g. Frontier, 1997; Hawkins & Towell, 2010; Judge & Healey, 1983; Lang & Perez, 1996; L'Huillier, 1999):

(6) a. *Je doute que tu sois heureux* ('I doubt that you are happy')
    b. *Je cherche une femme qui connaisse la vérité* ('I'm looking for a woman who knows the truth')
    c. *Ainsi soit-il* ('So be it')

In *que*-clauses (as in example (6a)), the subjunctive is triggered by the following:

(7) a. Affirmative constructions expressing will, order, advice and desire, such as:
           Il veut que... ('He wants that...')
           Il souhaite que... ('He wishes that...')
           Il est important que... ('It is important that...')
           Il faut que... ('It is necessary that...')
    b. Affirmative constructions expressing emotions and feelings:
           Il aime que... ('He likes that...')
           Il regrette que... ('He regrets that...')
           Il est dommage que... ('It is a shame that...')
           Il a peur que... ('He is scared that...')
    c. Affirmative construction expressing opinion, possibility and doubt:
           Il accepte que... ('He accepts that...')
           Il doute que... ('He doubts that...')
           Il est possible que... ('It is possible that...')
           Il semble que... ('It seems that...')

d. Negative and question constructions, such as:
   Il ne croit pas que... ('He does not believe that...')
   Croit-il que... ? ('Does he believe that... ?')
   Il ne pense pas que... ('He does not think that...')
   Pense-t-il que...? ('Does he think that... ?')

In adverbial clauses, conjunctions that specify the subjunctive deal with establishing hypothetical and conditional situations, including: *afin que* ('so that'), *bien que* ('although'), *malgré que* ('despite'), *soit que* ('whether'). Certain time conjunctions also trigger the subjunctive (e.g. *avant que* 'before', *jusqu'à ce que* 'until'). It has also been noted, however, that when opinion verbs such as *croire* ('believe') and *penser* ('think') are used in negative and question constructions, there is some degree of optionality with the indicative, as noted by Lang and Perez (1996: 127): 'Croire and penser are also followed by the subjunctive if they are interrogative or negative. Today, however, this rule is not always observed.' This subjunctive-indicative optionality is illustrated by Abouda (2002: 1) with the verb *croire* in affirmative (8a), interrogative (8b) and negative (8c) constructions:

(8) a. *Il croit que Pierre est / *soit revenu.*
   'He believes that Pierre returned-INDIC / returned-SUBJ'
   b. *Croit-il que Pierre est / soit revenu?*
   'Does he believe that Pierre returned-INDIC / returned-SUBJ'
   c. *Il ne croit pas que Pierre est / soit revenu.*
   'He does not believe that Pierre returned-INDIC / returned-SUBJ'

Some prescriptive grammars indicate that opinion verbs such as *croire* ('believe') license the indicative in affirmative constructions (8a), whereas in negative (8c) and interrogative (8b) constructions only the subjunctive is licensed (Hawkins & Towell, 2010; L'Huillier, 1999), but, as the sentences in (8b) and (8c) illustrate, optionality between the subjunctive and the indicative appears possible in modern French. According to Abouda (2002), subjunctive-indicative optionality with opinion verbs in negative and interrogative constructions is due to the truth-value entailment of the proposition expressed by the complement clause, which then has repercussions in the syntax. When the main verb in the subordinate clause expresses a truth value, the indicative is licensed; but when hypotheticality (or no truth value) exerted the subjunctive is licensed. In (8c), for example, the indicative is licensed if the semantics of negation extend over the entire proposition (e.g. I do not believe Pierre is coming and I know he is not because he is at home), but when the semantics of negation do not extend beyond the speaker's own doubt then the subjunctive is licensed (e.g. I do not believe Pierre is coming but he might be).

SLA of Modality

Few studies have focused on the acquisition of the French subjunctive. The dearth of research in this area is likely due to the challenging factors associated with the French subjunctive already outlined, including (1) the infrequency of the form in spontaneous speech and (2) the difficulty in clearly identifying subjunctive from indicative forms. However, despite these difficulties, two studies are insightful in indicating patterns in the use and acquisition of this form.

Howard (2008) investigated the acquisition of the subjunctive in French L2 by analysing English-speaking university learners' ($n = 12$) performance in sociolinguistic interviews. In his cross-sectional study, learners differed in terms of level of instruction: Group 1 ($n = 6$) had completed two years of university-level French and Group 2 ($n = 6$) had completed three years. The analysis showed that learners produced very few subjunctive tokens at all, irrespective of level of instruction. Furthermore, when only clearly identifiable subjunctive morphemes were considered (i.e. subjunctive forms distinct from the indicative), less than 10 tokens were found in the whole sample (approximately 18 hours of speech). However, when the number of potential subjunctive tokens was taken into consideration, this figure rose to 100 tokens. This pattern clearly indicates the difficulty in sampling subjunctive forms that are morphologically and phonologically distinct from the indicative. Overall, the study's findings show that the most frequent triggers for the subjunctive were: *falloir que* ('necessary that') and *vouloir que* ('want that'). Similar findings are reported by Bartning (forthcoming) for Swedish-speaking university learners ($n = 8$) who completed a series of oral tasks (e.g. interviews, story retells). In agreement with Howard, her learners produced very few subjunctive tokens; for all eight learners, 25 clearly identifiable subjunctive tokens were found. Bartning argues that because the subjunctive is also infrequent in native-speaker French (based on her own native speaker [NS] corpus, [$n = 4$]), learners' similarly infrequent use of this form is not an avoidance strategy but reflects its low frequency in the target language community. In terms of how learners use the subjunctive, her findings are in line with those of Howard: the most frequent subjunctive triggers were *que* clauses, especially *falloir que* ('necessary that'). Additional uses included the subjunctive with (1) adverbial clauses (e.g. *avant que* 'before') and (2) negated verbs of opinion (e.g. *ne pas penser que* 'do not think that'). She additionally suggests an order of acquisition based on the subjunctive's local syntactic context: the subjunctive is used with affirmative before negative constructions.

The Spanish subjunctive is also reported to be relatively infrequent in spontaneous speech (Collentine, 1995, 2010). For example, Collentine (2010) reports on data from the *Corpus del Español*, a corpus of spoken and written language of over 20 million words (Biber *et al.*, 2006; Davies, 2002), showing that 'the proportion of subjunctive forms native speakers produce is small compared to other paradigms/conjugations [...]. The subjunctive, whether in the present or the imperfect, comprises only about 7.2% of all verb forms' (Collentine, 2010: 39). Compared to French SLA research, however, studies focusing on L2 Spanish report fewer difficulties eliciting the subjunctive. Gudmestad (2012), as an example, designed three oral tasks to elicit the subjunctive in her study of 130 English-speaking university learners from different Spanish proficiency levels (assessed independently). As a result of her study design, Gudmestad reports that learners produced 2573 subjunctive tokens, with results demonstrating a gradual increase in use of the subjunctive in line with proficiency. Furthermore, the results indicated that learners' use of the subjunctive can be predicted by the clause's semantic category. The subjunctive was most frequent with volition clauses, followed by clauses expressing comment, uncertainty and temporality.

In sum, previous L2 research on the subjunctive has indicated that in tasks not specifically designed to elicit it, its frequency in learner output is likely to be low. In French L2, even when learners produce subjunctive triggers (e.g. *falloir que*), subordinate verb forms are likely to be ambiguous because not all indicative forms are morphologically or phonologically distinguishable from the subjunctive (e.g. regular *–er* verbs). With methodologies not designed to elicit this form (e.g. analysis of smaller semi-spontaneous learner corpora), it is possible that learners' knowledge of the subjunctive may be under-represented. This shortcoming could be addressed not only by drawing on large data samples, but also by data elicited by different means. Indeed, as advocated by Chaudron (2003: 763), triangulating different data-collection techniques 'is feasible, if not desired, in order for the researcher to obtain the best sample of learners' performance potential'. Because of a reliance on semi-spontaneous oral production, previous research on the acquisition of the French subjunctive has not been able to reliably ascertain the difference between (1) structures that are not yet acquired and (2) structures that are not produced. In such cases, a combination of different elicitation tasks, such as production and judgment, is desirable.

Research Questions

The current study investigates the acquisition of the subjunctive in French L2 with respect to differences in oral L2 proficiency and local syntactic context. The following research questions guide this study:

(9) *Research question 1*: Do differences in L2 proficiency and local syntactic context (affirmatives, adverbials, negatives) affect learners' use of the French subjunctive in oral and written production?
Research question 2: Do differences in L2 proficiency and local syntactic context affect learners' knowledge of the French subjunctive?

These research questions were investigated using data collected from two production tasks (a semi-structured oral interview and an argumentative writing task) and a timed grammaticality judgment task (GJT). Following performance on an oral proficiency test (described below), learners were split into two significantly different groups: a low group and a high group. A native-speaker group also served as a control. Participants' knowledge and use of the subjunctive was then analysed in the two production tasks and the GJT according to proficiency group and local syntactic context. If L2 proficiency influences the acquisition of the French subjunctive, performance differences between learners of different proficiency levels would be expected. If differences in local syntactic context influence the acquisition of the subjunctive, performance differences between affirmative, adverbial and negative subjunctive triggers would be expected.

Methodology

Participants

This study involves 23 English-speaking university learners of French recruited from a university in England (mean age = 20 years, SD = 0.87). They were all participants in a larger ongoing longitudinal project that focuses on the acquisition of French and Spanish before, during and after a nine-month stay abroad (http://langsnap.soton.ac.uk). Overall, data were collected at six different points over 23 months. All learners were recruited from the same level of instruction and were spending year three (of a four-year degree program) abroad in France. Previous classroom instruction ranged from 8 to 15 years (mean = 10.4 years, SD = 2.4). All learners also reported informal exposure to French prior to data collection, mostly through family holidays and language exchanges. Because learners from the same level of instruction are typically not homogeneous in their L2 proficiency (Callies *et al.*, this volume; Tremblay, 2011; Tremblay & Garrison, 2010), learners' oral proficiency in L2 French was independently measured by an elicited imitation (EI) test. In this proficiency measure, learners are judged on their repetition attempts for 30 French sentences of differing complexities (for a detailed presentation of this measure, see Tracy-Ventura *et al.*, this volume). Each participant is scored out of 120, with the 23 participants in the current study scoring from 36 to 85 (mean score = 58.7, SD = 15.79). Scores on the EI test were used to divide learners into two groups; those scoring below the mean were placed in a 'low group' (scores of 36–58, $n = 13$) and those scoring above the mean in a 'high group' (scores of 61–85, $n = 10$). In addition, data were collected from 10 native speakers of French. All French native speakers were recruited from the same English university where they were taking part in an ERASMUS university exchange program. Data were collected within two weeks of their arrival in England.

Test instruments

For the present study, participants completed a total of three tasks (in addition to the EI test): an argumentative writing task, a semistructured oral interview and a GJT.

Argumentative writing task

The argumentative writing task was computer-based, and required learners to respond to an essay-style question in French. Responses from two essay questions are used in the present study: *Pensez-vous que les couples homosexuels ont le droit de se marier et d'adopter des enfants?* ('Do you think homosexual couples have the right to marry and adopt children?') and *Pensez-vous que la marijuana devrait être légalisée?* ('Do you think that marijuana should be legalized?'). Participants were provided with the essay question and then given 3 min to plan their answer before beginning their response. The task was timed and participants had up to 15 min to write approximately 200 words.

Oral interview

The oral interview was conducted on a one-to-one basis in French between the participant and a native/near-native speaker of French. Each interviewer was provided with a list of questions designed to elicit responses on living abroad, daily routines at work/university, free time activities and so on. The interview also solicited opinions and hypotheticality, and lasted approximately 20 min. All interviews were transcribed and analyzed morphologically using the CLAN software suite (MacWhinney, 2000).

Timed grammaticality judgment task

The timed GJT was designed specifically to assess learners' knowledge of the subjunctive. Each stimulus sentence consisted of a main clause and a subordinate clause (see Appendix 9A for examples). In order to assess learners' knowledge of the subjunctive – in particular learners' knowledge of the triggers and local syntactic contexts that license use of the subjunctive – the test sentences were squared in a 2 × 2 design, which is illustrated in Table 9.1 (* indicates not grammatical and √ grammatical).

This design tests two conditions: (1) knowledge that a subjunctive trigger in the main clause takes a subjunctive verb form in the following subordinate clause, and (2) knowledge that an indicative trigger takes an indicative

Table 9.1 GJT design for test sentences

Form	Trigger	
	Subjunctive	*Indicative*
Indicative	*	√
Subjunctive	√	*

verb form. The test contained 30 test items (affirmatives, adverbials, negatives and questions) and 12 distractors, but the current analysis is only based on 24 of these test items (affirmative, adverbial and negative constructions). Only verbs that morphologically distinguish the subjunctive from the indicative were used (e.g. *faire* 'do': *il fait*-INDIC versus *il fasse*-SUBJ). Participants were instructed to indicate on a three-point Likert scale whether the test sentence was 'grammatical', 'don't know', or 'not grammatical'. The task was computer-administered using a program specially designed by the project team (available to download from IRIS: http://www.iris-database.org). There was an overall time limit of 20 min to complete the test.

Data Collection and Analysis

As previously mentioned, this study is part of a larger longitudinal project with data collected at six different points over 23 months: Pre-test (before departure abroad), three on-site tests (whilst Abroad), Post-test and Delayed post-test (after residence abroad). For the purposes of the present study, we analyzed argumentative writing and oral interview data collected at both the Pre-test (May 2011) and Visit 1 Abroad (November 2011). EI data were collected at the Pre-test and GJT data were collected at Visit 1 Abroad.

The main goal of the analyses was to determine the respective influences of L2 proficiency and different local syntactic contexts on the acquisition of the French subjunctive. Audio data from the oral interviews were orthographically transcribed in CHAT (CHILDES; MacWhinney, 2000). Data from the writing task were also converted into CHAT format. All CHAT files were checked and syntactically tagged using the MOR program in CLAN. All obligatory subjunctive contexts were coded, and frequency counts were undertaken on suppliance in obligatory contexts. In terms of scoring on the GJT, for a grammatical sentence, one point was awarded for selecting 'grammatical' and zero points for selecting 'don't know' or 'not grammatical'. For an ungrammatical sentence, one point was awarded for selecting 'not grammatical' and zero points for selecting 'don't know' or 'grammatical'. Consequently, the maximum score for the GJT was 24. A test of internal consistency (Cronbach's alpha) was conducted and at 0.72, this demonstrated acceptable reliability by testing standards.

Results

Elicited production

To investigate our first research question, whether differences in L2 proficiency and local syntactic context (affirmatives, adverbials, negatives) affect learners' use of the French subjunctive in oral and written production, we identified all obligatory subjunctive contexts in the argumentative writing and oral interview tasks. Tables 9.2 to 9.4 show the total number of subjunctive contexts participants produced, in addition to the number of contexts produced where subjunctive usage was target-like (showing raw counts and percentages). Within target-like suppliance, the counts are separated into those subjunctive forms identical to the indicative (e.g. *je joue* 'I play') and those that are unique to the subjunctive (e.g. *je fasse* 'I do'). Table 9.2 displays the results for the low group learners, Table 9.3 the high group learners and Table 9.4 the native speakers.

Table 9.2 Use of subjunctive by low group learners (*n* = 13)

		Target-like suppliance of subjunctive		
Task	All subjunctive contexts	Total target-like production in subjunctive contexts	Identical indicative	Unique subjunctive
Argumentative writing				
Pre-test	11	7 (63.6%)	3	4
Visit 1 Abroad	7	4 (57.1%)	2	2
Oral interview				
Pre-test	6	2 (33.3%)	0	2
Visit 1 Abroad	9	3 (33.3%)	2	1

Note: For the argumentative writing task, the subject was 'Gay rights' for the pre-test and 'Marijuana' for Visit 1 Abroad.

Table 9.3 Use of subjunctive by high group learners (*n* = 10)

		Target-like suppliance of subjunctive		
Task	All subjunctive contexts	Total target-like production in subjunctive contexts	Identical indicative	Unique subjunctive
Argumentative writing				
Pre-test	12	7 (58.3%)	0	7
Visit 1 Abroad	8	6 (75%)	1	5
Oral interview				
Pre-test	20	12 (60%)	10	2
Visit 1 Abroad	18	16 (88.8%)	7	9

Note: For the argumentative writing task, the subject was 'Gay rights' for the pre-test and 'Marijuana' for Visit 1 Abroad.

Table 9.4 Use of subjunctive by French native speakers control group (n = 10)

Task	All subjunctive contexts	Target-like suppliance of subjunctive		
		Total target-like production in subjunctive contexts	Identical indicative	Unique subjunctive
Argumentative writing				
Gay rights	11	10 (90.9%)	8	2
Marijuana	8	7 (87.5%)	3	4
Oral interview	8	7 (87.5%)	3	4

In total, 91 subjunctive contexts were identified in the learner data, 33 in the low group and 58 in the high group. The native speakers produced 27 subjunctive contexts. Frequency differences between low and high learner groups are not evident in the argumentative writing task, but only in the oral interview, both at the Pre-test and at Visit 1 Abroad. The results in Tables 9.2 to 9.4 also show that a subjunctive context was not produced by every participant. For example, in the oral interview, low group learners (n = 13) produce only six subjunctive contexts at the Pre-test and then nine at Visit 1. Also, despite a seemingly higher number of subjunctive productions in the advanced group's interviews, the 20 contexts were produced by eight (out of the 10) high group learners at the Pre-test, whereas only four learners were responsible for producing the 18 contexts provided at Visit 1.

Considering the frequency information just provided, the results presented in Tables 9.2 to 9.4 are largely exploratory. Nonetheless, noteworthy patterns emerge. In particular, the high group's target-like suppliance in writing is proportionally higher than the low group's at Visit 1 Abroad. On the oral interview, on the other hand, the high group's target-like suppliance started higher and increased over time, whereas the low group showed no improvement from the Pre-test to Visit 1 Abroad.

A syntactic analysis of subjunctive use in the elicited production tasks was also carried out to investigate the range of subjunctive triggers produced in the different syntactic contexts (affirmatives, adverbials and negation). Tables 9.5 and 9.6 show that across writing and speaking the most frequently used subjunctive triggers are found in affirmative constructions (e.g. *je veux que...* 'I want that...') and the least frequent triggers are in negative constructions (e.g. *je ne suis pas sûr que...* 'I am not sure that...'). A type/token analysis of subjunctive use additionally reveals that the most frequent subjunctive triggers in speaking are *falloir que* ('be necessary that') and *vouloir que* ('want that') (see Table 9.6a,b). However, in writing, it appears that across the groups more adverbial and negative constructions are used than in speaking (see Table 9.5a,b).

Table 9.5a Subjunctive triggers used in writing by group and time (affirmative contexts)

Group	Affirmative contexts										
	Falloir que	Être probable que	Être possible que	Sembler que	Être nécessaire que	Être dommage que	Être important que	Le fait que	Dire que	Demander que	Vouloir que
Low											
Gay rights	2	–	2	2	1	–	1	–	–	–	–
Marijuana	1	–	–	–	–	–	–	–	–	1	1
High											
Gay rights	–	1	1	–	–	1	5	–	–	–	–
Marijuana	1	1	1	–	–	–	–	–	1	–	1
Control											
Gay rights	–	–	1	–	2	–	–	2	–	–	–
Marijuana	–	–	1	–	–	–	–	–	–	–	1

Note: The subject was 'Gay rights' for the Pre-test and 'Marijuana' for Visit 1 Abroad; *falloir que* ('necessary that'), *être probable que* ('be probable that'), *être possible que* ('be possible that'), *sembler que* ('seem that'), *être ncessaire que* ('be necessary that'), *être dommage que* ('be a shame that'), *être important que* ('be important that'), *le fait que* ('the fact that'), *dire que* ('say that'), *demander que* ('ask that'), *vouloir que* ('want that').

Table 9.5b Subjunctive triggers used in writing by group and time (adverbial and negative contexts)

	Adverbial contexts						Negative contexts					
Group	Bien que	Pour que	A condition que	Autant que	Quoique	Sans que	Ne pas penser que	Ne pas comprendre que	Ne pas impliquer que	Ne pas être sûr que	Total tokens	Total types
Low												
Gay rights	2	–	–	–	–	–	1	–	–	–	11	6
Marijuana	2	–	–	1	–	–	1	–	–	–	7	6
High												
Gay rights	2	2	–	–	–	–	–	–	–	–	12	7
Marijuana	1	1	–	–	1	–	–	–	–	1	8	8
Control												
Gay rights	1	1	1	–	–	–	–	1	2	–	11	7
Marijuana	2	–	–	–	–	1	3	–	–	–	8	15

Notes: The subject was 'Gay rights' for the Pre-test and 'Marijuana' for Visit 1 Abroad; *bien que* ('although'), *pour que* ('so that'), *à condition que* ('provided that'), *autant que* ('as much as'), *quoi que* ('although'), *sans que* ('unless'), *ne pas penser que* ('not think that'), *ne pas comprendre que* ('not understand that'), *ne pas impliquer que* ('not imply that'), *ne pas être sûr que* ('not sure that'). The columns Total tokens and Total types present results for all subjunctive forms in writing (affirmative, adverbial and negative contexts, combined).

Table 9.6a Subjunctive triggers used in the oral interviews by group and time (affirmative contexts)

Affirmative contexts

Group	Falloir que	Vouloir que	Préférer que	Être important que	Être possible que	Être content que	Avoir peur que	Souhaiter que	Le fait que	Dire que	Le problème que
Low											
Pre-test	2	1	–	–	–	–	–	–	–	–	–
Visit 1	1	4	1	–	–	–	–	–	–	–	–
High											
Pre-test	4	8	1	1	1	–	1	–	–	–	–
Visit 1	13	1	–	–	–	3	–	1	–	–	–
Control	2	1	–	–	–	–	–	–	2	1	1

Note: Falloir que ('necessary that'), *vouloir que* ('want that'), *préférer que* ('prefer that'), *être important que* ('be important that'), *être possible que* ('be possible that'), *être content que* ('be happy that'), *avoir peur que* ('be scared that'), *souhaiter que* ('wish that'), *le fait que* ('the fact that'), *dire que* ('say that'), *le problme que* ('the problem that').

Table 9.6b Subjunctive triggers used in the oral interviews by group and time (Adverbial and negative contexts)

Group	Adverbial contexts			Negative contexts		Total tokens	Total types
	Bien que	Avant que	Pour que	Ne pas penser que	Ne pas être sûr que		
Low							
Pre-test	1	–	1	1	–	6	5
Visit 1	–	1	1	–	–	9	6
High							
Pre-test	2	–	–	2	1	20	8
Visit 1	–	–	–	–	–	18	4
Control	–	–	1	–	–	8	5

Note: *Bien que* ('although'), *avant que* ('before'), *pour que* ('so that'), *ne pas penser que* ('not think that'), *ne pas être sûr que* ('not sure that'). The columns Total tokens and Total types present results for all subjunctive forms in oral interviews (affirmative, adverbial and negative contexts, combined).

Timed grammaticality judgment task

Our second research question investigated whether differences in L2 proficiency and local syntactic context affect learners' knowledge of the French subjunctive as measured using the timed GJT. Table 9.7 displays descriptive statistics by group for overall scores on this task.

To investigate whether there are effects of proficiency and local syntactic context (i.e. affirmatives, adverbials, negatives) on subjunctive knowledge, participants' accuracy scores for each syntactic context were compared. Figure 9.1 displays learners' performance on the GJT, with results presented by group and local syntactic context.

As Figure 9.1 illustrates, low group learners consistently performed less accurately overall than high group learners on the GJT, i.e. across all syntactic contexts. This same observation is also found for the differences between high group learners and native speakers. To test whether these differences were statistically significant, a mixed between–within subjects analysis of

Table 9.7 Descriptive statistics for the GJT

Group	Mean ($k = 24$)	SD	Score range
Low group ($n = 13$)	12.92	4.07	7–19
High group ($n = 10$)	16.70	3.06	12–21
Native speaker control ($n = 10$)	22.4	1.3	21–24

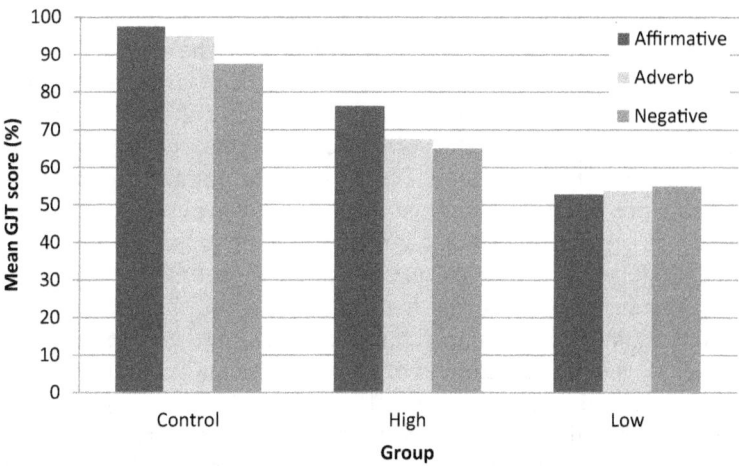

Figure 9.1 Participants' mean scores (in percent) on the GJT analyzed according to local syntactic context

variance (ANOVA) was carried out with syntactic context as the within-groups factor (affirmatives, adverbials and negation) and group as a three-level between-groups factor. A significant main effect was found for group only ($F[2, 30] = 25.643$, $p = 0.000$, partial $\eta^2 = 0.63$). No significant main effect was found for local syntactic context (Wilks' lambda = 0.930, $F[2, 29] = 1.088$, $p > 0.05$, partial $\eta^2 = 0.07$), nor was an interaction effect found between syntax and group (Wilks' lambda = 0.918, $F[4, 58] = 0.637$, $p > 0.05$, partial $\eta^2 = 0.04$). These results demonstrate that scores on the GJT differed by proficiency level only. The various local syntactic contexts of the subjunctive did not have a statistically significant influence on learners' scores.

Discussion

The goal of this study was to investigate the effects of oral L2 proficiency and local syntactic context on the acquisition of the subjunctive in French L2, using two different elicited production tasks, one spoken and one written, and a timed GJT. In line with Bartning's (forthcoming) and Howard's (2008) findings, very few tokens of the subjunctive were found in elicited production, and this was also true for our French native speaker group (see also O'Connor DiVito, 1997).

Research question 1 investigated whether there were differences in subjunctive use by proficiency level and local syntactic context in an argumentative essay and an oral interview. It was predicted that if L2 proficiency influences the acquisition of the subjunctive, performance differences between learners of different proficiencies would be expected. This hypothesis was generally confirmed. Despite the general infrequency of subjunctive contexts in the elicited production tasks, the high group produced more subjunctive contexts and tokens in the oral interview compared to the low group. The results also show that the high group (with scores ranging from 58.3% to 88.8%) was more accurate in terms of target-like suppliance of the subjunctive than the low group (33.3% to 63.6%). However, as previously noted, a large number of subjunctive tokens were mainly produced by a limited number of participants (i.e. not the whole group), therefore any claims drawn solely from the production data are tentative. With respect to the role of local syntactic context on subjunctive use, the limited number of tokens again makes it difficult to conclude whether this factor significantly affected learners' production. The elicited production results showed that learners' most frequent use of the subjunctive was with affirmatives, followed by adverbials and negatives, but differences between the three are small. There is some indication that native speakers use the subjunctive more frequently in writing than in speech; that is, they are sensitive to genre in respect of production of subjunctive triggers/subjunctive forms. There is no indication that the learners in either group show genre sensitivity.

Research question 2 investigated the effect of proficiency and local syntactic context on learners' knowledge of the French subjunctive, using results from a timed GJT. It was hypothesized that if differences in the subjunctive's local syntactic context influence the acquisition of the French subjunctive, performance differences between different syntactic contexts (affirmatives, adverbials, negatives) would be expected. This hypothesis was not confirmed. No main effect was found for local syntactic context (i.e. affirmatives, adverbials, negatives), but there was a significant main effect for proficiency level. Furthermore, no interaction effect was found between syntax and group. These results suggest that performance on the timed GJT was not influenced by the subjunctive's local syntactic context, but rather by overall levels of oral L2 proficiency.

Taken together, proficiency level appears to account better for knowledge of the French subjunctive (as measured by performance on the GJT) than local syntactic context. As noted, previous research on this form has documented use, finding that in spoken French certain subjunctive triggers appear to be used more frequently than others (e.g. *falloir que*). However, the findings from Bartning (forthcoming) and Howard (2008) on subjunctive use are based on a combined total of 35 tokens from a small sample of participants. The present study's findings suggest that when learners are tested on a range of different subjunctive triggers in different local syntactic contexts, a somewhat different picture emerges: the subjunctive's local syntactic context does not influence performance, but proficiency level does. As a result, the present study demonstrates how triangulating different data collection techniques can contribute to obtaining a more reliable sample of learners' performance potential. This kind of triangulation is particularly relevant when investigating aspects of language that not only are infrequent in the input, but are also morphologically and phonologically variable in production, as is the case with the French subjunctive. By designing a GJT using verbs that were unambiguously subjunctive (i.e. showing morpho-phonological differences between subjunctive and indicative), we were able both to work with a larger sample of data and draw conclusions on clearly identifiable subjunctive forms. This research design, in particular, allowed us to examine both more and less frequent subjunctive forms (as documented by O'Connor DiVito, 1997), such as *soit* versus *finisse*, as well as both frequent and infrequent triggers, such as *falloir que* ('necessary that') versus *souhaiter que* ('wish that').

We would also like to emphasize that the learners who participated in this study came from the same institutional level (end of year two/start of year three of university French), yet when separated into different groups using an independent measure of oral proficiency, differences in their knowledge and use of the French subjunctive were found, thus reinforcing the view that the subjunctive is late-acquired and still developing among this relatively advanced group. This finding highlights the importance of using independent measures of proficiency in SLA research, a stance also advocated by numerous contributions to the current volume, including those by Leclercq and Edmonds, Tracy-Ventura *et al.*, Ankerstein, Gertken *et al.* and Callies *et al.*

Although this study has revealed important factors in the acquisition of the French subjunctive, further research on the influence of both proficiency and syntax is required. First, although our learners' L2 oral proficiency was independently measured, the numbers in each group were fairly low (10 in the high group and 13 in the low group), and replication with larger numbers is desirable. Further research on subjunctive triggers exhibiting optionality is also required to be able to verify the present study's findings. Particular attention should be paid to question and negative constructions. Additionally, this study only investigated the effect of local syntactic context on knowledge and use of French subjunctive, but studies on the Spanish subjunctive, in particular, (see Gudmestad, 2012) have suggested that the semantics of the trigger may also play a role. Future research is required to substantiate the present study's findings and also to investigate how semantics influences learners' use of the French subjunctive.

Conclusions

The goal of this study was to test the effects of proficiency level and syntactic context on the acquisition of the subjunctive in French L2 using two different elicited production tasks and a timed GJT. Overall, our findings suggest that the French subjunctive is indeed relatively late acquired. Our two groups of advanced university learners were still in the process of acquiring it, their usage was less accurate than that of the native speaker group, and even the 'high' group was not using the subjunctive in the range of contexts used by native speakers. Second, our findings suggest that the acquisition of the subjunctive reflects the general development of L2 oral proficiency, while no significant main effects on performance were found for differences in local syntactic context (affirmatives, adverbials, negatives).

In terms of a contribution to the assessment of language proficiency, this study therefore suggests that the use of a range of subjunctive contexts and accurate subjunctive use in elicited production can be taken as a positive indicator of advanced proficiency. However, to assess adequately learners' mastery of this particular domain of morphosyntax, focussed tests will continue to be required. In terms of a contribution to research methodology, this study has also demonstrated that triangulating different data-collection techniques is especially beneficial for forms that are infrequent in spontaneous speech (such as the subjunctive). The use of a GJT not only takes into consideration that the form may be infrequent in a speech sample, but it also allows knowledge of the subjunctive to be properly assessed by using forms that are clearly subjunctive.

Acknowledgments

This study is supported by the UK Economic and Social Research Council (ESRC; research grant RES-062-23-2996) and is part of the Languages and Social Networks Abroad Project (LANGSNAP). We would like to thank all the people involved in the project, including fieldworkers and transcribers, and in particular the learners who kindly agreed to participate in the study. We are also grateful to two anonymous reviewers for their useful comments and suggestions for improvement.

References

Abouda, L. (2002) Negation, interrogation et alternance indicatif-subjonctif. *Journal of French Language Studies* 12, 1–22.
Ayoun, D. (2005) The acquisition of tense and aspect in L2 French from a universal Grammar perspective. In D. Ayoun and M.R. Salaberry (eds) *Tense and Aspect in Romance Languages* (pp. 79–127). Amsterdam: John Benjamins.
Bartning, I. (2009) The advanced learner variety: Ten years later. In E. Labeau and F. Myles (eds) *The Advanced Learner Varieties: The Case of French* (pp. 11–40). Bern: Peter Lang.
Bartning, I. (forthcoming) Late morphosyntactic features in very advanced L2 French – a view towards the end state. In S. Habberzettl (ed.) *The End State of L2 Acquisition*. Berlin: Mouton de Gruyter.
Bartning, I. and Schlyter, S. (2004) Itinéraires acquisitionnels et stades de développement en français L2. *Journal of French Language Studies* 14, 281–299.

Bartning, I., Forsberg Lundell, F. and Hancock, V. (2009) Resources and obstacles in very advanced L2 French: Formulaic language, information structure and morphosyntax. In L. Roberts, D. Véronique, A. Nilsson and M. Tellier (eds) *EUROSLA Yearbook 9* (pp. 185–211). Amsterdam: John Benjamins.

Bartning, I., Forsberg Lundell, F. and Hancock, V. (2012) On the role of linguistic contextual factors for morphosyntactic stabilization in high-level L2 French. *Studies in Second Language Acquisition* 34, 243–267.

Bassano, D. and Mendes-Maillochon, I. (1994) Early grammatical and prosodic marking of utterance modality in French: A longitudinal study. *Journal of Child Language* 21, 649–675.

Biber, D., Davis, M., Jones, J.K. and Tracy-Ventura, N. (2006) Spoken and written register variation in Spanish: A multi-dimensional analysis. *Corpora* 1 (1), 1–37.

Butt, J. and Benjamin, C. (2000) *A New Reference Grammar of Modern Spanish*. London: Arnold.

Chaudron, C. (2003) Data collection in SLA research. In C.J. Doughty and M.H. Long (eds) *The Handbook of Second Language Acquisition* (pp. 762–828). Oxford: Blackwell.

Coates, J. (1980) *The Semantics of the Modal Auxiliaries*. London: Croom Helm.

Collentine, J. (1995) The development of complex syntax and mood-selection abilities by intermediate-level learners of Spanish. *Hispania* 78 (1), 122–135.

Collentine, J. (2010) The acquisition and teaching of the Spanish subjunctive. An update on current findings. *Hispania* 93 (1), 39–51.

Davies, M. (2002) Un corpus anotado de 100.000.000 palabras del español histórico y moderno. *Sociedad Española para el Procesamiento del Lenguaje Natural*, 21–27.

Frontier, A. (1997) *La grammaire du français*. Paris: Editions Belin.

Gudmestad, A. (2012) Acquiing a variable structure: An interlanguage analysis of second-language mood use in Spanish. *Language Learning* 62, 373–402.

Hawkins, R. and Towell, R. (2010) *French Grammar and Usage*. London: Hodder Education.

Howard, M. (2005) Les contextes prototypiques et marqués de l'emploi de l'imparfait par l'apprenant du français langue étrangère. In E. Labeau and P. Larrivée (eds) *Nouveaux développements de l'imparfait*. (pp. 175–197). New York: Rodopi.

Howard, M. (2008) Morpho-syntactic development in the expression of modality: The subjunctive in French L2 acquisition. *Canadian Journal of Applied Linguistics* 11 (3), 171–192.

Isabelli, C.A. and Nishida, C. (2005) Development of the Spanish subjunctive in a nine-month study – abroad setting. In D. Eddington (ed.) *Selected Proceedings of the 6th Conference on the Acquisition of Spanish and Portuguese as First and Second Languages* (pp. 78–91), Somerville, MA: Cascadilla Proceedings Project.

Judge, A. and Healey, F.G. (1983) *A Reference Grammar of Modern French*. London: Edward Arnold.

L'Huillier, M. (1999) *Advanced French Grammar*. Cambridge: Cambridge University Press.

Labeau, E. (2005) *Beyond the Aspect Hypothesis: Tense-Aspect Development in Advanced L2 French*. Berlin: Peter Lang.

Lang, M. and Perez, I. (1996) *Modern French Grammar: A Practical Guide*. New York: Routledge.

MacWhinney, B. (2000) *The CHILDES project: Tools for analyzing talk – Electronic edition. Part 1: The CHAT transcription format*. See http://childes.psy.cmu.edu/ (accessed 18 September 2012).

McManus, K. (2013) Prototypical influence in second language acquisition: What now for the Aspect Hypothesis? *International Review of Applied Linguistics in Teaching* 51 (3), 299–322.

O'Connor DiVito, N. (1997) *Patterns across Spoken and Written French: Empirical Research on the Interaction among Forms, Functions and Genres*. Boston, MA: Houghton Mifflin.

Poplack, S. (1992) The inherent variability of the French subjunctive. In C. Lauefer and T. Morgan (eds) *Theoretical Studies in Romance Linguistics* (pp. 235–263). Amsterdam: John Benjamins.

Poplack, S. (2001) Variability, frequency and productivity in the irrealis domain of French. In J. Bybee and P. Hopper (eds) *Frequency Effects and Emergent Grammar* (pp. 405–428). Amsterdam: John Benjamins.

Rowlett, P. (2007) *The Syntax of French*. Cambridge: Cambridge University Press.

Tremblay, A. (2011). Proficiency assessment standrds in second language acquisition research: 'Clozing' the gap. *Studies in Second Language Acquisition* 33, 339–372.

Tremblay, A. and Garrison, M.D. (2010) Cloze tests: A tool for proficiency assessment in research on French L2. In M.T. Prior, Y. Watanabe and S.-K. Lee (eds) *Selected Proceedings of the 2008 Second Language Research Forum: Exploring SLA Perspectives, Positions and Practices* (pp. 73–88). Somerville, MA: Cascadilla Proceedings Project.

Appendix 9A

Table 9.1A Test items used in the GJT

Items	Grammaticality	Items	Grammaticality
Adverbial		**Affirmative**	
Amandine est heureuse jusqu'à ce que ses amies vont au cinéma 'Amandine is happy until her friends go to the cinema'	U	*Elle veut que son ami finit ses devoirs tôt* 'She wants her friend to finish her homework early'	U
Bien qu'il a souvent raison, cette fois il se trompe 'Although he is often right, this time he is mistaken'	U	*Il est douteux que ma sœur fait ses courses aujourd'hui* 'It is doubtful that my sister will go shopping today'	U
Bien que Luc sache épeler mon nom, je vais l'écrire 'Although Luc knows how to spell my name, I'm going to write it'	G	*Il est possible que nous rentrions à Marseille* 'It is possible that we are going back to Marseille'	G
Le prisonnier a été exécuté avant que l'avocat ait prouvé son innocence 'The prisoner was executed before the lawyer proved his innocence'	G	*Il faut qu'on fait des courses ce soir* 'It is necessary that we go shopping tonight'	U
Le professeur mange une pomme avant que nous arrivons en classe 'The teacher eats an apple before we arrive in class'	U	*Il faut que vous ayez la monnaie exacte* 'It is necessary that you have the correct change'	G
Pierre a persisté jusqu'à ce qu'elle sorte avec lui 'Pierre persisted until she went out with him'	G	*Je doute que tu sois heureux* 'I doubt that you are happy'	G

(Continued)

Table 9.1A (Continued)

Items	Grammaticality	Items	Grammaticality
Prends tes baskets pour que nous puissions jouer au foot! 'Take you trainers so that we can play football!'	G	*Le professeur souhaite que Jacques finisse ses devoirs avant les cours de grammaire* 'The teacher wishes that Jacques would finish his homework before the grammar classes'	G
Trouve la gare pour qu'ils peuvent aller à Londres! 'Find the station so that we can go to London!'	U	*On veut que tu réussisses* 'We want you to succeed'	G
Negative			
Christophe n'accepte pas que vous arriviez en retard 'Christophe does not accept that you arrive late'	G		
Il n'aime pas que tu sais parler français 'He does not like that you can speak French'	U		
Il n'est pas certain que nous avons la clé 'It is not certain that we have the key'	U		
Je n'ai pas besoin qu'il vienne 'I do not need that he come'	G		
Je ne demande pas que vous achetez deux voitures 'I am not asking that you buy two cars'	U		
Je ne pense pas que Jeannette est contente 'I do not think that Jeanette is happy'	U		
Je ne pense pas que vous puissiez arriver à 6h 'I do not think that you can arrive before six o'clock'	G		
Je ne suis pas sûr que tu es patient 'I am not sure that you are patient'	U		

Note: G = grammatical, U = ungrammatical.

10 Testing L2 Listening Proficiency: Reviewing Standardized Tests Within a Competence-Based Framework

Naouel Zoghlami

Introduction

Testing second language (L2) proficiency is a fundamental part of teaching, because it informs instructional programs and very often delineates the starting point for describing students' profiles in terms of language levels, competence and needs. Although language ability, or a learner's level of linguistic and communicative competence, has been defined variously in the literature, there is a consensus to include listening as a major component of language competence (e.g. Prince, this volume, agrees that listening is an important part of language competence and provides an example of classroom-based assessment of the listening component). We spend a large amount of our communication time (45%) performing this skill (Feyten, 1991). Moreover, language acquisition/learning is based on listening, and the development of this skill is highly correlated with progress in other skills (Dunkel, 1991; Rost, 2002; Vandergrift, 2004). The majority of standardized language tests today include a listening section, illustrating the importance of this component. Standardized tests generally cover academic goals, and compete with each other commercially. They are published tests that have been submitted to cautious and expert preparation, and have undergone detailed statistical analysis to estimate and guarantee their validity and reliability. A test is valid when it really measures what it claims to measure and it is considered reliable when it produces similar results over time and under consistent conditions. Thus, while reliability refers to the overall consistency of a measure, validity concerns the degree to which test scores can be accurately interpreted in relation to the proposed uses of the tests.

When it comes to selecting a listening test, teachers and researchers need solid criteria upon which to base their choice. Choosing which test to administer is not simple and straightforward: apart from the price and length of the test, aspects related to test purpose, content and procedure need to be taken into consideration. This chapter claims that high-quality testing needs to be theory-driven and seeks to acquaint readers with relevant issues that must be considered prior to testing. It also attempts to contribute to the field of listening assessment by incorporating the competence-based model initially proposed by Buck (2001), which has not been taken up by all testing researchers, and which we develop further here. Within this competence-based framework, the listening segments of two specific off-line norm-referenced measures of English ability are analyzed and evaluated in order to determine the degree to which these two tests, the *Oxford Placement Test* (OPT) and the *First Certificate in English* (FCE), might function as predictors of overall English listening proficiency. Before starting test analysis, a definition of the listening construct and a description of the competence model are provided.

The Nature of L2 Listening Proficiency: Defining the Construct

Hulstijn (2011), among many other researchers, stresses the fact that we should be very specific about what we mean by 'language proficiency' and that we need to formulate a clear construct. This was also stated in 1993 by Dunkel and colleagues, who explained that '[p]rior to designing and utilizing a possible framework for the assessment of L2 listening comprehension proficiency, we must first attempt to understand and articulate the nature of the listening comprehension construct so that we have a clear understanding of what it is that we are attempting to assess' (Dunkel *et al.*, 1993: 181). It follows that understanding what constitutes listening proficiency in an L2 is necessary prior to testing. However, the fact that the listening process is quite complex and not directly observable, coupled with the temporal nature of listening and the different variables involved in listening ability, make it arguably the most difficult skill not only to develop for some language learners, as reported by Graham (2003, 2006) and Grosjean and Frauenfelder (1997), but also to define (Wagner, 2004). A final clear-cut definition of what constitutes L2 listening competence has not yet been formulated. In the literature, however, the necessity of specifying the construct has been emphasized and several descriptive attempts have been provided.

Wipf (1984) described listening as the skill of discriminating between sounds, understanding vocabulary and grammar, interpreting text stress and intonation and relating this to the wide sociocultural context of the discourse. However, listening is more complex than simply paying attention to and perceiving speech sounds and assigning meaning to that linguistic input. Listening is an active multifaceted process that involves the activation of linguistic, pragmatic and psycholinguistic processes. Coakley and Wolvin (1986), for example, describe listening as ongoing interactive communication processes occurring inside the listener. The listener, in fact, plays a significant role in understanding spoken language. Meaning is not in the text but rather has to be constructed by the listener; its construction involves both pragmatic and psycholinguistic processes. Listening research describes comprehension as an inferential process, where listeners' linguistic, world and strategic knowledge interact to create mental representations and interpretations of the aural input (Anderson & Lynch, 1988; Buck, 2001; Hulstijn, 2003; O'Malley et al., 1989; Rost, 1991, 2002; Taylor & Geranpayeh, 2011).

When it comes to testing, the construction of meaning is all the more complex because it will be influenced by variables related to the setting and demands of the test experience (answer type, time constraints and additional stress), and the often decontextualized nature of the task. The construct of listening that is being tested is determined by the identification of both the target language use situation and the purpose of the test (Buck, 2001). Theoretical perspectives on the listening process have inspired test designers in developing L2 listening constructs in assessment such as Buck (2001) with his default listening framework, Wagner (2002) with his explicit–implicit model created for video listening, and more recently Xiaoxian and Yan (2010) with their interactive listening model and Taylor and Geranpayeh (2011) with their socio-cognitive construct for academic listening. In the assessment field, there seems to be no consensus on a unified model. What these constructs show, however, is that there are interacting processes underlying L2 listening comprehension. Because the focus in this chapter is on standardized proficiency tests of general listening ability, test-users are urged first to define what the components of listening are for them, identify the features inherent in the published tests, then operationalize and convert them into real sets of test items (Buck, 2001). This is quite a complicated mission, as test-users are often teachers with little training on testing and what it entails, and with limited time for test design. It is therefore probably more efficient to adopt the opposite approach: to start from the tests available, identify the language theory and listening processes implicit in the techniques used in the tests, and match them to the construct to be measured. A legitimate question then arises: 'On what listening construct is a given test based?' This is what we seek to investigate in this study, for two well-known and widely available instruments, the OPT and the *First Certificate Listening* paper.

The Competence-based framework

One way to define what is being assessed is to identify the underlying competencies the testees should possess. Chapelle (1998) refers to this as the *trait* perspective of construct-definition, which she opposes to the behaviorist and interactionalist definitions. A person's performance on a test is the reflection of his competence, i.e. certain knowledge, skills and abilities that he would show across different tasks and contexts. This echoes previous attempts to describe comprehensively what encompasses L2 listening ability. A few researchers saw in the development of skill taxonomies the solution to the difficult task of defining listening competence (Lund, 1990; Peterson, 1991; Richards, 1983; Weir, 1993). Although these taxonomies have been criticized with regard to their validity in testing (Buck, 2001), their usefulness in defining and operationalizing listening constructs cannot and should not be overlooked, as they offer a possibility for researchers to fill the gaps in L2 listening model operationalization. Recent assessment approaches (e.g. the communicative approach) have put emphasis on the kind of ability that reveals effective language use instead of 'mere' linguistic knowledge. Buck (2001) was the first to offer a definite framework for describing the competence-based listening construct, in which listening ability is based on aspects of linguistic and strategic competence that support automatic language processing. However, to our knowledge, this framework has not been used in the literature on listening assessment. Given the wide variety of testing situations and uses (education, certification, research), standardized listening tests should be based on a competence model for describing listening ability that incorporates basic skills and strategies. For the purposes of the present test review, this comprehensive listening framework constituted the starting point for the operationalization of the listening model we propose here. Our model is depicted in Figure 10.1

An L2 listener's competence encompasses linguistic, pragmatic and strategic competence; however, it is almost impossible to disconnect language knowledge from cognitive abilities, even in L2 processing. The L2 listener would bring to the listening task a whole set of knowledge and executive resources that also reflect the social dimensions of language use. All of these processes are inter-related and executed concurrently. Consequently, and following Buck's (2001) recommendations, a broad communicative competence description of listening comprehension ability is proposed in this study. The outcome of this linguistic and strategic processing would be that listeners exhibit the following basic skills or behaviors.

(1) Basic skills or behaviors exhibited by listeners:
    - to perceive and discriminate sounds and words;
    - to identify and distinguish minor and major elements in discourse;
    - to recognize details (unknown vocabulary, numbers, names, etc.);

Testing L2 Listening Proficiency   195

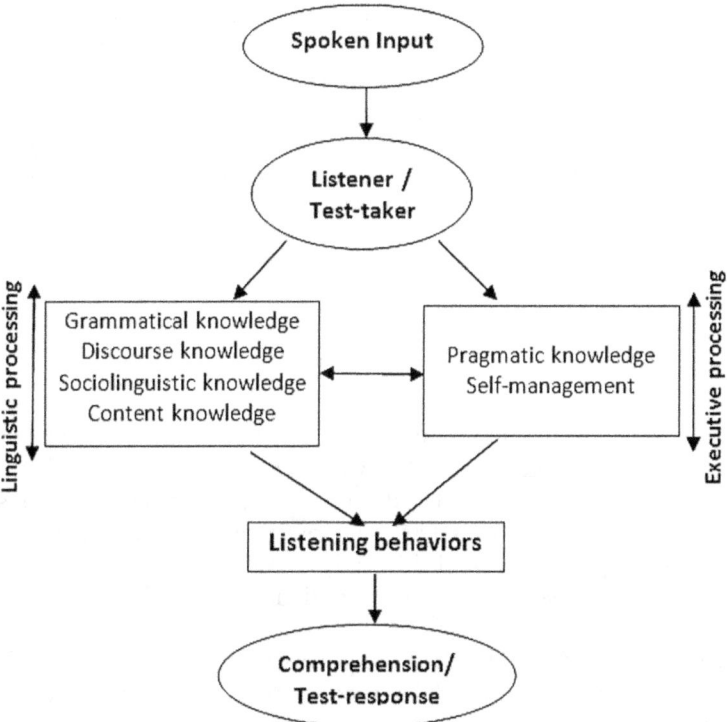

Figure 10.1 A competence L2 listening comprehension ability model (inspired by Buck, 2001 and Weir, 2005)

- to understand and discriminate between literal and implied meanings;
- to make suitable inferences about participants, attitudes and situations;
- to build content-based meanings;
- to use background knowledge to form suitable interpretations;
- to deduce possible discourse outcomes;
- to apply any compensatory strategy for discourse comprehension;
- to engage in ongoing monitoring of one's own listening;
- to evaluate one's own effectiveness in the performance of the task.

This list is definitely not an exhaustive one. These abilities are however, from our perspective, the main components of listening comprehension, taking into account both 1980s communicative-based and more formal psycholinguistically validated aspects of listening. Test developers no longer focus on testing knowledge of the language system (such as its phonetics), but rather on testing the ability to use the target language (Geranpayeh & Taylor, 2008). We agree with Buck (2001) that this framework should only have a guiding role, leaving test developers with some degree of freedom in defining those elements of listening comprehension that would correspond to their particular testing purpose and context. Although in other frameworks, such as those that are task-based, the default and the socio-cognitive models (Buck, 2001; Taylor & Geranpayeh, 2011) have been proposed, we feel that the present competence model is broad enough to suit most of those interested in testing listening, whether for academic or research purposes. This framework can be very useful not only in validating but also in evaluating commercially available L2 listening tests. It provides a systematic tool with which we can measure the appropriateness of the activities of a certain test in a certain context.

The Study

The goal of the present study was to compare the listening segments of two commercialized measures of English ability within a competence-based framework, and to investigate the degree to which these listening tests can function as predictors of overall listening proficiency in the French context. More specifically, the interest of this study is to ally qualitative and quantitative analyses to answer two research questions:

(2) *Research question 1*: What listening construct(s) do the OPT and FCE standardized tests assess? i.e. what particular listening abilities are reflected in these tests?
Research question 2: Which construct, and therefore which test, best reflects the competence-based model?

Procedure and analysis

The study took place in the English department of the Université de Savoie in Chambéry, France. The participants ($n = 110$) were French-speaking students learning English as an L2 at university level. Their average age was 18.5 years. The informants were enrolled in the first year of a language program (Langues Etrangères Appliquées, LEA), leading to a BA in Applied Foreign Languages. The OPT was administered to the students, followed by the FCE, as well as other tests and questionnaires as part of a larger study conducted to investigate the listening comprehension problems encountered by French learners of English. The listening tests took approximately 50 mins, and were administered collectively, in a pencil-and-paper format.

As the main purpose of this study was to evaluate the effectiveness of these two standardized tests of listening proficiency, descriptive and inferential statistical measures were conducted using SPSS version 17. On each of the tests, the extent to which listening scores were normally distributed was estimated through the mean, standard deviation, kurtosis, skewness and standard error values. These were calculated with and without outliers in order to check the effect of extreme scores on the distributions. In fact, because these two standardized proficiency tests are norm-referenced, they 'should produce scores which fall into a normal distribution' (Brown, 2005: 5). Cronbach's alpha, the index of reliability, was measured for the OPT, the FCE and subsections of FCE listening. An analysis of the correlation coefficients between scores was undertaken to test the hypothesis that a student obtaining a high score on the OPT would obtain a high score in FCE (as both tests claim to assess global listening proficiency). A factor analysis was conducted to account for the statistical correlations between scores and their underlying explanations/factors.

Test descriptions

The present study deals with the listening sections of the OPT and the FCE listening paper. An overview of the test batteries from which these are extracted indicates the place and importance attributed to the listening skill in these instruments. It also points to the view of language underlying the tests. Table 10.1 presents a brief summary and description of the contents of these tests in their complete version.

OPT listening

The OPT was developed by Dave Allan and first published by Oxford University Press in 1992; a later version, published in 2004, was used in this study. The OPT was designed as a placement instrument but it is also widely used as a general ability test in academic and research contexts (Ahmadi et al., 2012; Brooke et al., 2012; Morell Moll, 1999; Tahriri & Yamin, 2010). It includes two sections: a grammar test and a listening test assessing 'language skills as well as knowledge of English as language system' (Allan, 2004: 1). The listening part (10 mins) does not display any variety in format (only one type of question). It involves 100 short isolated sentences that present discursively contextualized minimal pairs. According to Buck (2001), this phoneme discrimination task is a special technique for assessing knowledge of the sound system of the L2 where the testee has to discriminate two items that differ by one phoneme. Here are three examples from the test:

(3) 'I gather you've been having trouble with your *earring / hearing*'
    'You can get quite a *view / few* from up here'
    'I've just heard that these tests have been *pirated / piloted* in Japan'

The sentences are taken from a synthesis of authentic instances of 'slips of the ear' or mishearing and are spoken by different native speakers, men and women having the British Received Pronunciation (RP) accent. Allan (2004: 2) asserts that the sentences were carefully selected as representing concrete examples of the 'adaptation to a test format of actual situations

Table 10.1 Description of two standardized English language tests (based on Allan, 2004, and UCLES, 2008)

Test	Test focus	Audience	Time	Subtests/subparts
OPT General	To establish a rank order for placement and other purposes	Learners at all levels	70 min	Two parts: grammar, listening
Listening	To test reading, listening and vocabulary size		10 min	100 sentences containing minimal pairs
FCE General	To assess general ability in English	Learners at upper-intermediate level	4 h 30 min	Five parts: reading, writing, use of English, listening, speaking
Listening	To assess understanding of detail and gist, and deduction of meaning		40 min	Four parts/30 questions: multiple choice, sentence completion, multiple matching, true/false

Note: The OPT is published by Oxford University Press (2004); the FCE by ESOL Examinations, University of Cambridge (2007).

when a non-native speaker's listening skills proved to be inadequate, and so caused a failure of communication or resulted in the transmission of the wrong meaning'. Despite the unique question format of the test, the items are quite varied: some show common sound confusion, such as between /l/ and /r/, /t/ and /d/ or /f/ and /v/, while others require thorough knowledge of stress and lexical segmentation as in 'personal / personnel' and 'holiday / horrid day'. The sentences are played only once and at a normal speaking speed. Before the actual test begins, three examples are provided to clarify the test procedure and scheme. The author of the OPT claims that all the items were piloted on several groups of natives and the item reliability was high across these groups. He also maintains that the OPT has recently been calibrated with the *Common European Framework of Reference* (CEFR), and hence can be accurately correlated to various international L2 examinations including TOEFL, TOEIC, IELTS and Cambridge ESOL.

FCE listening

The FCE, in its complete form, is one of the most established products in the domain of ESL testing. It is a certification of L2 competence awarded by the testing service of Cambridge University – ESOL Examinations – which is internationally recognized in commerce and industry as well as in universities, some of which use the FCE for entrance requirements. This test in its entirety is composed of five distinct parts called 'papers': reading, writing, use of English, listening and speaking. Each paper contains from two to four sub-sections.

The listening paper has a radically different focus and format (allotted time and range of texts and tasks) from the OPT. It is a proficiency test aiming at unraveling the potential ability of L2 listeners to understand gist, details, attitudes, opinions, functions, relationships and process inferential meanings. It lasts about 40 min and has four sub-sections representing different text and task types with 30 questions overall. The FCE listening texts are composed of authentic or semi-authentic extracts from lectures, phone messages, advertisements and everyday transactions. In the 2007 listening paper used for this study, the audio passages included 15 short unrelated monologues and dialogues reflecting real-life situations, sections of radio programs and interviews. These are presented in a variety of native speaker accents, which is another point that distinguishes FCE from OPT. Answer formats used are multiple-choice (three options), completion of sentences summarizing passages, multiple matching and sentence evaluation (true/false). The recordings are played twice and each correct answer is worth one point.

The FCE has, since its inception in the 1980s, attempted to reflect a more communicative type of testing. It is a test that 'better simulates the characteristics of target-language use in the real world [...] an attempt to test a richer, more realistic listening construct' (Buck, 2001: 92). Like the OPT, FCE scores can be linked to CEFR levels. However, this test was designed specifically to assess candidates' abilities at an upper-intermediate level, i.e. level B2 of the CEFR. This standardized test has undergone several reviews over the years, and its validity and reliability are now established.

Findings

The normality of the data was the first thing observed. Table 10.2 displays the descriptive statistics of the listening sections of both tests. The variance and standard deviation measuring the spread of a distribution around its mean show that a random FCE score is distributed near the mean value $M = 76.17$. However, given the kurtosis and skewness values, the FCE listening scores were less normally distributed than OPT listening scores.

Skewness (a measure of the asymmetry of the statistical distribution of a variable in relation to the mean) and kurtosis (a measure of its peakedness) are useful in defining the extent to which a distribution differs from a normal

Table 10.2 Descriptive statistics for the total scores of the FCE and OPT

Test	Participants	Min.	Max.	Mean	SD	Variance	Skewness	Kurtosis
OPT	110	62	96	76.17 (0.593)	6.22	38.71	0.232 (0.23)	0.46 (0.457)
FCE	110	4	26	12.52 (0.497)	5.21	27.17	0.663 (0.23)	0.02* (0.457)

Note: *$p < 0.05$.

one. The skewness index obtained from the total scores in the FCE (0.663) is positive but less than the arbitrary +1. This indicates that the distribution of FCE scores was moderately skewed to the right, whereas the skewness value for OPT scores points to more symmetrical data because it is close to zero (0.232). When looking at kurtosis estimates, the significant FCE kurtosis value (0.02*) further supported the fact that FCE data were not normal. No deviations from normality were observed for the OPT skewness and kurtosis estimates. The distribution of test scores, presented graphically in Figure 10.2, parallels the information observed in the descriptive Table 10.2.

Kolmogorov–Smirnov (KS) and Shapiro–Wilk (SW) tests of normality confirmed that, for OPT scores, the distribution did not meaningfully deviate from normality (KS = 0.062, SW = 0.987, $p > 0.05$). However, for the FCE set of scores, KS = 0.115 and SW = 0.953, which were significant at a p-level of <0.001, meaning that scores were not normally distributed. This result was confirmed by Q–Q plots of both tests' scores, as shown in Figure 10.3. This figure displays the observed values in our data (represented by the dots) and compares them to the expected normal distribution represented by the straight lines. OPT scores seem to sit solidly on the line, whereas, for the

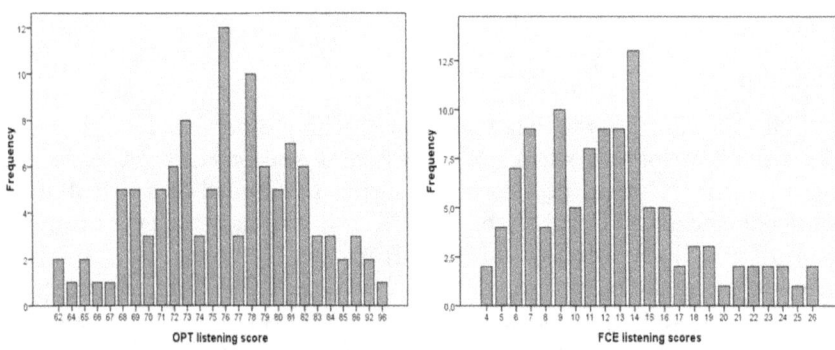

Figure 10.2 Frequency distributions of OPT and FCE Scores ($n = 110$)

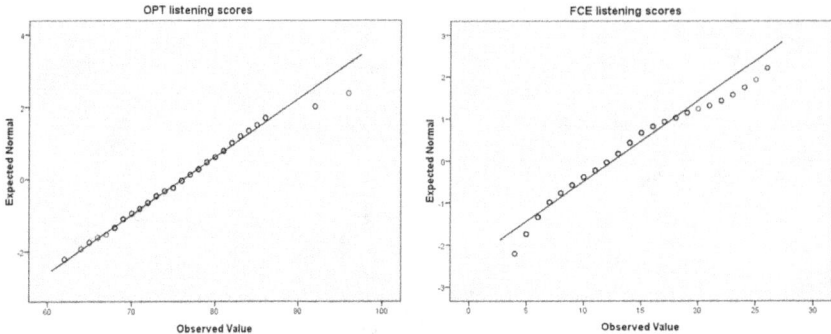

Figure 10.3 Normal Q-Q plots of OPT and FCE scores

FCE, the plot reveals that the distribution deviates somewhat from normality at both ends. Extreme FCE scores were obtained, and a more significant difference between students was observed. Certain students' performance on the FCE test stood out from the sample. A few students obtained very high scores and others very low scores. This was not the case for the OPT. It appears then that, given the range of results in both tests and as far as students' abilities and skills in listening are concerned, the skills assessed by the OPT would have less tendency to provide outlier scores at least in a population of French subjects whose listening proficiency may be broadly similar.

Aside from normality issues, we also considered the internal consistency of and the correlation between the listening variables assessed in our tests. The reliability estimates were satisfactory, because Cronbach's alpha (α) was 0.807 and 0.729 for the total test scores of the OPT and the FCE, respectively. However, when considering the reliability of the four sub-sections of the FCE, a small inconsistency was revealed. The reliability index of the third section of this test was relatively lower ($\alpha = 0.519$) than the other FCE subsections.

Looking at the correlation coefficient (r), which estimates the strength and the direction of a relationship between two variables, the results indicated that there was a positive, weak and statistically significant correlation between the OPT and the FCE ($r = 0.46$, $p < 0.001$). The calculation of the coefficient of determination (r^2), which provides the proportion of the variance of one variable that is predictable from the other variable, gave us additional evidence for our claim that the tests measure different aspects of listening proficiency. We found that $r^2 = 21.16$, which means that only 21.16% of the total variation in students' listening ability as conveyed in FCE scores can be explained by the linear relationship between FCE and OPT listening scores. Thus, the correlation coefficient of the tests accounts for quite a low percentage of variation.

A factor analysis was conducted to investigate the construct validity of the items included in each test and to measure the extent to which these

Table 10.3 Result of PCA for FCE responses

Factor	Initial eigenvalues	Percent of variance	Cumulative %
1	2.011	59.08	59.08
2	1.016	16.60	75.68
3	0.586	14.64	90.32
4	0.387	9.682	100

reflect the characteristics of listening proficiency the tests were supposed to assess. Before conducting the factor analysis, we speculated on the number of possible factors underlying the OPT and FCE tests. According to what we know about the tests – our interpretation of their underlying constructs and the listening behaviors of the competence-based framework listed earlier in this chapter – we initially hypothesized that OPT items would basically test language knowledge and load on one factor only – phoneme discrimination. For the FCE, we hypothesized three relevant factors: comprehension of gist, comprehension of detail, and inference. In fact, these FCE variables are sociolinguistically theorized reasons for listening that encompass language knowledge, discourse knowledge and pragmatic knowledge.

We used the default extraction method for factor analysis, principal component analysis (PCA), and we set it to extract the number of factors we identified for each test. PCA confirmed that the OPT measured only one factor corresponding to the ability to distinguish two words or phrases based on the phoneme heard (phoneme discrimination). PCA yielded a two-factor solution for the FCE, presented in Table 10.3. Here, two factors present an eigenvalue superior to 1, explaining 75.7% of the variance observed in the FCE scores.

According to the results of the PCA, we retained a two-factor solution for the FCE listening test and we revised the factors we proposed earlier. The ability to identify the gist and details of discourse, initially two separate abilities in our proposal, would actually represent the ability to understand literal meanings, i.e. explicit information in the listening passage. The ability of inferring meanings, attitudes and opinions refers to the ability to comprehend non-literal meanings, i.e. implicit information. This result implies that the subsections of the FCE measure a slightly broader range of listening skills than the OPT.

Discussion

A rapid qualitative analysis of the tests will illustrate the fact that the OPT listening section fails to account for higher-order listening skills. In terms of the list in (1), we can say that the proposed task assesses the constituent sub-skills of segmenting and discriminating sounds. The available options (minimal pairs) are both structurally and semantically plausible in the sentence given. Choosing the right word is based on phonological perception and orthographic recognition. Testees need to have not only a thorough knowledge of the phonetic and prosodic system of English, but also the corresponding graphemes and lexical orthography. This is mainly a test of reading, listening and vocabulary size, as asserted by the test designer himself (Allan, 2004: 2). Almost all L2 listening tests presented in written formats concurrently assess reading skills at different levels. The validity of these tests is therefore partially compromised. This is especially true for the OPT, which also assesses the ability to read fast while listening. The recorded sentences run one after the other with no pause between them. The OPT candidates are not given time to go through the sentences prior to listening. The speed seems to us inappropriate for the stated purpose of the test. In addition, a recent study (Brooke *et al.*, 2012) argues that some vocabulary in the OPT is low frequency and can be quite distracting. Given the structure of the utterances, the vocabulary used and the speed involved, it is argued here that learners would not need to understand the sentences to be able to give a correct answer. A correct response is synonymous with successful aural recognition. The OPT measures students' mastery of 'lower-level' linguistic processes, namely the recognition of prosodic and phonological patterns, referred to as 'grammatical knowledge' in the competence-based model we developed earlier in this chapter. The listening section of the OPT therefore operationalizes a restricted linguistic aspect of listening proficiency. Phoneme discrimination, the principal listening skill assessed in the OPT, and segmentation skills tested in some items of this test do not cover the complexity of the listening process and the listening abilities needed to function satisfactorily in academic and professional contexts. The test seems to assess only two listening sub-skills and, therefore, reflects a very limited model of what constitutes listening proficiency – too limited for a competence framework perspective on listening.

The FCE, on the other hand, seems to focus on higher-order abilities. Test items measured both global and detailed comprehension of spoken input that is varied and semi-authentic. The tasks require not only linguistic, but also discursive, pragmatic and sometimes sociolinguistic knowledge, as well as strategic processing at the cognitive and metacognitive levels. FCE test items require takers to get the gist of the texts, attend to details like numbers and names, identify speakers' opinions and intentions, infer certain information, take notes, comprehend and complete summaries and paraphrases, and finally evaluate statements. These are among the skills that would be necessary in study and business contexts, and fit nicely in a competence model of listening comprehension. The variety of tasks and response types included in the FCE correspond to recommendations given in some research on assessment (Chalhoub-Deville & Turner, 2000). Because testees' performance is affected by test methods, task diversity helps neutralize the advantages or disadvantages of certain item types for certain test-takers. It might also, of course, decrease reliability across tasks. This has been confirmed in our results, because item statistics reveal that the group average and the reliability index of section three of the test were lower than for the other sub-sections.

Quantitative comparison of these two instruments also provides some interesting results. According to Brown (2005), scores obtained on standardized tests of global proficiency should be normally distributed. All the normality tests proved that the OPT listening section displayed a more normal distribution than FCE, around the central score of 76 points. Compared to the FCE listening test, the OPT has less tendency to generate outlier values. The students did not perform in equivalent fashion on both tests, as also illustrated by the low correlation between the two series of scores. The OPT does not seem to reflect the overall listening proficiency of some students, who obtained low FCE scores but above-average OPT scores. One student's score on the OPT should not be interpreted as a reflection of his/her general ability in listening to English, but rather as a measure of his/her ability in the two formal sub-skills of listening, phoneme distinction and to some extent word recognition and discourse segmentation. Listening proficiency involves more than these formal recognition processes, of course, and it would therefore not be judicious to base pedagogical or research decisions concerning learners' listening proficiency on OPT scores only. The proficiency components measured by the FCE appear to be basically different from those measured by the OPT, and better aligned with the competence-based perspective we adopt here in this review. From our standpoint, the FCE listening test, even if it does not fit very closely with our model, seems a more valid tool for studies requiring a more complete measure of listening proficiency. Teachers and researchers who wish to use the FCE listening section with their subjects must, however, first submit it to a test of normality, and be cautious when running parametric statistical analyses.

Although one might expect that a learner who obtains a high score on one listening task (the OPT) will also score well on a second set of listening tasks (the FCE), the results from the current study only partially confirm this hypothesis. We found a moderate positive correlation between the results on the two tests ($r = 0.46$), illustrating the possibility that they measure different listening sub-skills. They could be used for different purposes: the OPT listening test when one is interested in measuring subjects' formal decoding processes (namely knowledge of the English sound and orthographic system), and the FCE (as stipulated by UCLES, 2008), for a more global assessment of listening proficiency in English (including both formal and higher-order processes). According to our findings, we believe the FCE to reflect the listening proficiency in English of a French population within a competence-based model. It might be of interest to use both tests together, for a more complete reflection of L2 learners' listening abilities.

Conclusion

This chapter has raised a number of issues regarding the L2 listening proficiency construct and its assessment. It has argued that the identification of a valid instrument depends on factors other than price and length. Apart from considering the purpose, the target population, the spoken input, and task format, test-users also need to keep in mind that there is always a certain degree of error due to testing conditions that might ultimately affect the scores obtained. Test-users also need to be aware of what the test really measures: for example, both tests reviewed here indirectly assess learners' reading skills. The format of the OPT also measures the ability to read very quickly and knowledge of low-frequency words.

Both the OPT and FCE listening sections proved to be reliable measures of certain aspects of listening proficiency. Yet, within the competence-based model, the FCE seems to be more effective for measuring the English listening proficiency of the population investigated. It remains for teachers, researchers and educational organizations to choose the appropriate test, given their view of the listening construct and the purpose of the test, as has already been argued in the literature (Bachman, 2002; Brown, 2005; Buck, 2001; Rost, 2002). If no standardized test matching the skills one wishes to assess is available, then designing a test that would meet specific needs becomes necessary. A thorough knowledge of the listening construct and its components should guide test designers in the design process.

Although our analysis yielded satisfactory responses to the objectives of this study, we are currently engaged in a thorough investigation of the effectiveness of all the items included in each test (item discrimination/difficulty analysis). Replications of the study are also encouraged in other English learning contexts.

References

Ahmadi, K., Ketabi, S. and Rabiee, R. (2012) The effect of explicit instruction of metacognitive learning strategies on promoting Iranian intermediate language learners' writing skills. *Theory and Practice in Language Studies* 2 (5), 938–944.
Allan, D. (2004) *Oxford Placement Test 1*. Oxford: Oxford University Press.
Anderson, A. and Lynch, T. (1988) *Listening*. New York: Cambridge University Press.
Bachman, L.F. (2002) Some reflections on task-based language performance assessment. *Language Testing* 19 (4), 453–476.
Brooke, K., Aden, M., Al-Kuwari, N., Christopher, V., Ibrahim, M., Johnson, B. and Souyah, O. (2012) Placement testing in an EFL context. *TESOL Arabia Perspectives* 19 (2), 13–20.
Brown, J. D. (2005) *Testing in Language Programs*. New York: McGraw-Hill.
Buck, G. (2001) *Assessing Listening*. New York: Cambridge University Press.
Chalhoub-Deville, M. and Turner, C. (2000) What to look for in ESL admission tests: Cambridge certificate exams, IELTS, and TOEFL. *System* 28, 523–539.

Chapelle, C.A. (1998) Construct definition and validity inquiry in SLA research. In L.F. Bachman and A.D. Cohen (eds) *Interfaces between Second Language Acquisition and Language Testing Research* (pp. 32–70). New York: Cambridge University Press.

Coakley, C.G. and Wolvin, A.D. (1986). Listening in the native language. In B.H. Wing (ed.) *Listening, Reading, Writing: Analysis and application* (pp. 11–42). Middlebury, VT: Northeast Conference on the Teaching of Foreign Languages.

Dunkel, P. (1991) Listening in the native and second/foreign language: toward an integration of research and practice. *TESOL Quarterly*, 25, 431–457

Dunkel, P., Henning, G. and Chaudron, C. (1993) The assessment of an L2 listening comprehension construct: A tentative model for test specification and development. *The Modern Language Journal* 77 (2), 180–191.

Feyten, C.M. (1991) The power of listening ability: An overlooked dimension in language acquisition. *The Modern Language Journal* 75 (2), 173–180.

Geranpayeh, A. and Taylor, L. (2008) Examining listening: Developments and issues in assessing second language listening. *Cambridge ESOL: Research Notes* 32, 2–5.

Graham, S. (2003) Learner strategies and advanced level listening comprehension. *Language Learning Journal* 28, 64–69.

Graham, S. (2006) Listening comprehension: The learners' perspective. *System* 34 (2), 165–182.

Grosjean, F. and Frauenfelder, U. (eds) (1997) *A Guide to Spoken Word Recognition Paradigms: Special Issue of Language and Cognitive Processes*. East Sussex, Hove: Psychology Press.

Hulstijn, J.H. (2003). Connectionist models of language processing and the training of listening skills with the aid of multimedia software. *Computer Assisted Language Learning* 16, 413–425.

Hulstijn, J.H. (2011) Language proficiency in native and nonnative speakers: An agenda for research and suggestions for second-language assessment. *Language Assessment Quarterly* 8, 229–249.

Lund, R.J. (1990) A taxonomy for teaching second language listening. *Foreign Language Annals* 23, 105–115.

Morell Moll, T. (1999) A linguistic needs analysis for EFL at the university level. *Revista Alicantina de Estudios Ingleses* 12, 117–125.

O'Malley, J.M., Chamot, A.U. and Küpper, L. (1989) Listening comprehension strategies in second language acquisition. *Applied Linguistics* 10 (4), 418–437.

Peterson, P. (1991) A synthesis of methods for interactive listening. In M. Celce-Murcia (ed.) *Teaching English as a Second or Foreign Language* (2nd edn) (pp. 106–122). New York: Newbury House.

Richards, J.C. (1983) Listening comprehension: Approach, design, procedure. *TESOL Quarterly* 17 (2), 219–240.

Rost, M. (1991) *Listening in Action*. London: Prentice Hall.

Rost, M. (2002) *Teaching and Researching: Listening*. London: Longman.

SPSS (2009) *SPSS 17.0 for Windows*. Chicago, IL: SPSS Inc.

Tahriri, A. and Yamin, M. (2010) On teaching to diversity: Investigating the effectiveness of MI-inspired instruction in an EFL context. *The Journal of Teaching Language Skills* 2 (1), 165–183.

Taylor, L. and Geranpayeh, A. (2011) Assessing listening for academic purposes: Defining and operationalising the test construct. *Journal of English for Academic Purposes* 10, 89–101.

University of Cambridge ESOL Examinations (UCLES) (2007) *Cambridge First Certificate in English* (n° 0102). New York: Cambridge University Press.

University of Cambridge ESOL Examinations (UCLES) (2008) *First Certificate in English: Handbook for Teachers*. New York: Cambridge University Press.

Vandergrift, L. (2004) Listening to learn or learning to listen? *Annual Review of Applied Linguistics* 24, 3–25.

Wagner, A. (2002) Video listening tests: A pilot study. *Working Papers in TESOL and Applied Linguistics, Teachers College, Columbia University* 2 (1). See http://journals.tc-library.org/index.php/tesol/article/view/7 (accessed 31 March 2009).

Wagner, E. (2004) A construct validation study of the extended listening sections of the ECPE and MELAB. *Spaan Fellow Working Papers in Second or Foreign Language Assessment* 2, 1–25.

Weir, C.J. (1993) *Understanding and Developing Language Tests*. London: Prentice Hall.

Weir, C.J. (2005) *Language Testing and Validation: An Evidence-Based Approach*. Houndgrave: Palgrave–Macmillan.

Wipf, J.A. (1984) Strategies for teaching second language listening comprehension. *Foreign Language Annals* 17, 345–348.

Xiaoxian, G. and Yan, J. (2010) Interactive listening: Construct definition and operationalization in tests of English as a foreign language. *Chinese Journal of Applied Linguistics* 33 (6), 16–39.

11 Assessing Language Dominance with the Bilingual Language Profile

Libby M. Gertken, Mark Amengual and David Birdsong

Introduction

The construct of dominance in the bilingual context covers many dimensions of language use and experience. Proficiency, fluency, ease of processing, 'thinking in a language', cultural identification, frequency of use and so forth are among the notions associated with this construct. Dominance is properly understood in relativistic, not absolute, terms. That is, a person is not simply dominant in a given language, but is dominant in that language to a certain measurable degree. And this person can be more dominant or less dominant in that language than some other person.

Language dominance is a variable of interest in a number of domains, including academic research, education, public policy, commerce and clinical settings. Among its influences on language behavior, cognition and emotion, dominance may predict cross-linguistic transfer in syntactic processing (Rah, 2010), influence code-switching patterns (Basnight-Brown & Altarriba, 2007), govern bilingual lexical memory representation (Heredia, 1997), affect language choice for self-directed and silent speech (Dewaele, 2004), determine the language of mental calculations (Tamamaki, 1993) and shape perceptions of the usefulness, richness and colorfulness of a bilingual's two languages (Dewaele, 2004). Educators and administrators use the construct of language dominance to determine the language in which tests of academic and linguistic ability should be carried out and as a classification tool for bilingual education planning (e.g. Brunner, 2010). In commerce, data on the language dominance of consumers informs decisions about the language of packaging and nutrition labels (B. Watson, Nestlé USA, personal communication, 11 May 2012). Language dominance also plays a notable role in clinical research: Alzheimer's disease has been found to differentially affect dominant and non-dominant languages (Gollan et al., 2010), for instance, and the severity of a person's stuttering may be influenced by language dominance (Howell et al., 2004; Lim et al., 2008a). Moreover, dominance is a key issue when deciding in which language to deliver the most effective language therapy treatment (Lim et al., 2008b).

Given the importance of dominance in these various arenas, its proper measurement takes on special significance. Dominance is primarily assessed via self-evaluations or objective tests within research on bilingualism and language acquisition. Self-evaluation, in various forms, is perhaps the most common method (e.g. Cutler et al., 1992; Dussias, 2003; Golato, 2002b; Li et al., 2006; Lim et al., 2008b; Mägiste, 1979; Rah, 2010; Tokowicz et al., 2004). In conventional self-assessment approaches, such as that used by Tokowicz et al. (2004), bilingual dominance corresponds to relative self-reported proficiency for the two languages. Tokowicz and colleagues classified participants as dominant in either Spanish or English based on self-reported abilities in reading, writing, comprehension and speaking. Cutler et al. (1992) used a different method, asking English–French bilinguals a simple question: If you had to lose one of your languages to save your life, which language would you choose? The language kept was taken to be dominant. In yet another approach, Rah (2010) asked trilingual participants to give self-ratings of language dominance directly.

Objective measures of dominance offer an alternative to self-evaluations that minimize the influence of subjective reflection. For example, Flege et al. (2002) implemented a sentence repetition task to determine the language dominance of Italian–English bilinguals. A similar processing task was used by Golato (2002a), along with a number of other psycholinguistic measures, including recall of words in sentences presented in noise, read-aloud speed with distracter noise, and grammaticality judgments (see Bairstow et al., this volume, for a psycholinguistic study on bilingual memory using an innovative translation recognition task). In a more recent study, Treffers-Daller (2011) allocated Dutch–French and French–English bilinguals to dominance groups according to lexical diversity scores from elicited speech samples.

Why a chapter about dominance in a volume concerned with proficiency? For one thing, dominance and proficiency, although conceptually overlapping in some respects, need to be distinguished (Birdsong, 2006). Although dominance is often associated with language proficiency (e.g. Tokowicz et al., 2004), proficiency does not alone define language dominance: One can be dominant in a language without being highly proficient in that language. This said, as one component of dominance, proficiency is duly examined here. Second, dominance and proficiency have assessment issues in common. A reinvigorated discussion about both proficiency and dominance assessment in the study of bilingualism is now taking place in prominent journals and international conferences (e.g. Dunn & Fox Tree, 2009; Gollan *et al.*, 2012; Hulstijn, 2012; Marian *et al.*, 2007; Tremblay, 2011; see special issue of *International Journal of Bilingualism* (2011) 15; *L2 Proficiency Assessment Workshop*, Montpellier, France, February 2012). Researchers are calling for standards and guidelines that would increase comparability and replicability in bilingual research, enhance interpretation of results, and ultimately help to clarify effects of bilingualism on social interaction, academic success, cognition and other human activity (Bedore *et al.*, 2012; Birdsong, 2006; Dunn & Fox Tree, 2009; Gollan *et al.*, 2012; Grosjean, 1998; Lim *et al.*, 2008b; Tremblay, 2011).

As with proficiency assessment, there is considerable diversity in the selection of variables pertinent to measuring language dominance and the weighting of these variables (Hulstijn, 2012; Lim *et al.*, 2008b). Underlying the various forms of dominance assessment is little consensus about what it means to be dominant, which can be attributed to the theoretical orientations of the creators and administrators of these assessments, the context of assessment and to matters of practicality and feasibility. We hope to shed some light on the construct of dominance and its testing through an understanding of language dominance as a multi-faceted, gradient and dynamic construct that includes but is not equivalent to language proficiency. Our conception of dominance aims to be broad enough to be useful for a variety of purposes and at the same time precise enough to give clarity to the construct.

In this chapter, we present the Bilingual Language Profile (BLP), a tool for measuring language dominance through self-reports and a questionnaire that delivers a general bilingual profile taking into account a variety of language-related variables. Our aim with the BLP project is to describe the notion of language dominance and to address some of the drawbacks of existing dominance assessment methods. The BLP is not intended to replace all previous forms of dominance assessment, but rather to offer a reliable, valid and highly practical instrument that can be used to describe bilingual participants within and outside academic research. We envision use of the BLP by researchers, educators and administrators wishing to quickly and easily gather information about the functional language abilities of bilingual populations. In the discussion to follow, we will address the construct of dominance, existing dominance assessment tools and the creation of the BLP instrument. Finally, we offer some concluding remarks on the BLP and dominance assessment in general.

Conceptualizing Dominance

The primary and most crucial step of language testing is to specify the construct under investigation (Alderson & Banerjee, 2002). A construct is simply what we are trying to measure – here, language dominance. However, as we have highlighted in the preceding section, this task is not uncomplicated given the many dimensions and dynamics of bilingualism.

The construct of dominance versus proficiency

The constructs of language dominance and proficiency are easily conflated and often correlated (Birdsong, 2006). As mentioned above, measures of relative proficiency in reading, writing, speaking and listening are often used to determine language dominance. In these cases, the construct of proficiency relates to 'the largely implicit, unconscious knowledge in the domains of phonetics, prosody, phonology, morphology and syntax' and 'the largely explicit, conscious knowledge in the lexical domain (form-meaning mappings)' (Hulstijn, 2010: 186).[1] We would like to establish, however, that dominance is conceptually distinct from proficiency. Dominance is a construct that derives from the nature of bilingualism – of having two languages in one's mind (Grosjean, 1998). It involves the relationship between competencies in two languages and is thus inherently relativistic. Proficiency, on the other hand, does not require a bilingual context for its definition. Indeed, the language proficiency of monolinguals is often assessed, and a range of proficiency scores is observed (e.g. Dabrowska, 2012; Pakulak & Neville, 2010).

Consider also that two equally balanced bilinguals may yet differ in their proficiency, with one individual showing high proficiency in both languages, and the other showing lower proficiency in both languages (Treffers-Daller, 2011). Balanced bilingualism does not entail high proficiency, only a state of equilibrium (Hamers & Blanc, 2000). Dominance may also shift within a bilingual's lifetime, independent of proficiency: 'For immigrants with many years of immersion in their second language, the second language can come to be the most dominant language, even if it remains the less proficient language, as measured by tests of grammar and vocabulary.' (Harris *et al.*, 2006: 264).

Components of dominance

In our view, proficiency (where proficiency concerns the types of knowledge described in Hulstijn's, 2010, definition) is an essential component of dominance but does not alone define it. For those researchers who distinguish proficiency and dominance, whether explicitly or not, dominance is commonly described in psycholinguistic terms. For instance, from a psycholinguistic perspective, Birdsong (2006) observed that relative dominance can be conceptualized in terms of differences in processing abilities between the two languages of a bilingual. For Harris *et al.* (2006: 264), 'language dominance refers to which language is generally most accessible in day-to-day life. It is the language that is most highly activated, and can be the default language for speaking and thinking.' Heredia (1997) likewise describes the dominant language as the 'active' language, determined by frequency of use. Dewaele (2004) also relies on psycholinguistic concepts (e.g. automaticity) for his description of a change from first to second language dominance, which he describes as characterized by slower access to the first language (regardless of proficiency). Other studies, such as that by Bahrick *et al.* (2004), have shown that differences in processing alone cannot account for differences in dominance. In their study of dominance, Bahrick and colleagues examined four measures – lexical decision, category generation, vocabulary and oral comprehension – and found that tasks that address processing and those that address competence or representation convey different information about language dominance. Processing and competence are thus two distinct and important aspects of dominance.

In addition to psycholinguistic and proficiency-related components, dominance is shaped by language attitudes. Factors such as cultural identification (Marian & Kaushanskaya, 2004) and motivation (Piller, 2002) play a role in forming language attitudes, which in turn influence language dominance. We argue, like Pavlenko (2004), that language dominance is not independent of psychosocial factors: 'Rather, [it is a corollary] of complex linguistic trajectories of individuals who make choices about what language to use, when and with whom' (Pavlenko, 2004: 189). We thus view dominance as a global construct that is informed by many factors relating to knowledge, processing and effect.

For the BLP project, we set about distinguishing several primary dimensions of dominance based on these three components, with a goal to providing a dominance assessment instrument useful for both academic research and non-research settings. In keeping with our goal, we balanced comprehensiveness with economy to establish four dimensions of language dominance that both reflected the main components of dominance and were suitable for self-assessment: language history, use, proficiency and attitudes.

We also acknowledge that bilinguals are not necessarily dominant in one language across the board, and it is often the case that a bilingual will show dominance in one language only for certain topics or within certain speech settings (e.g. Grosjean, 2001; Lim *et al.*, 2008b). We addressed this issue by including items in the questionnaire that contribute information about language practices in multiple settings, including home, work/school and social settings. By taking into account various contexts of language experience in both languages, we feel that the BLP, while still providing an overall (context-independent) dominance assessment, is a fair representation of dominance that meets our criteria of efficiency and practicality.

Dominance as a continuum

Another important aspect of language dominance, as we conceive it, is gradation. Gradient dominance highlights the fact that, although it may be useful in some instances to classify bilinguals as dominant in one or the other language, dominance is not necessarily dichotomous (Grosjean, 2001). Indeed, discrete classifications of language dominance can obscure rich data about variation within groups, a point that Grosjean (1998) underscores in his discussion of the complexity of the bilingual individual. A bilingual may be more or less dominant in one language relative to the other, and the relative strength of the two languages can change over a lifetime (e.g. Harris *et al.*, 2006). We thus draw a principled distinction between binary and continuous conceptions of dominance. Development of the BLP was in part motivated by the observation that practical ways of measuring dominance along a continuum are scarce.

Dominance Assessment Tools

Why self-reports?

A thorough review of self-report methodology is beyond the scope of this chapter, but it is worth noting that there are several benefits to using self-evaluations for bilingual dominance assessment. First, there is ample evidence that bilinguals are able to assess their language experience and language abilities in a way that corresponds with behavioral measures of linguistic performance (Bairstow *et al.*, this volume; Flege *et al.*, 2002; Golato, 2002a; Gollan *et al.*, 2012; Langdon *et al.*, 2005; Lim *et al.*, 2008b; Marian *et al.*, 2007). As opposed to objective tests of language ability, they succeed in accounting for certain non-linguistic factors, such as language attitudes, which are crucial aspects of dominance (e.g. Pavlenko, 2004). Self-reports are efficient in that they take less time to complete than linguistically based tasks, they are easier to interpret, and they do not require complex scoring or statistical calculations. Nor is specialized training required to administer them. Additionally, self-report questionnaires can be completed by testees offsite before arriving at an experimental session, saving researchers valuable time.

Existing bilingual self-report surveys

Although a number of *ad hoc* techniques have been used to measure bilingual language dominance, there exist several reliable, valid and widely accessible self-report instruments. The Language Experience and Proficiency Questionnaire (LEAP-Q) (Marian *et al.*, 2007), the Bilingual Dominance Scale (BDS) (Dunn & Fox Tree, 2009) and Lim *et al.*'s (2008b) Self-Report Classification Tool (SRCT) are recently developed instruments that provided the foundation upon which the BLP was built. The LEAP-Q, BDS and SRCT are self-report questionnaires that probe aspects of language experience, proficiency and, in the case of the LEAP-Q, attitudes. While the BDS and SRCT are expressly aimed at determining language dominance, the LEAP-Q provides descriptive information for each language.

The LEAP-Q instrument is excellent for eliciting descriptive data because it is comprehensive and amenable to multilingual populations, but it is not a dominance assessment per se. The LEAP-Q provides independent data for each of a multilingual's languages rather than a composite score relating strengths in one language with the other language. A shortcoming of the LEAP-Q's comprehensiveness is that it contains many items, some of which are lengthy and complex. One question in particular stands out as quite difficult to process: 'When choosing to read a text available in all your languages, in what percentage of cases would you choose to read it in each of your languages? Assume that the original was written in another language, which is unknown to you.' (LEAP-Q; Marian *et al.*, 2007).

The BDS stands at the opposite end of the spectrum with its brevity and conciseness. The BDS elicits self-reports for a number of factors known to influence language dominance in just 12 questions. It has the advantage of being quick to administer, containing short and comprehensible questions, and being adaptable to illiterate populations. The BDS's scoring method can be used to obtain a dominance score along a continuum by subtracting one language score from the other.

One drawback to the BDS involves the free response format for responding to questions. When using the questionnaire for another research project, we found a considerable amount of variability in responses to questions such as 'Do you feel that you have lost any fluency in a particular language', ranging from 'yes/no' to anecdotes about fluency loss that were difficult to quantify. Another drawback involves the BDS's scoring procedure. Different weights are assigned to each item in the questionnaire, although we do not see sufficient motivation for assigning higher point values and thus more influence to some factors over others. For example, five points are assigned, with little justification, to the language predominantly used at home, but only four points are given to the language of the region where the participant is currently living.

Finally, it seems that the BDS may work best as a dominance assessment tool for particular bilingual populations, such as simultaneous bilinguals (see Amengual & Blanco, 2011). When administered to late L2 learners, dominance calculations can actually become invalid. Late L2 learners tend to receive low total scores for their L2 based on the weights assigned to the questions in the BDS. If a respondent indicates that he has lost fluency in the L2 as well, points are subtracted from these low scores, and the resulting total score for the L2 becomes negative. When the negative number is subtracted from the higher total score for the first language, this actually results in an erroneously inflated dominance score.

The SRCT was developed by Lim *et al.* (2008b) to assess language dominance in multilingual Asian communities for clinical purposes. Importantly, the authors wanted to avoid equating proficiency classifications with dominance and to highlight the roles that frequency and context of language use play in determining dominance. The SRCT is a brief pencil-and-paper survey that elicits rankings of a bilingual's two languages, as well as scalar proficiency assessments, and information about frequency and context of use. A scoring system based on rating differences in the two languages can be used to determine dominance in one language or another.

A drawback to the SRCT is its narrow focus on one community of bilinguals. Specifically, the authors created the questionnaire for English–Mandarin bilinguals living in Singapore, so one section of the survey probes school examination grades uniquely relevant to the education system in Singapore. It is unclear how the items on the SRCT would apply to other bilingual contexts. The authors note, however, that the format of the questionnaire and criteria for scoring dominance may be adaptable to other bilingual groups and contexts.

The scoring procedure for the SRCT is somewhat problematic. According to Lim *et al.* (2008b), a language is interpreted as dominant if differences between language scores (e.g. Mandarin scores subtracted from English scores) are similar in directionality on two out of three criteria, including (1) the difference in total rating score; (2) the difference in scores on combined understanding, speaking and reading modalities; and (3) the difference in scores on combined understanding, speaking and writing modalities. What remains uncertain is how total rating scores are derived and whether these total scores take into account items pertaining to age of first exposure and language use in addition to the proficiency scores that make up criteria (2) and (3). Aside from the details of the scoring procedure, a final drawback of the SRCT is that the product of scoring is discrete dominance groups rather than a continuous score of bilingual language dominance.

There are differences in the accessibility of the LEAP-Q, BDS and SRCT questionnaires. The BDS and SRCT are available as a pencil-and-paper questionnaire that must be scored by hand. Because the BDS contains simple questions, it can be administered in oral format as well, and the administrator can record testees' responses. The LEAP-Q is available in writable PDF and Word document form and retrievable online as a free download.

The BLP owes much to the LEAP-Q, BDS and SRCT in its design and theoretical orientation, but is intended to address what we view as shortcomings in the format and accessibility of these instruments. The BLP underwent several rounds of pilot testing in order to refine, shorten and clarify questionnaire items, with a view to making them relevant for diverse bilingual populations (Treffers-Daller, 2011). We chose to elicit only multiple-choice scalar responses to questionnaire items, which avoids ambiguity in responses and is in keeping with the notion of a scalar dominance score. Unlike Dunn and Fox Tree (2009), we decided not to differentially weight the four components of the BLP. To weight, say, the scores on the proficiency module above those on the other modules would bias the global scores for dominance (and, effectively, our operationalization of dominance and users' interpretation of dominance) toward reflecting proficiency at the expense of the other components. This said, those users who wish to concentrate on proficiency assessment are able to do so – either independently of, or relative to, scores on the other components. (There are instructions on the BLP website for this purpose; Birdsong *et al.*, 2012).

We developed the BLP as both a pencil-and-paper questionnaire and an online questionnaire for maximum flexibility. It can be accessed freely in its online version as a template in Google Docs.[2] Within this template is an adjoining Excel spreadsheet that automatically tabulates scores for each respondent.

Depending on the context in which it is used and the needs of the administrator, any one of the aforementioned self-report questionnaires may be the best choice for dominance assessment. The comparison in Table 11.1 can serve as a reference guide when choosing which instrument to use.

The Bilingual Language Profile

Creation of the BLP

The BLP was developed in cooperation with the Center for Open Educational Resources and Language Learning (COERLL).[3] COERLL is one of 15 National Foreign Language Resource Centers funded by the US Department of Education. COERLL's mission is to produce resources to improve the teaching and learning of foreign languages and to disseminate these resources to a variety of settings. The BLP is one of many Open Educational Resources sponsored by COERLL.

Creation of the BLP took place over two and a half years and involved a series of steps in accordance with those outlined in Dörnyei's (2003: 66–69) *Questionnaires in Second Language Research*. First, we reviewed and discussed the construct of dominance and previous dominance assessments as part of an inter-disciplinary bilingual dominance reading group. Following this, the authors collaborated to prepare a pool of questionnaire items drawing on previous research in language dominance and on items previously used in the LEAP-Q, BDS and SRCT. The initial questions were trimmed and matched to one of four dimensions of dominance: history, use, proficiency and attitudes. The resulting question pool was piloted in English on bilingual colleagues. On the basis of participants' responses and feedback (Alderson & Banerjee, 2002; Brown, 1993), the BLP was revised for clarity and succinctness (e.g. rewording, elimination of redundant or irrelevant items). Questionnaires were then translated into other languages in consultation

Table 11.1 Comparison of the bilingual language profile, bilingual dominance scale, language experience and proficiency questionnaire, and self-report classification tool

Characteristics	BLP (Birdsong et al., 2012)	BDS (Dunn & Fox Tree, 2009)	LEAP-Q (Marian et al., 2007)	SRCT (Lim et al., 2008b)
Administration	Online and pencil-and-paper formats	Pencil-and-paper questionnaire; can be administered orally	Writeable PDF format and pencil-and-paper versions for some languages	Pencil-and-paper questionnaire
Languages	Arabic, ASL, Catalan, English, French, Spanish, Russian	English	12 languages	English
Completion time	Less than 10 min	Less than 5 min	15–25 min to complete (more for each language evaluated)	Less than 5 min
Self-report components	• 19 items • Multiple-choice responses • All scalar responses	• 12 items • Fill-in-the-blank responses • No scalar responses	• 31 items • Pull-down menu for responses • Some scalar responses	• 24 items • Fill-in-the-blank and multiple-choice responses • Some scalar responses • Rankings
Scoring system	Four equally weighted modules	Weighted point system for each item	No scoring procedure for each language	Point system based on language score differences for three criteria
Result	Continuous dominance score; descriptive profile for each module	Continuous dominance score	No dominance index; descriptive profile	Discrete dominance groups
Procedure	Self-scored	Scored by hand	No scoring procedure	Scored by hand
Website	http://sites.la.utexas.edu/bilingual/	No website	http://comm.soc.northwestern.edu/bilingualism-psycholinguistics/leapq/	No website

with native speakers. Next, we worked with COERLL to create the online version of the questionnaire in Google Docs. The resulting BLP was piloted with 16 bilinguals who were either simultaneous bilinguals or L2 learners (Spanish–English, Arabic–English, French–English). We once again revised the questionnaire for clarity, online use and appropriate scoring based on feedback and results.

We undertook testing and validation of the BLP based on questionnaires completed by 68 English–French bilinguals residing in the US and in France. We performed a factor analysis in order to determine whether the items in the BLP that were designed to reflect the distinct concepts of language history, use, proficiency and attitudes patterned together. Next we measured internal consistency within these modules with Cronbach's alpha reliability (e.g. Dewaele, 2004). Finally, we established criterion-based validity by comparing BLP scores with linguistic performance on a psycholinguistic naming task and a standardized test of proficiency. The details of these analyses are beyond the scope of this chapter but conclusions are briefly summarized in the following (for a full description see Amengual et al., in preparation).

The factor analysis yielded desirable component groupings that reflected the underlying dimensions of dominance that we identified initially. Based on the observation that the factor analysis groupings accounted for the majority of the variance in English–French bilinguals' self-reports, we concluded that our questionnaire items were sufficiently broad to capture variability within the English–French bilinguals sampled for this analysis. Cronbach's alpha – a test of reliability – for each module was found to be moderately to highly reliable, indicating that the items within each module measure the same variable while still contributing unique information.

We also compared BLP scores of self-rated proficiency with the *Oxford Placement Test* (OPT) of proficiency in French. A correlation analysis between self-assessed proficiency in French on the BLP and OPT scores for French revealed a strong positive correlation, suggesting accurate self-reporting on the BLP. Finally, we evaluated the extent to which a subset of the original 68 participants' dominance scores on the BLP related to performance on *A Quick Test of Cognitive Speed* (AQT; Wiig et al., 2002), a timed test that requires participants to identify 40 images on a page as quickly as possible. We found a moderate positive correlation between the two measures, indicating that dominance scores on the BLP reflect performance on an objective psycholinguistic dominance test. We attribute the moderate (as opposed to large) amount of variance on the AQT that was explained by the BLP to the fact that the two instruments assess different aspects of dominance. The former looks at dominance in terms of executive control in lexical retrieval, while the BLP provides a more comprehensive assessment of dominance that includes experiential and attitudinal factors.

Features of the BLP

Sample screen shots from the online version of the BLP appear in Appendix 11A. The BLP contains an introductory section for collecting biographical information about testees[4] and four modules designed to assess different dimensions of dominance. The instrument contains a total of 19 items, which elicit responses about each of a bilingual's languages (Figure 11.1). Bilingual testees may choose the language in which to complete the questionnaire.

The four modules of the BLP questionnaire treat different aspects of dominance. The Language History module gathers information about the age of acquisition of each language, the age at which the testee felt comfortable using each language, the number of years of schooling in each language, the time spent in a country or region in which each language is predominantly used, the time spent in a family where each language is used, and the time spent in a work environment where each language is used. Language Use questions probe the percentage of use in an average week for each language in various contexts: with friends, with family, and at school or work. This section also asks testees to relate how often they talk to themselves in each language and how often they use each language when counting. In the Language Proficiency portion of the questionnaire, testees are asked to rate how well they speak, listen, read and write in each language on a scale from 0 ('not well at all') to 6 ('very well') for each language. The final module investigates Language Attitudes, asking the degree to which testees feel like themselves when speaking each language, how much they identify with cultures that speak each language, the importance of using each language like a native speaker and the importance of being taken for a native speaker.

Using the BLP

The BLP is an open-source language profile instrument. We developed a website (Birdsong *et al.*, 2012) that provides detailed information about the instrument (with tabs such as 'Using the BLP', 'About the Project' and 'Connect and Share') to facilitate accessing and administering the BLP, as well as to encourage contributions and feedback from the research community.

Step-by-step instructions and an explanatory video on how to use the online BLP questionnaire can be found at the BLP website (Birdsong *et al.*, 2012). In brief, questionnaires in each language pair are available as templates in Google Docs that can be transferred to your personal Google Docs account. Introductory comments and biographical information questions can be adjusted to suit the needs of the administrator, and the questionnaire can then be emailed to participants. The administrator can view responses and automatically tabulated scores within the Google Docs form

Biographical information
• Name • Age • Sex • Place of residence • Highest level of formal education

Module 1: Language history
• At what age did you start learning ENGLISH? (SPANISH)[5] • At what age did you start to feel comfortable using ENGLISH? (SPANISH) • How many years of classes (grammar, history, math, etc.) have you had in ENGLISH (primary school through university)? (SPANISH) • How many years have you spent in a country/region where ENGLISH is spoken? (SPANISH) • How many years have you spent in a family where ENGLISH is spoken? (SPANISH) • How many years have you spent in a work environment where ENGLISH is spoken? (SPANISH)

Module 2: Language use
• In an average week, what percentage of the time do you use ENGLISH with friends? (SPANISH; OTHER LANGUAGES) • In an average week, what percentage of the time do you use ENGLISH with family? (SPANISH; OTHER LANGUAGES) • In an average week, what percentage of the time do you use ENGLISH at school/work? (SPANISH; OTHER LANGUAGES) • When you talk to yourself, how often do you talk to yourself in ENGLISH? (SPANISH; OTHER LANGUAGES) • When you count, how often do you count in ENGLISH (SPANISH; OTHER LANGUAGES)

Module 3: Language proficiency
• How well do you speak ENGLISH? (SPANISH) • How well do you understand ENGLISH? (SPANISH) • How well do you write ENGLISH? (SPANISH) • How well do you read ENGLISH? (SPANISH)

Module 4: Language attitudes
• I feel like myself when I speak ENGLISH. (SPANISH) • I identify with an ENGLISH-speaking culture. (SPANISH) • It is important to me to use (or eventually use) ENGLISH like a native speaker. (SPANISH) • I want others to think I am a native speaker of ENGLISH. (SPANISH)

Figure 11.1 Format of the Bilingual Language Profile (sample English–Spanish questionnaire)

in their personal account. This information is not available to respondents. Responses and scores can be downloaded as Excel files for further analysis. If using the pencil-and-paper version of the BLP, it will be necessary to score the questionnaire by hand. The manual scoring procedure can also be found on the website.

The BLP is designed to assess bilinguals from a variety of linguistic and cultural backgrounds. We define bilingual in the broadest sense, to include people who use two (or more) languages. The BLP can thus be used in such bilingual contexts as L2 acquisition, heritage learning, attrition, *in situ* or immigrant contexts, and sequential or simultaneous bilingualism. Because items on the BLP require a certain amount of introspection and literacy skills, the instrument should be administered to bilinguals who are at least of high-school age.

Concluding Remarks

The BLP project has both practical and theoretical objectives. We sought to create an easy-to-use instrument for dominance assessment that tapped as many aspects of dominance as possible without sacrificing efficiency. We also wanted to design an instrument suitable to a variety of bilingual settings for a variety of purposes. As Bachman and Eignor (1997) have pointed out, validation is an ongoing process. The BLP has been used recently in several projects involving sentence processing by English-French bilinguals in the US and France (Gertken, 2013) and phonetic transfer in the production and perception of Spanish-Catalan bilinguals in Majorca, Spain (Amengual, 2013). We hope that as more members of the community use the BLP, the more reliability and validity testing there will be to help understand the value of the BLP in diverse contexts (Li *et al.*, 2006).

Already, users have contributed to its development by submitting new translations. We welcome these updates and report them regularly to the BLP website (Birdsong *et al.*, 2012). Comments and suggestions concerning the BLP can be submitted through the website's 'Give us feedback' link.

We also sought to contribute to a discussion of what it means to be dominant in a language, which we see as an obstacle to establishing standards and guidelines concerning dominance assessment. In this respect we are building on Bedore *et al.* (2012), Dunn and Fox Tree (2009) and Gollan *et al.* (2012). In addition, we have offered a comprehensive and multi-factorial understanding of language dominance that is measurable by scores on the BLP along four crucial dimensions: language history, use, proficiency and attitudes.

We do not claim this instrument is superior to others or appropriate for all contexts of bilingual assessment. However, the BLP has in its favor free access, ease of use and adaptability, and has been validated against other measures (see Amengual *et al.*, in preparation). We look forward to further development of the BLP questionnaire across a variety of languages, as well as to users' feedback, which will be crucial to the refinement of the instrument.

Notes

(1) Hulstijn (2010: 186) also includes a processing component in his definition of proficiency: 'the automaticity with which [various] types of knowledge can be processed'. We make a distinction between this psycholinguistic component and implicit and explicit knowledge in various linguistic domains.
(2) Google Docs, Google's online document-sharing service, is now a part of Google Drive, the company's cloud storage initiative with upgraded storage capacity. With an older Google Docs account or a newer Google Drive account, users may collaborate in real time on documents such as the BLP as well as share media including movies, images and music.
(3) See http://www.coerll.utexas.edu/coerll/
(4) The section of the BLP questionnaire collecting biographical information can be modified to suit administrators' needs.
(5) Questions are repeated for the items in parentheses.

References

Alderson, J.C. and Banerjee, J. (2002) State-of-the-art review: Language testing and assessment (part two). *Language Teaching* 35, 79–113.
Amengual, M. (2013) An experimental approach to phonetic transfer in the production and perception of early Spanish–Catalan bilinguals. PhD thesis, University of Texas at Austin, TX.
Amengual, M. and Blanco, C. (2011) *The use of the Spanish imperfect subjunctive in monolingual and bilingual populations*. Paper presented at the 15th Hispanic Linguistics Symposium (HLS). University of Georgia. Athens, GA, October 8, 2011.
Amengual, M., Birdsong, D. and Gertken, L.M. (in preparation) The Bilingual Language Profile: An easy-to-use instrument to assess language dominance.
Bachman, L.F. and Eignor, D.R. (1997) Recent advances in quantitative test analysis. In C.M. Clapham and D. Corson (eds) *Encyclopedia of Language and Education, Volume 7. Language Testing and Assessment* (pp. 227–242). Dordrecht: Kluwer Academic.
Bahrick, H.P., Hall, L.K., Goggin, J.P., Bahrick, L.E. and Berger, S.A. (2004) Fifty years of language maintenance and language dominance in bilingual Hispanic immigrants. *Journal of Experimental Psychology* 123, 264–283.
Basnight-Brown, D.M. and Altarriba, J. (2007) Code-switching and code-mixing in bilinguals: Cognitive, developmental, and empirical approaches. In A. Ardila and E. Ramos (eds) *Speech and Language Disorders in Bilinguals* (pp. 69–89). New York: Nova Science Publishers.
Bedore, L.M., Peña, E.D., Summers, C.L., Boerger, K.M., Resendiz, M.D., Greene, K., Bohman, T.M. and Gillam, R.B. (2012) The measure matters: Language dominance profiles across measures in Spanish–English bilingual children. *Bilingualism: Language and Cognition* 15, 616–629.
Birdsong, D. (2006) Dominance, proficiency, and second language grammatical processing. *Applied Psycholinguistics* 27, 46–49.
Birdsong, D., Gertken, L.M. and Amengual, M. (2012) Bilingual Language Profile: An easy-to-use instrument to assess bilingualism. COERLL, University of Texas at Austin, TX. See https://sites.la.utexas.edu/bilingual/ (retrieved 4 March 2014)

Bohman, T.M. and Gillam, R.B. (2012) The measure matters: Language dominance profiles across measures in Spanish–English bilingual children. *Bilingualism: Language and Cognition* 15, 616–629.
Brown, A. (1993) The role of test-taker feedback in the test development process: Test-takers' reactions to a tape-mediated test of proficiency in spoken Japanese. *Language Testing* 10, 277–303.
Brunner, J. (2010) *Bilingual Education and English as a Second Language Programs Summary Report, 2009–2010*. Austin Independent School District, Department of Program Evaluation. See http://archive.austinisd.org/inside/docs/ope_09_67_Bilingual_Education_and_English_as_a_Second_Language.pdf (accessed 29 May 2012).
Cutler, A., Mehler, J., Norris, D. and Segui, J. (1992) The monolingual nature of speech segmentation by bilinguals. *Cognitive Psychology* 24, 381–410.
Dabrowska, E. (2012) Different speakers, different grammars: Individual differences in native language attainment. *Linguistic Approaches to Bilingualism* 2, 219–253.
Dewaele, J.-M. (2004) Perceived language dominance and language preference for emotional speech: The implications for attrition research. In M.S. Schmid, B. Köpke, M. Kejser and L. Weilemar (eds) *First Language Attrition: Interdisciplinary perspectives on methodological issues* (pp. 81–104). Amsterdam/Philadelphia, PA: Benjamins.
Dörnyei, Z. (2003) *Questionnaires in Second Language Research*. Mahwah, NJ: Erlbaum.
Dunn, A.L. and Fox Tree, J.E. (2009) A quick, gradient Bilingual Dominance Scale. *Bilingualism: Language and Cognition* 12, 273–289.
Dussias, P.E. (2003) Syntactic ambiguity resolution in L2 learners: Some effects of bilinguality on L1 and L2 processing strategies. *Studies in Second Language Acquisition* 25, 529–557.
Flege, J.E., Mackay, I.R.A. and Piske, T. (2002) Assessing bilingual dominance. *Applied Psycholinguistics* 23, 567–598.
Gertken, L.M. (2013) Priming of relative clause attachment during comprehension in French as a first and second language. PhD thesis, University of Texas at Austin, TX.
Golato, P. (2002a) Operationalizing 'language dominance' in late bilinguals. *Working Papers in Linguistics* 1, 26–35.
Golato, P. (2002b) Word parsing by late-learning French–English bilinguals. *Applied Psycholinguistics* 23, 417–446.
Gollan, T.H., Salmon, D.P., Montoya, R. and Peña, E. (2010) Accessibility of the nondominant language in picture naming: A counterintuitive effect of dementia on bilingual language production. *Neuropsychologia* 48, 1356–1366.
Gollan, T.H., Weissberger, G.H., Runnqvist, E., Montoya, R.I. and Cera, C.M. (2012) Self-ratings of spoken language dominance: A Multilingual Naming Test (MINT) and preliminary norms for young and aging Spanish–English bilinguals. *Bilingualism: Language and Cognition* 15, 594–615.
Grosjean, F. (1998) Studying bilinguals: Methodological and conceptual issues. *Bilingualism: Language and Cognition* 1, 131–149.
Grosjean, F. (2001) The bilingual's language modes. In J.L. Nicol (ed.) *One Mind, Two Languages: Bilingual Language Processing* (pp. 1–22). Malden, MA: Blackwell.
Hamers, J.F. and Blanc, M.H. (2000) *Bilinguality and Bilingualism*. Cambridge: Cambridge University Press.
Harris, C.L., Gleason, J.B. and Aycicegi, A. (2006) When is a first language more emotional? Psychophysiological evidence from bilingual speakers. In A. Pavlenko (ed.) *Bilingual Minds: Emotional Experience, Expression, and Representation*. Clevedon: Multilingual Matters.
Heredia, R. (1997) Bilingual memory and hierarchical models: A case for language dominance. *Current Directions in Psychological Science* 6, 34–39.
Howell, P., Ruffle, L., Fernandez-Zuniga, A., Gutierrez, R., Fernandez, A.H., O'Brian, M.L., Tarasco, M., Vallejo Gomez, I. and Au-Yeung, J. (2004) Comparison of exchange

patterns of stuttering in Spanish and English monolingual speakers and a bilingual Spanish–English speaker. In A. Packman, A. Meltzer and H.F.M. Peters (eds) *Theory, Research and Therapy in Fluency Disorders. Proceedings of the 4th World Congress on Fluency Disorders, Montreal, Canada* (pp. 415–422). Nijmegen: Nijmegen University Press.

Hulstijn, J.H. (2010) Measuring second language proficiency. In E. Blom and S. Unsworth (eds) *Experimental Methods in Language Acquisition Research* (pp. 185–200). Amsterdam: Benjamins.

Hulstijn, J.H. (2012) The construct of language proficiency in the study of bilingualism from a cognitive perspective. *Bilingualism: Language and Cognition* 15, 422–433.

Langdon, H., Wiig, E. and Nielsen, N. (2005) Dual dimension naming speed and language-dominance ratings by bilingual Hispanic adults. *Bilingual Research Journal* 29, 319–336.

Li, P., Sepanski, S. and Zhao, X. (2006) Language history questionnaire: A web-based interface for bilingual research. *Behavior Research Methods* 38, 202–210.

Lim, V.P.C., Lincoln, M., Chan, Y.H. and Onslow, M. (2008a) Stuttering in English–Mandarin bilingual speakers: The influence of language dominance on stuttering severity. *Journal of Speech, Language, and Hearing Research* 51, 1522–1537.

Lim, V.P.C., Rickard Liow, S.J., Lincoln, M., Chan, Y.K. and Onslow, M. (2008b) Determining language dominance in English–Mandarin bilinguals: Development of a self-report classification tool for clinical use. *Applied Psycholinguistics* 29, 389–412.

Mägiste, E. (1979) Recall of abstract and concrete sentences in bilinguals. *Scandinavian Journal of Psychology* 20, 179–185.

Marian, V. and Kaushanskaya, M. (2004) Self-construal and emotion in bicultural bilinguals. *Journal of Memory and Language* 51, 190–201.

Marian, V., Blumenfeld, H. and Kaushanskaya, M. (2007) The Language Experience and Proficiency Questionnaire (LEAP-Q): Assessing language profiles in bilinguals and multilinguals. *Journal of Speech, Language, and Hearing Research* 50 (4), 940–967.

Pakulak, E. and Neville, H. (2010) Proficiency differences in syntactic processing of monolingual native speakers indexed by event-related potentials. *Journal of Cognitive Neuroscience* 22, 2728–2744.

Pavlenko, A. (2004) Stop doing that, ia komu skazala!: Emotions and language choice in bilingual families. *Journal of Multilingual and Multicultural Development* 25, 179–203.

Piller, I. (2002) Passing for a native speaker: Identity and success in second language learning. *Journal of Sociolinguistics* 6, 179–206.

Rah, A. (2010) Transfer in L3 sentence processing: Evidence from relative clause attachment ambiguities. *International Journal of Multilingualism* 7, 147–161.

Tamamaki, K. (1993) Language dominance in bilinguals' arithmetic operations according to their language use. *Language Learning*, 43, 239–261.

Tokowicz, N., Michael, E.B. and Kroll, J.F. (2004) The roles of study-abroad experience and working memory capacity in the types of errors made during translation. *Bilingualism: Language and Cognition* 7, 255–272.

Treffers-Daller, J. (2011) Operationalizing and measuring language dominance. *International Journal of Bilingualism* 15, 1–17.

Tremblay, A. (2011) Proficiency assessment standards in second language acquisition research: 'Clozing' the gap. *Studies in Second Language Acquisition* 33, 339–372.

Wiig, E., Nielsen, H., Minthon, L. and Warkentin, S. (2002) *A Quick Test of Cognitive Speed (AQT)*. San Antonio, TX: PsychCorp.

Appendix 11A

Sample screen shots from the online Bilingual Language Profile

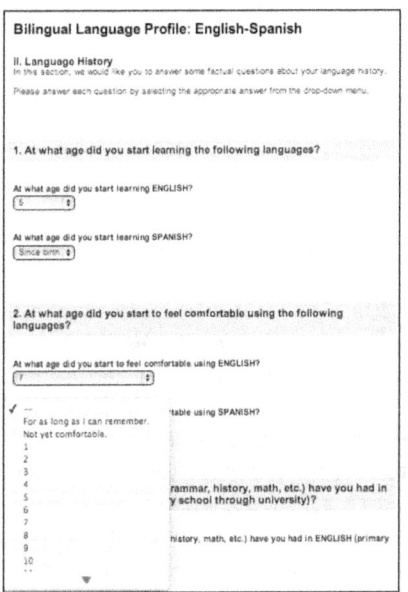

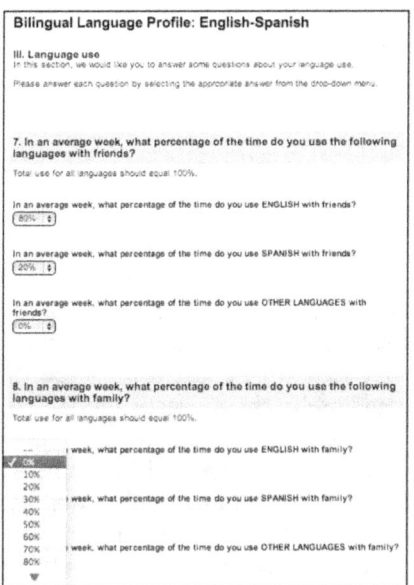

Epilogue

Our initial goal in this volume was to provide a clearer definition of what it means to be proficient in a second language (L2), so as to be able to measure L2 proficiency in a valid, reliable and practical manner. Thomas (1994), Norris and Ortega (2003: 717), Pallotti (2009) and many others have made it clear that there was a need for trustworthy L2 proficiency assessment tools that second language acquisition (SLA) researchers and language teachers could use in their investigations.

We sought (1) to present recent research projects developing new tools that are innovative, reliable and easy to use, for the evaluation of learners' language level, in particular with respect to productive and receptive skills, to be used both in research contexts and in larger educational settings; and (2) to narrow the gap between SLA research and language teaching with respect to evaluation by proposing concrete applications of advancements in SLA research for language teachers as well as classroom perspectives on L2 assessment.

The eleven chapters of this volume, which all deal with L2 proficiency assessment from an SLA perspective, contribute to a deeper understanding of the proficiency construct, and provide a variety of answers to the question of how to assess L2 proficiency. As Hulstijn (2010: 185)[1] puts it, choosing a testing instrument is a complicated issue, which largely depends on the assessment purpose, the type of population targeted, and the expected outcome of the evaluation. Practicality issues also constrain the choice of assessment instrument. SLA is a wide-ranging field, with some researchers studying language production from a rather linguistic perspective (McManus *et al.*, Callies *et al.*, this volume), others exploring the cognitive dimension of L2 learning (Hilton, Bairstow *et al.*, Ankerstein, this volume), while others choose to adopt an educational stance in order to study L2 learning (Osborne, Gertken *et al.*, Prince, Zoghlami, this volume). However, the readers will have noticed that there is no strict boundary between those approaches, and that most papers in this volume make use of common linguistic and cognitive concepts, thus highlighting diverse but convergent aspects of L2 proficiency assessment.

We therefore hope that the wide range of research tools presented here (corpus analysis, collaborative platform, BLP questionnaire, standardized test, elicited imitation, coefficient of variation and so on) will inspire researchers and teachers and help them adapt their assessment practices when necessary.

This volume provides by no means an exhaustive account of assessment tools for SLA research nor for language assessment in an educational context. It would be particularly interesting to more thoroughly explore classroom practices, as such an investigation would no doubt shed interesting light on current evaluation practices; and, at the other end of the SLA spectrum of investigation methods, to keep looking for psycholinguistic indicators/predictors of L2 proficiency.

We hope this volume will be a source of inspiration for L2 researchers and teachers. We feel there is a need for a greater cooperation between research and the language teaching world. We are, however, fully aware that there is still a long way to go from the research lab to the classroom, and we call for the establishment of methodological guidelines for valid, reliable and practical assessment of L2 proficiency in SLA research. We strongly believe there is room for future research in this field.

Pascale Leclercq and Amanda Edmonds
December 2013

Note

(1) See conclusion of Chapter 1 for the complete quotation.

References

Hulstijn, J.H. (2010) Measuring second language proficiency. In E. Blom and S. Unsworth (eds) *Experimental Methods in Language Acquisition Research* (pp. 185–200). Amsterdam: Benjamins.
Norris, J. and Ortega, L. (2003) Defining and measuring SLA. In C.J. Doughty and M.H. Long (eds) *The Handbook of Second Language Acquisition* (pp. 717–761). Oxford: Blackwell Publishing.
Pallotti, G. (2009) CAF: Defining, refining and differentiating constructs. *Applied Linguistics* 30, 590–601.
Thomas, M. (1994) Assessment of L2 proficiency in second language acquisition research. *Language Learning* 44, 307–336.

Index

Accuracy, 8–9, 56, 59–60, 61–63, 67, 72, 76, 78, 110, 118, 119, 132, 136, 182
Automaticity, 7, 18, 29, 37, 38, 43, 44, 97, 109–112, 118–119, 126, 129, 194, 212, 222

Basic language cognition (BLC), 7–8, 105, 144, 145, 156, 158
Bilingualism, 4, 18, 20, 29–30, 146, 208–210, 211–213, 218, 219, 221
Bilingual memory, 18, 122–123, 124–127, 130, 137, 208, 209

Classroom, 6, 11, 18, 45, 94, 95, 99, 104, 136, 145, 148, 191, 226, 227
Cluster analysis, 4, 17, 76, 84–85, 157
Coefficient of variation, 4, 18, 110–113, 117–120, 227
Collaborative assessment, 11, 14, 17, 55–56, 58, 59, 61, 73, 98, 226
Common European Framework of Reference for Languages (CEFR), 6, 13–15, 17, 54, 56–58, 59–68, 73, 75, 77–83, 86, 87, 97–98, 99, 104, 198, 199
Competence, 5–8, 15, 19, 20, 33, 56, 72, 87, 97, 145, 147, 158, 191–192, 194–196, 199, 202, 203–205, 211, 212
Comprehension, 18, 19, 28, 30, 93, 96–98, 99, 103, 105, 109, 110, 119, 131, 132, 146, 192–193, 194–196, 202, 203, 209, 212
Complexity, 8–9, 72, 78, 137, 146, 153, 154
Corpus, 4, 9, 13–15, 17, 28, 29–33, 34, 35–36, 45, 61, 63, 71–78, 86–87, 169–170, 172, 226
Crosslinguistic, 19, 144, 146, 147, 148, 156–157, 158

Descriptor, 6, 13, 14, 15, 17, 21, 45, 54, 56–58, 60–68, 72, 75, 76, 78, 83, 84, 85, 86, 98

Elicited imitation (EI), 4, 16, 19, 102, 143, 145–148, 149–153, 155–157, 161–166, 174, 176, 227

Fluency, 4, 8–9, 16–17, 28–30, 33–34, 35–46, 52, 56, 57, 58, 59, 60, 63–64, 66, 67, 72, 78, 118, 119, 127, 128, 208, 214

Grammar, 5, 6, 7, 9, 11, 13, 14, 20, 30, 31, 33, 34, 41, 44, 57, 61–63, 79, 94, 96, 103, 120, 143–149, 155, 164–166, 171, 174, 175, 176, 182, 189–190, 193, 197, 198, 203, 209, 211, 220

Higher language cognition (HLC), 7–8, 105, 144, 145, 156, 158

Inter-rater reliability, 14, 17, 31, 58–60, 80, 81, 101, 150

Language dominance, 13, 20, 123, 208–216, 221
Language teachers, 3, 15, 20, 66, 68, 120, 226
Lexical retrieval, 36, 39, 109, 218
Lexicon, 5, 9, 30, 61, 109, 119, 122–123, 127
Listening, 5, 7, 10, 11, 18, 19, 20, 28, 31, 33, 34, 93–98, 101, 103–105, 144, 156, 157, 191–197, 198, 199, 201, 202–205, 211
Listening proficiency, 18, 19, 97, 102, 105, 192–193, 196–197, 201, 202, 203, 204–205

Oral proficiency, 11, 14, 27, 45, 56, 63, 143, 146, 154, 155–157, 174, 185, 186

Performance, 9, 10, 11, 12, 14, 15, 18, 29, 45, 54, 55, 60, 61, 62, 66, 67, 72, 75, 86, 95, 99, 100, 101–103, 110, 112, 126, 136, 146, 149, 156, 168, 173, 174, 185, 186, 194, 195, 203, 213, 218
Practicality, 10–11, 13, 19, 119, 123–124, 143, 210, 212, 226, 227
Pragmatic, 6, 7, 13, 20, 29, 46, 96, 109, 193, 194, 202, 203
Processing, 5, 8, 9, 16–18, 20, 28, 29, 33, 35–36, 37–44, 45, 46, 93–98, 103–105, 109–113, 118–120, 123, 124, 125, 126–127, 144, 194, 203, 208, 209, 211, 212, 221, 222
Production, 9, 14, 16–17, 19, 28–30, 31–41, 45, 52–53, 54–60, 62, 66, 67, 73, 78, 79, 82, 93, 94, 101, 103, 131, 132, 147, 173–174, 176–178, 183–186, 221, 226
Pronunciation, 5, 35, 61–62, 67, 197
Psycholinguistic, 15, 28, 29, 109–110, 114, 193, 195, 209, 211–212, 218, 222, 227

Reading, 5, 7, 62, 94, 103, 124, 129, 144, 198, 199, 203, 205, 209, 211, 215, 216
Reliability, 3, 4, 9, 10–11, 13, 14, 15, 16, 17, 19, 20, 28, 29, 31, 36, 72, 77, 78, 86, 123–124, 131, 146, 147, 150–151, 155–157, 167, 176, 191–192, 197, 198, 199, 201, 204, 205, 210, 213, 218, 221, 226, 227

Self-assessment/self-rated proficiency, 13, 14, 19, 20, 21, 55, 126, 130–133, 136–137, 143, 146, 209–210, 213–216, 218
Sociolinguistic, 6, 20, 172, 202, 203
Speaking, 5, 7, 11, 28, 31, 32, 45, 54, 124, 129, 144, 151, 156, 157, 178, 198, 199, 209, 211, 215, 219
Standardized tests, 16, 72, 83, 143, 144, 191, 193, 194, 196, 198, 199, 204, 205, 218, 226
Subjectivity, 12–14, 17, 57, 72, 125, 129, 132, 133, 209

Translation, 4, 18, 42, 109, 120, 122–127, 128–130, 135–137, 209, 221

Validity, 3, 4, 10–11, 13, 15, 18, 19, 20, 77, 94, 95, 97, 104, 105, 120, 123–124, 136, 147, 150–151, 155–157, 191–192, 194, 199, 201, 203, 204, 205, 210, 213, 218, 221–222, 226, 227
Vocabulary, 9, 61–62, 64, 67, 80–81, 97, 98, 109, 137, 143, 145, 148, 149, 156, 193, 194, 198, 203, 211–212

WebCEF, 17, 55–56, 58, 60, 61, 62, 66, 68
Working memory, 9, 18, 43, 46, 94, 103, 146
Writing, 5, 7, 11, 17, 28, 54, 72, 73, 75, 78–79, 81–86, 94, 99, 102, 105, 122, 144, 151, 156, 174, 175, 176, 177, 178, 179–180, 184, 198, 199, 209, 211, 215

For Product Safety Concerns and Information please contact our EU Authorised Representative:

Easy Access System Europe

Mustamäe tee 50

10621 Tallinn

Estonia

gpsr.requests@easproject.com